Pay the Rent or Feed the Kids

By the Same Author

The Betrayal of Canada
A New and Better Canada
At Twilight in the Country

Pay the Rent or Feed the Kids

THE TRAGEDY AND DISGRACE OF POVERTY IN CANADA

Mel Hurtig

Canadian Cataloguing in Publication Data

Hurtig, Mel
    Pay the rent or feed the kids : the tragedy and disgrace of poverty in Canada

Includes bibliographical references.
ISBN 0-7710-4213-2

1. Poverty – Canada.   2. Poor – Canada.   3. Family – Economic aspects
– Canada.   4. Canada – Economic conditions.   I. Title.

HC120.P6H87 1999   362.5'0971   C99-931519-6

We acknowledge the financial support of the Government of Canada through the Book Publishing Industry Development Program for our publishing activities. Canada

We further acknowledge the support of the Canada Council for the Arts and the Ontario Arts Council for our publishing program.

Every reasonable effort has been made to contact copyright holders of material used in this book. Any information regarding errors or omissions will be gratefully received.

Typeset in Times by M&S, Toronto
Text design by Ingrid Paulson

Printed and bound in Canada

McClelland & Stewart Inc.
The Canadian Publishers
481 University Avenue
Toronto, Ontario
M5G 2E9

1 2 3 4 5 6   04 03 02 01 00 99

This book is dedicated, with my gratitude and admiration, to all the committed, generous, and compassionate people that I have had the great privilege of meeting while writing this book.

I was very fortunate to have been able to spend time with and get to know so many remarkable men and women, inner-city school principals and teachers, food bank workers, ministers and priests, social workers, child care staff, academics, poverty and welfare organization members, and other caring, wonderful people.

Many of these men and women work fifty- to sixty-hour, stress-filled weeks for terribly inadequate wages. If one is ever disheartened, if one ever feels a loss of faith in our fellow human beings, the examples these people offer, on a daily basis, are enough to restore a great deal of any lost respect for the state of humanity.

I only wish that every adult Canadian could have been with me during my interviews for this book. I hope that in the following pages I can convey an adequate reflection of what I have encountered and discovered.

Contents

Acknowledgements ix

List of Figures xi

Introduction xiii

Part One: A Nation of Hypocrites

But What About the Poor? 2

"No Measurable Progress" 6

How Does Canada Compare? 13

Number One – For Some 16

Poor Families: "A Disturbing Trend" 19

Single-Parent Families: The Poorest of Them All 22

"With the Wave of a Pen": Defining Poverty Away 25

To Market, to Market, to Buy a New Measure 31
    (And It Won't Cost Taxpayers a Dime!)

Hunger in Canada: "Pay the Rent or Feed the Kids" 35

From the Hungry to the Homeless 46

Part Two: Poor People Have Poor Children

Child Abuse by Politicians 56

On the Same Page in the Dictionary: Poverty and Power 61

Single Parents, Child Care, and Child Tax Benefits 70

Part Three: The Distribution of Income and Wealth

Rising Yachts and Sinking Rafts 82

The Rich Getting Richer, the Poor Getting Poorer 89

Trickle Down Has Fizzled Out 99

Wealth: The Numbers That Really Count 107

Part Four: Why Are People Poor?

The Bottom Line Has Replaced the Golden Rule 114

The Great Free Trade Hoax 127

UI, EI, Oh! 137

Part Five: Work, Wages, Profits, and Hypocrisy
    The Working Poor and the Big Bonus Bankers   144
    Eighty-Seven Dollars for Me, One Dollar for You   154
    Laughing All the Way to the Bank   159
    "Ripping the Heart Out of Democracy"   166

Part Six: Six Reasons the Poor Are Ignored
    The Poor Must Sing for Their Supper   174
    Government Spending: In the Middle of the Pack   185
    "We Can't Afford to Help the Poor"   189
    Brain Drain or Brain Gain?   196

Part Seven: The War Against the Poor
    Hostility, Extremists, and the Denial of Need   208
    "Building Bigger Prisons to House the Poor"   227
    The Quality of Life and the Quality of Death   240
    Sometimes They Come Back Dead   249

Part Eight: Under Poor Management
    The Country Is Humming, Money Is on the Move,   260
        We're on a Roll
    Debt, Savings, and Disposable Income   267
    Treading Water or Sinking   273

Part Nine: What Can We Do About Poverty in Canada?
    "At a Crossroad" – The Best Possible Investment   280
    "Where the Hell Are We Going to Get the Money?"   303
    The Big Disconnect   318

Conclusion   325

Appendix One: Measuring Poverty   335
Appendix Two: Canada's Trade Balance and the   344
    Free Trade Agreement
Appendix Three: Measuring Poverty in the United States   347
Appendix Four: Avoiding Paying Taxes in Canada   349
Appendix Five: Organizations and Abbreviations   352

Acknowledgements

I am most grateful to all of the following who have helped me with this book: my wife Kay Hurtig, my publisher Doug Gibson, Avie Bennett, David Perry, Julie Maloney, Brian Bechtel, Doug McNally, Neil Brooks, Jonathan Webb, John Kenneth Galbraith, Pamela Coates, Gordon Anderson, Peter Ibbott, Andrew Sharpe, Seth Klein, Michael Goldberg, Garnett Picot, Michael Hatfield, Betty Dean, John Strick, Joanne Currie, Andy Mitchell, Richard Shillington, Ele Gibson, Barry Hicks, Ross Finnie, Linda Grisley, Charles Beach, David Ross, Michael Wolfson, Emily Westwood, Jasmin Hoeven, Bill Irwin, Steve Kerstetter, Marjorie Bencz, Reny Clericuzio, Julia Bass, Sue Cox, Lana Sampson, Avril Pike, Martha Friendly, Sandra Woitas, Bill Gillespie, Midge Cuthill, Bruce Miller, Lynn McIntyre, Armine Yalnizyan, Erminie Cohen, Deborah Landry, Deborah Sunter, Deborah Wood, Carmel Forbes, George Jackson, Peter DeVries, Angela Petton, Susan Crandall, Bill Potter, Sherrie Tingley, Ken Battle, Bev Oldham, Mike Farrell, Danielle Hay, Ron Chalmers, Anne Golden, Robert Bragg, Pat Burns, Janet Fast, Deborah Norris, Stephen Lewis, Dalton Camp, Maryanne Webber, Walter Stewart, Arthur Donner, Christine Feaver, Frank Denton, Byron Spencer, Graham Riches, Canadian Institute for Health Information, Terrance Carson, Jared Bernstein, Cherry Murray, Saleem A. Ganam, Gayle Gilchrist James, Sherri Torjman, Tiina Burns, Gail Sharland, Aron Spector and Jennifer Whatley.

List of Figures

1. Unemployment Rate – Seasonally Adjusted — xv
2. Incidence of Low-Income Persons in Canada — 3
3. Number of Low-Income Persons in Canada — 4
4. Low-Income Rates for Families with Children — 14
5. United Nations Poverty Comparisons, 1989-1994 — 17
6. Incidence of Low Family Income — 19
7. Poverty Rates for Single Women with Children — 23
8. Poverty Rates for Single-Parent Families — 23
9. Child Poverty Rates Since the House of Commons Resolution — 58
10. Share of Aggregate Income, U.S.A. — 84
11. Family Income, Late 1970s to Mid 1990s — 85
12. Gross Domestic Product at Market Prices — 87
13. Change in Average Market Income for Families with Children, 1984 to 1994 — 92
14. Income Before Transfers – Income Share — 96
15. Average Total Change in Family Market Income, 1980 to 1996 — 97
16. Distribution of Market Income, Percentage Change, 1975 to 1994 — 100
17. Income Under $20,000 — 101
18. Average After-Tax Income — 103
19. Average Total Money Income — 104
20. Average Income After Transfers and Income Tax, 1996 — 105
21. Average Annual Unemployment Rates by Decade — 116
22. Unemployed Persons in Canada — 117
23. Unemployment as a Percentage of the Labour Force — 119
24. The Labour Force Participation Rate — 131
25. Part-Time Employment as a Percentage of Total Employment — 131
26. Youth Employment — 133
27. Employment, Average Annual Growth — 134
28. Exports and Jobs Since the Free Trade Agreement — 134
29. Percentage of Unemployed Receiving EI Benefits — 140
30. Changes in Annual Labour Income in Canada — 149
31. Wage Settlements — 150
32. Changes in Real Annual Earnings by Decile, 1981 to 1995 — 151

33. Changes in Hourly Earnings, 1989 to 1998   151
34. Indexed Real Annual Earnings of Paid Male Workers,
    Aged 18 to 24, 1979 to 1995   152
35. Wage and Salary Increases Per Unit of Output   157
36. Corporate Operating Profits   160
37. Average Percentage Return on Capital, 1970 to 1979   161
38. Bank Operating Profits   163
39. Major Transfers as a Percentage of GDP   170
40. Persons in Low Income After Tax, 65+   176
41. Public Social Expenditures as a Percentage of GDP, 1995   182
42. General Government Outlays as a Percentage of Nominal GDP   186
43. General Government Total Outlays to GDP   186
44. Net Government Current Expenditures on Goods and Services
    Ratio to Real GDP   187
45. Current Government Receipts to GDP, 1960 to 1995   191
46. Total Tax Revenue as a Percentage of GDP   192
47. Immigrants as a Percentage of Canada's Population,
    1901 to 1996   202
48. Five-Year Percentage Labour Force Growth Rates   204
49. International Homicides by Men Per 100,000 People,
    1985 to 1990   241
50. Incarcerations Per 100,000 People   245
51. Net Official Aid, Disbursements as a Percentage of GDP   257
52. GDP Growth, Annual Percent Change   263
53. Trends in Economic Well-Being and GDP Per Capita Indexes   265
54. Personal Debt as a Percentage of Disposable Income   268
55. Household Debt as a Percentage of Personal Disposable Income   269
56. Household Savings Ratio as a Percentage of Disposable Income   269
57. Savings Ratios, International Comparisons   270
58. Annual Percentage Changes in Personal Disposable Income   271
59. Aggregate Income Deficiency   274
60. Capital Consumption Allowances as a Percentage of GDP   308
61. Total Personal Income, Percentage Changes from Previous Year   318
62. Relative Poverty Rates for Children, Mid-1980s to Mid-1990s   320

Introduction

How is it possible that we now have millions of Canadians living in poverty when a great many less fortunate countries have poverty rates that are but a fraction of our own?

How is it that, as our country's economy has expanded, as our gross domestic product (GDP) has increased every year, there have been growing numbers of poor men, women, and children in Canada?

How is it that somehow Canadians seem prepared to tolerate so much hunger, homelessness, and suffering in such a relatively well-to-do country?

How is it that, as the country's economy has grown, the income gap between the rich and the poor has widened?

And how is it that, while our government tells us repeatedly how well we're doing, there are growing numbers of families and individuals across Canada who are increasingly insecure about their future?

I started out, over two years ago, to write a different book. It was to be called "The Good Country: Myth and Reality in Pursuit of the Canadian Dream." The book was going to look at what our political and corporate leaders tell us, and what their think tanks and institutes report, and then it was going to look at how the media handles this information and how reality frequently differs substantially from what we read and what we are told.

The first chapter of the book was supposed to be about poverty in Canada, the second about child poverty, the third about distribution of income, and so on. But, after I began doing daily interviews across the country for the first two chapters, the more people I talked to, the more research I did, the angrier I became. And then the sadder I became.

This book is the result. In a way it's a book about how much Canada has changed. As I write these words, a new national public-opinion poll has been published. It tells us that when Canadians were asked to name the issues that concerned them the most, poverty was not even mentioned.

This book is about social justice. It's about social responsibility and fairness in society. It's also about hungry children, about the homeless, about the eroding social safety net, and it's about political and elite hypocrisy and indifference to human suffering.

In the following pages you will find many numbers, tables, charts, definitions, international comparisons, and analysis. But you will also find many examples of *what poverty really means*. Sometimes we miss the trees because of the forest. When you finish reading this book, I hope you will be as angry as I am about how we have allowed so many of our fellow citizens to live in misery and deprivation, with little hope for the future.

Mother Teresa said, "You and I will be judged by what we have done for the poor." On that basis, Canada must be truly ashamed.

I have always distrusted short-term statistical analysis. You can prove almost anything you want by selecting the right base year to validate your point. For example, Figure 1 shows what has been happening to our unemployment rate. Looks pretty good, doesn't it? Yet when you come to the chapters in this book on employment and unemployment, you will find quite a different picture.

With this in mind, for the most part, I have provided a look at what has happened in Canada during the past two decades, the years 1979 to 1998 inclusive. At the same time, this will allow an interesting comparison between the decade before the Free Trade Agreement came into effect in 1989 and the first ten years of the FTA and the first years of the North American Free Trade Agreement (NAFTA). I'm certain, regardless

FIGURE 1

Unemployment Rate – Seasonally Adjusted

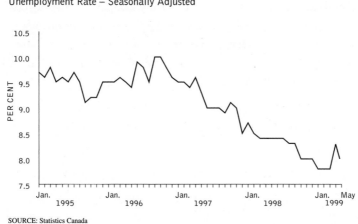

SOURCE: Statistics Canada

The unemployment rate has fallen over the past few years – but the apparent good news is misleading, as we shall see.

of your political orientation, you will find the comparisons remarkable, and for many quite unexpected and disturbing.

Those of you who may find that the numbers in this book do not match what you may have read elsewhere should know that Statistics Canada has made major revisions to its national accounts, as well as corrections and updates. I am especially grateful to all the excellent people at Statistics Canada who have been so cheerfully and patiently helpful in providing the information and the sources that I have required. Readers who may wish additional information about sources should feel free to write to me, care of the publisher.

I have made every effort to gain permission to use the items quoted, where such permissions are required. In a few cases I have not been successful because of returned mail, unanswered faxes, or inability to locate certain individuals.

For the most part, the notes contain sources and exact dates. In a few cases I have failed to locate an exact date and for this I apologize.

I am especially grateful to all those from different parts of Canada who gave me personal interviews and talked freely about the problems they have faced. For obvious reasons, as you will see, I have protected their identities.

I believe that poverty in Canada is truly a tragedy and a national disgrace. I hope that you will agree when you finish reading this book, and I hope you will do everything you can to help make the important changes in society that are necessary, and do whatever you can to help those who are less fortunate.

PART ONE

A Nation of Hypocrites

But What About the Poor?

One of my first interviews was with the principal of an inner-city school. It was an old three-storey brick building with creaky linoleum floors and small classrooms. My appointment was for noon and I got there just a few minutes early. We sat talking in her tiny second-floor office. Suddenly she got up from her desk and moved to the window. She motioned for me to join her. I pressed my head to the glass as she instructed and down below I could just barely see a little girl hiding under the stairs. Just then the noon bell went off. The little girl leapt to her feet, ran along the side of the building, disappeared into a door, quickly reappeared and motioned across the schoolyard. Immediately, two small children, a boy and a girl, maybe five and four years of age, came running across the yard. All three vanished into the school.

The principal told me that the older girl, who was seven, was sneaking her younger brother and sister into the school's hot-lunch program. She did this several times near the end of each month. One of the new teachers noticed what was happening and, in a non-confrontational way, questioned the girl, who began to cry with shaking shoulders, deep sobs, and tears rolling down her face. There was no father in the family. Their

mother had been sick in bed for months. They always ran out of
food before the end of the month. The utility bill had to be paid;
if it wasn't, child welfare would take the kids away from their
mother. There was nothing in the house to eat.

I would be grateful if you would take the time to have a good look at
Figure 2. I wish I could be with you when you do so, for I would like to
be able to ask you what your first reaction is.

FIGURE 2

Incidence of Low-Income Persons in Canada

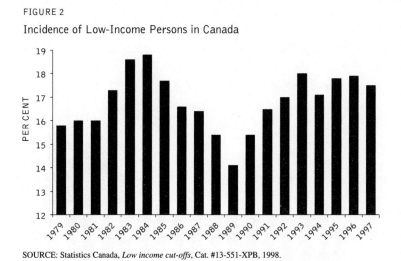

SOURCE: Statistics Canada, *Low income cut-offs*, Cat. #13-551-XPB, 1998.

The percentage of poor Canadians is higher than it was twenty years
ago. (Note that "persons" includes unattached individuals plus all
adults and children in families.) The comparatively low figure for 1989
was due to five years of exceptionally strong economic growth preced-
ing 1989, a period during which real GDP grew by an average of over 4.7
per cent annually.

The Croll report, *Poverty in Canada*,* was published almost thirty
years ago. Senator David Croll wrote, "No nation can achieve true
greatness if it lacks the courage and determination to undertake the

---

* The official report (published in 1971) for the Special Senate Committee on Poverty which was chaired
by Senator David Croll. The committee's mandate was to inquire into the causes of poverty in Canada and
to make recommendations for its elimination.

surgery necessary to remove the cancer of poverty from its body politic." I hope that when you look at Figure 2 you say to yourself something like "Good grief!" Despite all the fatuous rhetoric and all the pious pronouncements, despite all the House of Commons committees and Senate reports, despite all the warnings from anti-poverty organizations and from the growing numbers of food banks across the country, despite the inquiries and the commissions and all the published studies, the situation is even worse than it was thirty long years ago and much worse today than it was twenty years ago.

There's another way of counting low-income persons in Canada, not in percentage terms, but in actual numbers (see Figure 3).

FIGURE 3

Number of Low-Income Persons in Canada

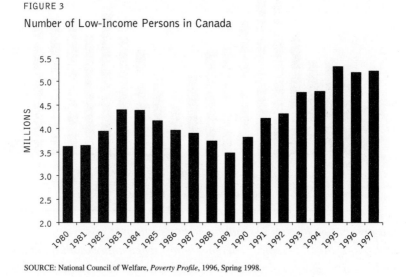

SOURCE: National Council of Welfare, *Poverty Profile*, 1996, Spring 1998.

In 1995, 1996, and 1997 more than 5.2 million Canadians lived below the low income line, more than ever before.

In April 1997, the National Council of Welfare reported that there were more Canadians living in poverty than "during the depths of the last two recessions. . . . Bluntly put, the modest economic growth was simply not filtering down to the ranks of the poor."*

---

* *Poverty Profiles 1995* published in April 1997.

Just over a year later, in May 1998, the council reported: "Although the last recession ended in 1991, poverty rates have risen steadily since then. . . . We expected that poor people would share in the return of prosperity; instead we found that poverty rates crept up after the recession. . . ." Using Statistics Canada's Low Income Cut-Off measurements, the council said: "The poverty rate . . . rose to 17.6 per cent, which meant that 5,190,000 people were living in poverty. The child poverty rate jumped to 20.9 per cent, or 1,481,000 children," in 1996. Moreover, while the poverty rate for single mothers under twenty-five was a terrible 83 per cent, "by 1996 it had leaped to 91.3 per cent."

How is this possible? The Canadian economy has gone through a sustained period of recovery. Exports have been booming. Interest rates are low. Unemployment is down. The banks have had record profits almost every year. According to Prime Minister Jean Chrétien, Finance Minister Paul Martin, and Bank of Canada Governor Gordon Thiessen, we're doing just great.

But what about the poor?

"No Measurable Progress"

The preamble of the 1948 United Nations Universal Declaration of Human Rights refers to "the inherent dignity and . . . equal and inalienable rights of all members of the human family" and the obligation of signatory nations "to promote social progress and better standards of life. . . ."

Article XXII says, "Everyone, as a member of society, has the right to social security and . . . economic, social and cultural rights indispensable for . . . dignity and the free development of (their) personality." Article XXV reads, "Everyone has the right to a standard of living adequate for health and well-being of himself and of his family, including food, clothing, housing and medical care and necessary social services, and the right to security in the event of unemployment, sickness, disability, widowhood, old age or other loss of livelihood in circumstances beyond his control." As well, "Motherhood and childhood are entitled to special care and assistance. All children, whether born in or out of wedlock, shall enjoy the same protection."

Twenty-eight years later, in 1976, Canada signed the International Covenant on Economic, Social and Cultural Rights, pledging that our country would provide "adequate food, clothing and housing" as part of "an adequate standard of living for Canadians."

So what happened?

Another seventeen years later, in 1993, the United Nations Economic and Social Council Committee on Economic, Social and Cultural Rights issued a report on Canada's performance:

> The Committee expresses concern about the persistence of poverty in Canada. There seems to have been no measurable progress in alleviating poverty over the past decade, nor in alleviating the severity of poverty among a number of particularly vulnerable groups.
>
> In particular, the Committee is concerned about the fact that, according to the information available to it, more than half of the single mothers in Canada, as well as a large number of children, live in poverty.
>
> Of particular concern to the Committee is the fact that the federal government appears to have reduced the ratio of its contributions to cost-sharing agreements for social assistance.
>
> The Committee received information from non-governmental organizations about families being forced to relinquish their children to foster care because of inability to provide adequate housing or other necessities.
>
> A further subject of concern for the Committee is the evidence of hunger in Canada and the reliance on food banks operated by charitable organizations.
>
> Given the evidence of homelessness and inadequate living conditions, the Committee is surprised that expenditures on social housing are as low as 1.3 per cent of Government expenditures.

And standing out among these comments:

> The Committee recommends a concerted Government action to eliminate the need for food banks.

So, what was Canada's response?

Five years later, in November 1998, at about the time of the fiftieth anniversary of the United Nations Declaration of Human Rights,

Canada's National Anti-Poverty Organization (NAPO) presented a seventy-three-page submission in Geneva relating to Canada's Implementation of the International Covenant on Economic, Social and Cultural Rights. NAPO's document is a well-prepared, insightful condemnation of Canada's treatment of our underprivileged men, women, and children.*

The document's cover quotes Gro Harlem Bruntland, the three-time prime minister of Norway: "Poverty is lack of opportunity, lack of freedom. It is hunger and malnutrition, disease and lack of basic social services. It is a policy failure that degrades people – those who suffer it, and those who tolerate it. . . . Poverty is still the gravest insult to human dignity. Poverty is the scar on humanity's face." In page after page of clear prose, tables, and charts, NAPO itemized Canada's dismal performance in our sustained tolerance of and indifference to poverty. The NAPO submission quotes a poor person:

> Poverty is: Feeling self-conscious about the amount of generic products you have at the checkout, not being able to afford the large bag of powdered milk, only being able to afford hamburger as your meat, fasting one day a week, walking 30 blocks to apply for a job to save the bus fare, then walking back. Getting turned down for that dishwasher job. Finally getting your high school diploma and then finding out it makes no difference. Being turned down for an Emergency Food Voucher by a Social Worker who is making at least $20 an hour, in a union, with a pension and eating good tonight.

The NAPO document then quotes from the annual report of the Canadian Association of Food Banks, *Hunger Count, 1998*: "In 1984 there were 75 food banks in Canada, by 1998 there are over 625 food banks that provide food assistance. In March, 1998, 716,496 people . . . received assistance from a food bank. The use of food banks doubled from 1989 to 1997." It then goes on to quote from a 1997 report by the Canadian Council on Social Development (CCSD): "Families received $800 million less support for children in 1996 than they did in 1984. . . .

---

* *The 50th Anniversary of the UN Declaration: Human Rights Meltdown in Canada*, November 16, 1998.

In 1996 dollars, poor families with two children were receiving $ 2,042 compared to $2,183 in 1984."*

As for child poverty, NAPO is clear: "Child poverty does not exist in a vacuum. Poor children live in poor families. Cuts to social assistance programs and unemployment benefits, lack of affordable child care, scarce sources of affordable housing, high unemployment levels and low minimum wages all mean that families are poorer – therefore the children living in these families are poor."

Soon after NAPO's submission in Geneva, an official Canadian government group faced questions from the same U.N. committee. In the words of *Toronto Star* columnist Gordon Barthos,† the federal and Ontario governments appearing before the U.N. committee provided "brazen self-justification, half-truths, bafflegab, artful dodging and distortions. . . . It was a shameful performance."

Asked by the U.N. committee how many people are homeless in Ontario, the reply was, "The provincial government does not collect data that would reflect the extent of homelessness in Ontario cities."

According to the Canadian Press, "The Canadian [government] delegation left committee members shaking their heads in disbelief at the vagueness of Canadian replies to specific and pointed questions about homelessness, reductions in welfare payments, living conditions in First Nations communities and other social problems."**

Obviously most members of the U.N. committee were disturbed, even angry. "Maybe . . . they're embarrassed at answering the obvious – that there is a great deal of poverty in Canada and it's such a rich country."†† Committee members felt the Canadian delegation was "stonewalling," "waffling," and "avoiding the glaring facts." Several observers described the Canadian government delegation's responses as smug or evasive.

The next month, the United Nations again strongly condemned Canada for its human-rights record. The U.N. committee (which included eighteen human-rights experts from around the world) attacked Canada for permitting such extensive poverty, homelessness,

---

* *Backgrounder: Child Poverty – the Extent and Depth of the Problem*, Ottawa, January 1997.

† *Toronto Star*, December 11, 1998.

** *Edmonton Journal*, November 28, 1998.

†† Amranga Pillay, Chief Justice of the Supreme Court, Mauritius.

for such inadequate support for poor children, for single mothers, and for aboriginal Canadians. One U.N. representative summed the report up: "I would not be surprised to hear about these things from developing countries. But to hear about these things in a very well-developed country like Canada with so many resources . . . the degree of homelessness and poverty is really quite shocking."*

The condemnation of Canada was the strongest attack on *any* industrialized nation in many years. The report questioned Paul Martin and the Chrétien government's abandonment of the Canada Assistance Plan for the Canada Health and Social Transfer, an action which made worse the plight of so many low-income Canadians. Among the committee's recommendations is federal legislation to prevent the provinces from clawing back federal benefits for the poor, the restructuring of the Employment Insurance program to return it to the original intention of providing adequate unemployment insurance, and much more concentration on the provision of proper housing for the underprivileged.

The U.N. committee blasted Ottawa's official delegation to the Geneva meetings: "Too many questions failed to receive detailed or specific answers." While "Canadians enjoy a singularly high standard of living" and "Canada has the capacity to achieve a high level of respect for all Covenant rights . . . that this has not yet been achieved is reflected in the fact the United Nations Development Programme's Human Poverty Index ranks Canada tenth on the list for industrialized countries."†

Tenth!

The committee "notes that since 1994 . . . the State Party has not paid sufficient attention to the adverse consequences for the enjoyment of economic, social and cultural rights" of Canadians. And in particular "by vulnerable groups." In specific areas of concern, the committee protested the failure of Canadian governments to respond to the appeals to provide "children adequate food, clothing and housing" and to "complaints [about] the basic necessities of life," as well as their "failure to provide legal protection in Canada of women's rights which are guaranteed under the Covenant." Moreover, "The Committee is greatly concerned at the gross disparity between Aboriginal people and the

---

* *Globe and Mail*, December 5, 1998.

† United Nations' Committee on Economic, Social and Cultural Rights, *Consideration of Reports Submitted by States Parties Under Article 16 and 17 of the Covenant.*

majority of Canadians with respect to the enjoyment of Covenant rights," with "little or no progress in the alleviation of social and economic deprivation . . . in particular mass unemployment, shortage of adequate housing and the high rate of suicide, especially among youth in the Aboriginal communities. . . . The committee is concerned that . . . income assistance measures have clearly not been adequate to cover rental costs of the poor. In the last five years, the number of tenants paying more than 50% of income toward rent has increased by 43%." Meanwhile, large cuts to social assistance "create obstacles to women escaping domestic violence. Many women are forced . . . to choose between returning to or staying in a violent situation, on the one hand, or homelessness and inadequate food and clothing for themselves and their children, on the other."

With reference to "workfare," the committee attacked "compulsory employment schemes" that often result in "work without protection of fundamental rights," in programs that "constitute discrimination based on social status or age," in "clear violation of article 8 of the Covenant. . . ."

As well, "The Committee is concerned that the minimum wage is not sufficient for a worker to have an adequate standard of living, which also covers his or her family" and that "the number of food banks almost doubled between 1989 and 1997 in Canada and are able to meet only a fraction of the increased needs of the poor."

In a nutshell, "the State Party . . . adopted policies at federal, provincial and territorial levels which exacerbated poverty and homelessness among many vulnerable groups during a time of strong economic growth and increasing affluence."

So, what should be done? The committee recommended that Canada re-establish national programs "with designated cash transfers for social assistance and social services which include universal entitlements and national standards, specifying a legally enforceable right to adequate assistance for all persons in need. . . ."

Another of the committee's recommendations is "to establish social assistance at levels which ensure the realization of an adequate standard of living for all." Moreover, Canada should ensure "that services such as mental health care, home care, child care and attendant care, shelters for battered women, and legal aid for non-criminal matters, are available at levels that ensure the rights to an adequate standard of living."

There are other important recommendations relating to the welfare of children, Canada's inadequate Employment Insurance program, our aboriginal population, homelessness, people with disabilities, post-secondary education for low-income students, human-rights tribunals, workfare, and legal matters relating to Canada's frequently ignored obligations relating to the United Nations covenant.

Can *anything* be more clear?

Truly, a national tragedy and a national disgrace.

How Does Canada Compare?

The principal at the school told me that just before Christmas a businessman brought in six pairs of warm boots for kids who might need them. This was great, but of the 240 kids in the east-end school, about 150 probably needed boots badly. How do you select which students get the six pairs? The teachers finally settled on a system of trying to figure out sizes by age, and then holding a draw. A little dark-haired, round-eyed aboriginal girl of seven won a pair. Her face lit up, her smile was heartwarming. She had been coming to school in old, flimsy running shoes, even in minus-thirty-degree weather, through deep snowdrifts. But a week later one of the teachers reported a problem to the principal. The little girl just wouldn't take the boots off, even in gym class. Several teachers had tried, but without success. Finally, the principal took her aside, privately. Why wouldn't she take her boots off? Tears appeared in her eyes. After some hesitation, she whispered that she didn't have any socks.

Just before we get into a discussion of how poor families fare, let's look at how Canada compares with other countries. Here in Figure 4 are the low-income rates for families with children, based on standardized

poverty definitions for eight countries, from Organization for Economic Co-operation and Development (OECD) information and the
Luxembourg Income Study.

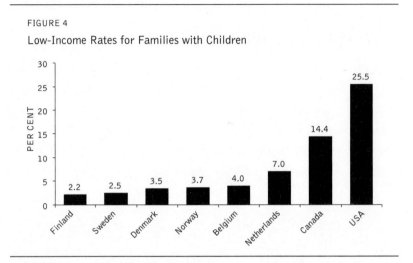

FIGURE 4

Low-Income Rates for Families with Children

*Canada has one of the worst rates of family and child poverty in the
developed world. The figures are for the early 1990s.*

In 1996, the United Nations' Children's Fund's (UNICEF) *Progress
of Nations* report showed that Canada had the second-highest number of
poor children among the eighteen leading industrialized nations.
(Second-highest of eighteen!) Not only is Canada's rate of child poverty
one of the highest among developed nations, but our country's assistance to children is well below that of many OECD nations. By 1997,
Canada was seventh in the world in GDP per capita, but in child benefits
we were fourteenth.

Economist Shelley Phipps, of Dalhousie University, compares children's well-being in Canada, Norway, and the United States. Her findings
show "rates of child poverty are much higher in Canada and particularly
in the U.S. than in most affluent countries." Some 18 per cent of young
children living with two parents were poor in the U.S. compared to some
13 per cent in Canada and only 5 per cent in Norway. For children living
with lone mothers, the rates were an appalling sixty 60 cent in the
U.S., 43 per cent in Canada, and only 16 per cent in Norway. "If we are

interested in improving the well-being of Canadian children, we should study policies available in Norway" where "all Norwegian children receive extremely generous, by Canadian standards, family allowances, maternity/parental leaves are very extensive and well-paid, very generous programmes are available to assist single mothers."*

Comparing Canada with the U.S., Phipps shows that poor children in the U.S. are almost always significantly worse off and "the extent of the deterioration is nearly always greater for the U.S. than for other countries." Of great interest is the fact that "despite very similar average incomes, there are very large differences in the absolute incomes received by the poorest twenty per cent of children in the three countries. For example, children in the bottom quintile (the lower fifth) of the Norwegian income distribution receive *double* the income of children in the bottom quintile of the U.S. income distribution."

Can governments make a difference? In 1996, the executive director of the UNICEF said, "There can be no doubt that millions of children are alive today because of the extra efforts set in motion since the World Summit for Children. In fact, one million fewer children will die this year than in 1990."†

Can government make a difference? Sweden once had a child-poverty rate of 23 per cent. Today it is down to only about 3 per cent. France reduced its child-poverty rate from over 25 per cent to 6.5 per cent. The Netherlands cut their rate from 14 per cent to 6 per cent. Decent full-time paying jobs are one key. Part-time jobs with benefits and proper low-cost daycare facilities are others. Raising minimum wages and child benefits are essential.

Today, in all the Nordic countries, child poverty has fallen dramatically. For that matter, it has for adults as well: "Poverty, although not quite abolished, has been reduced to near-invisibility," reports *The Economist* magazine.**

So governments *can* make a difference. If they want to. If they really care.

---

* *The Well-Being of Young Canadian Children in International Perspective*, October 1998.
† Carol Bellamy, *Globe and Mail*, October 17, 1996.
** January 23, 1999.

Number One – For Some

For the United Nations, "Poverty can mean more than a lack of what is necessary for material well-being. It can also mean the denial of opportunities and choices most basic to human development – to lead a long, healthy, creative life and to enjoy a decent standard of living, freedom, dignity, self-esteem and the respect of others."*

By now, most Canadians know about the U.N.'s Human Development Index, which for six consecutive years has ranked Canada the number-one country in the world. But very few Canadians have ever read the report. Few know that our number-one rating is based on a very narrow set of measurements, most of which are the direct result of Canada's progressive social programs before they were badly eroded by the Mulroney and Chrétien governments. We'll look more closely at social programs and government transfers shortly. But for now, let's consider the 1998 edition of the U.N. *Human Development Report*. The document doesn't mince words in its definition of poverty. Impoverishment is multidimensional. "Human poverty . . . looks at more than a lack of income." But poverty is unquestionably "deprivation in economic provisioning, leaving [people] unable to achieve the

---

* *Human Development Report*, 1997.

standard of living necessary to avoid hardship and to participate in the life of the community."

The 1997, 1998, and 1999 editions of the *Human Development Report* presented a new Human Poverty Index for industrial countries: "a multi-dimensional measure of human deprivation . . . appropriate to the social and economic conditions of the industrial countries." Note the words "human deprivation." Figure 5 shows the six-year average percentage of the population below the U.N.'s income poverty line. Not much for Canadians to be proud about. Bear in mind, too, that since 1994 the number of persons living in poverty in Canada has increased substantially.

FIGURE 5

United Nations Poverty Comparisons, 1989 to 1994

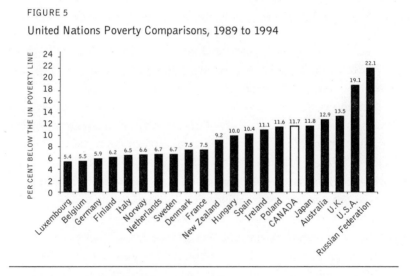

Even by this conservative international measure of poverty, Canada fares poorly.

For advocates of let-the-market-rule and trickle-down economics, the consistent and extremely high U.S. poverty rate is difficult to explain. Few, if any, will be surprised by the even more dismal showing of the Russian Federation. (The U.N. poverty comparisons are based on 50 per cent of a country's median personal disposable income as a poverty line – the median being the middle point in the total list.)

Note the remarkable comparisons between poverty levels and the national level of income. "The United States, with the highest per-capita income measured in purchasing power parity (PPP) among the 17 countries, also has the highest human poverty.* Sweden, which has [one of] the lowest poverty rates is far back at 13th in average income. . . . One might expect that the higher a country's GDP, the fewer poor people there would be." But the figure shows quite the opposite: "Poverty rates in higher-income countries are the same as – or higher than – rates in lower-income industrial countries." Clearly, then, distribution of income is an important factor. We'll look at that topic shortly.

In its 1997 *Human Development Report*, the U.N. told us: "In the past 50 years poverty has fallen more than in the previous 500." However, in recent years, "In some industrial countries, such as the United Kingdom and the United States, poverty has risen considerably." These "depressing developments" were not "inevitable. All can be reversed if countries take more seriously the commitment [they] already made to giving poverty reduction high priority. . . ."

For the U.N., "In every area of policy the state must advance the interest of poor people. . . . It is not the resources or the economic solutions that are lacking – it is the political momentum to tackle poverty head-on." What is required? The U.N. says, "The costs of eradicating poverty are less than people imagine. On a global basis, it would amount to some one percent of global incomes."

The report points out that "poverty can involve not only the lack of the necessities of material well-being, but the denial of opportunities for living a tolerable life. Life can be prematurely shortened. It can be made difficult, painful and hazardous. It can be deprived of knowledge and communication. And it can be robbed of dignity, confidence and self-respect – as well as the respect of others."

---

* Purchasing power parity measurements are used by economists to help make more valid international comparisons in determining the real purchasing power of currencies in buying similar baskets of goods and services in different countries.

Poor Families: "A Disturbing Trend"

One important way of measuring low incomes (see Figure 6) is to look at low-income families, using Statistics Canada numbers.

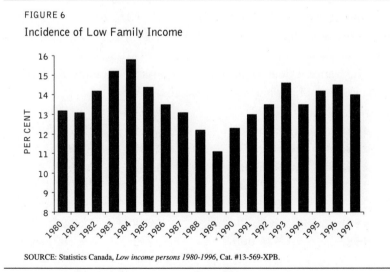

FIGURE 6

Incidence of Low Family Income

SOURCE: Statistics Canada, *Low income persons 1980-1996*, Cat. #13-569-XPB.

Family poverty rates fell from 1984 to 1989, but have now climbed back to higher levels than those of twenty years ago.

A report by Michael Hatfield of the Applied Research Branch of Human Resources Development Canada[*] indicates that the share of poor families now living in major Canadian cities represents a disturbing trend. "Since the onset of the 1981-1982 recession, income poverty and symptoms of economic and social marginalization such as homelessness, pan-handling, the share of children growing up in lone-parent families, and dependence on government transfer payments and food banks have tended to increase." Moreover, the proportion of poor families living in very poor urban neighbourhoods has increased from some 12 per cent to more than 18 per cent.

Here's a look at how the share of poor families living in very poor neighbourhoods has changed since 1980 in seven large metropolitan areas:

	1980	1995
Calgary	6.4%	8.7%
Edmonton	4.1%	18.8%
Montreal	30.1%	40.2%
Winnipeg	23.5%	36.1%
Quebec	20.8%	25.3%
Vancouver	7.2%	13.7%
Toronto	14.7%	29.8%

The National Council of Welfare also lists the numbers of poor families in Canada. Let's look at their annual figures:

1980	830,000	1989	786,000
1981	832,000	1990	874,000
1982	905,000	1991	949,000
1983	1,007,000	1992	991,000
1984	1,032,000	1993	1,116,000
1985	963,000	1994	1,108,000
1986	924,000	1995	1,187,000
1987	895,000	1996	1,230,000
1988	851,000	1997	1,175,160

---

[*] *Edmonton Journal*, October 27, 1998.

So, between 1980 and 1997, the number of poor families in Canada increased by 42 per cent.

Now let's turn to the poorest of them all.

Single-Parent Families:
The Poorest of Them All

Statistics Canada is clear about what group is the poorest in Canada: "Between 1973 and 1995, single-parent families experienced the highest low-income rate at the annual average of 56.5%." By comparison, the average low-income rate for unattached individuals was 37.9 per cent.* Figure 7 shows the poverty percentage rates for single women with children under eighteen:†

The National Council of Welfare explains, "The risk of poverty is higher for families of all types with very young children, since the job of caring for infants and toddlers often keeps mothers out of the labour force."

In terms of education, "Poor education can be either a cause of poverty or an effect. Young people who drop out of school may be poor because they lack the skills needed to get good jobs. On the other hand, young women who drop out of school if they get pregnant may be poor because of the hardships associated with single parenthood. The fact that they are poorly educated is a result of their family circumstances rather than an immediate cause of poverty." (The poverty rate in 1996

---

* Statistics Canada, *The Daily*, December 10, 1997.
† Andrew Sharpe and Lars Osberg, October 1998, and Statistics Canada, *Survey of Consumer Finance*.

FIGURE 7

Poverty Rates for Single Women with Children

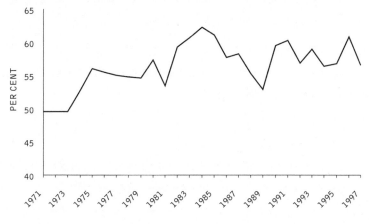

SOURCE: Statistics Canada, *The Daily*, December 10, 1997.

Despite extraordinarily high poverty rates, most poor single women with children have had their increased child benefits clawed back by the provinces.

FIGURE 8

Poverty Rates for Single-Parent Families

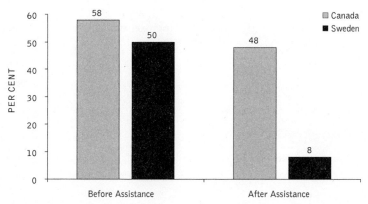

In most European countries poverty rates are well below Canada's thanks to government social programs.

for heads of families with a university degree was only 7.7 per cent.) For those who blame lone-parent poverty figures on increasing numbers of divorces and separations, it's interesting to note that the percentage of lone-parent families in Canada in 1997 was just about the same as it was in 1931. Of course divorce and separation lead to lone-parent families, and there have been sizable increases in both. But only the most extreme fundamentalists would consider legislation to keep husbands and wives together against their will.

The British Columbia Campaign 2000 produced an interesting comparison in its 1998 report (see Figure 8 on preceding page):

This one chart in itself speaks volumes.

The figures for unattached individuals below the Statistics Canada low-income line are also very high. Here are the percentages.*

1980	43.5%	1989	37.1
1981	42.0	1990	37.4
1982	42.6	1991	39.4
1983	46.3	1992	39.8
1984	43.8	1993	40.5
1985	43.2	1994	40.6
1986	41.5	1995	39.3
1987	40.6	1996	40.2
1988	40.4	1997	39.6

Not as bad as the figures for lone-parent families, but pretty appalling nevertheless.

---

* *Income distribution by size in Canada*, 1996, Cat. #13-207-XPB.

"With the Wave of a Pen":
Defining Poverty Away

I asked four inner-city school principals how things in their schools were different from schools in the wealthier districts in the city. They looked at each other, laughed for a moment, then began talking non-stop, frequently interrupting each other. In their schools the kids often came to school hungry. A great many were poorly dressed. In the winter few had adequate warm clothing. Many suffered severe emotional stress. There were no field trips. They couldn't afford to belong to the community leagues. No movies, no going to see hockey games. There were no computers in their homes. Few books. Some kids even came to school not knowing what a book is. In the summer there was no place to go. By mid-June many of the children became distressed; without the school lunch program, what would they eat?

The list went on and on and on. After about half an hour I asked them how many kids they had in their school, and how many played organized hockey. They answered quickly, one after the other: "240 – none." "220 – none." "306 – one." "198 – none."

What follows is a brief look at how poverty is defined in Canada.

Like many other countries, Canada does not have an official definition of poverty. A friend who works as a volunteer in a food bank says that the definition is easy: it's not having nearly enough money for food, rent, or clothing, or for things like personal-care needs, school supplies, and the like. She says:

> If you came to work with me you'd stop all the damn academic nonsense about low-income cut-offs, low-income measurements, market basket measures, absolute poverty, poverty gaps, and the rest of that garbage. I'm sick to death of bureaucrats and economists arguing whether the poor should be able to buy toothpaste, be entitled to bus passes, reading material, or school supplies. If they came to work with me for a few days they'd quickly forget all their fancy definitions and *finally* do something important about the poor.

For Brian Mulroney's Conservative governments (1984-1993), there wasn't much of a problem solving poverty in Canada. All you had to do was redefine it along the lines suggested by the far-right Fraser Institute's philosophy (poverty in Canada is greatly exaggerated) and the problem would be solved.

Now the Chrétien government, ever resolute and faithful followers of Brian Mulroney's policies, are considering a new Market Basket Measure as a possible official poverty line. We'll look at that measurement in the next chapter.

When the Fraser Institute commenced its assault against the poor in 1992, Andy Mitchell and Brigitte Kitchen nicely put the right-wing neo-neanderthals in perspective:

> The poor in Canada must have breathed a sigh of relief when they heard from the Fraser Institute that rather than being poor, the majority of them [had] . . . values and expectations that are too high.
>
> With the wave of a pen, the Fraser Institute attempts to redefine poverty so as to transport 70 per cent of Canada's poor into the middle class.

Its recent report, *Poverty in Canada*, creates a "poverty line" which strips the poor of anything more than the bare necessities of survival. . . .

Why launch an attack against the most vulnerable in society? The Fraser Institute, by [publishing] such a report, once again diverts us from the real issues we face as a nation: how to build a society which is productive and inclusive for all Canadians.*

Mitchell and social-policy analyst Richard Shillington of Ottawa elaborate further:

A close look at how the Fraser Institute assesses "basic needs" is chilling. A chapter devoted to costing the body's minimum caloric requirements estimates the weekly cost of food for an elderly woman at about $22, including 14 servings of fruit assumed to cost about $2.60.

Nothing is allocated for children's toys, books, writing materials or anything not considered to be a physical necessity. . . . No money is provided for school supplies.

Mitchell and Shillington suggest that there is little question about the motivation of the Fraser Institute in publishing the book.

The debate over the measurement of poverty is part of the attack of the right on the social programs that have defined us as Canadians and distinguished us from the Darwinian country to the south. The measure of poverty is a measure of society and of ourselves.

Poverty in a wealthy society calls for a response; a call that the siren voices of the Fraser Institute for lower taxes and less government don't want to hear.

So how do we fairly define poverty? We know that our right-wing fanatics, in columnist David Crane's words, "define most poverty out of

---

* *Toronto Star*, July 30, 1992.

existence." It's clear that the left, the centre, and the right have different concepts of what the necessities of life constitute. Crane puts the question well: "Most Canadians . . . would probably agree . . . that tackling poverty is about more than providing a bare subsistence existence. We want children, for example, to have a full opportunity to develop into healthy adults capable of realizing their potential. This is not only morally the right thing to want. It is also important for social and economic reasons because we are dealing with the quality of our future adult population."*

Michael Goldberg of the British Columbia Social Planning and Research Council (SPARC) and Jane Pulkingham produced an excellent paper, *Defining Poverty in Canada*, in January 1999. In defining poverty, several principles are imperative; among them, "the measures should be inclusive and include sufficient funds so that people can make choices on ways of participating in community life. . . ." The paper goes on to discuss various ideologies, including "the most dominant ideology . . . *laissez-faire* individualism" and the concept of "the deserving poor" and "the undeserving poor" whose circumstances were deemed to be "the result of personal failings or weaknesses." There is a need to avoid providing these undeserving poor "with sufficient income or other forms of assistance which would only encourage them in their already bad habits." This "dominant" ideology prevails in much of our society and "is reflected in the differing definitions and ways of measuring poverty."

The alternative "inclusive" approach considers "physical, emotional, social and spiritual needs of individuals and families . . . measures [that] argue that poverty is not simply about physical survival, but it is about being able to participate in the day-to-day life" of the community. Should poor people be able to subscribe to a newspaper? Afford a telephone? Afford the cost of continuing education? Should they be able to pay for a haircut or bus ticket? Or at least to be able to pay for some extracurricular school programs for their children?

Goldberg and Pulkingham conclude with an important "note of caution. All of the poverty-line measures in Canada have been based on the assumption that there was universal access to comprehensive health care, including prescription drugs; access to quality child care such that

---

* *Toronto Star*, November 4, 1998.

subsidies included the full cost of child care; and access to public education without fees. Any poverty line would have to be significantly modified if the trend to reducing core universal services in health care, child care, and public education was not reversed."

I will take only a brief look at the debate about the various measurements of poverty in Canada. Those who wish further details should consult Appendix One.

If we choose the Market Basket Measure now being touted as a likely official poverty line, will one less child go to school hungry? Will one more poor mother be able to afford quality child care? Will one more little boy or girl be able to afford to buy a few books? Will one more father be able to take his kids to a hockey game? Based on our dismal record in the past, I doubt it.

The new measure, if it is adopted, will magically reduce poverty rates in Canada. There are lots of politicians and government bureaucrats who like the idea, for obvious reasons. But, many, including myself, have grave reservations. Before reviewing the Market Basket Measure (see the next chapter), let's take a very quick look at some other poverty measurements.

For more than thirty-five years Statistics Canada has published Low income cut-offs (LICOs), which measure "the size, incidence and composition of the low income population. . . . LICOs reflect a well-defined methodology that identifies those who are substantially worse off than the average." Those are Statistics Canada's words. Note the word "substantially." We're not talking here about people who are moderately less well off. We're talking about the poor.

In the words of Dr. Ivan Fellegi, head of Statistics Canada, the goal in establishing the LICOs was to produce a measurement of Canadians "in the most straitened circumstances . . . the group who are the most disadvantaged."*

While Statistics Canada has never officially endorsed the LICOs as a specific measure of poverty, "substantially worse off than the average" and "the most straitened circumstances" surely speak for themselves.

An alternative, Low Income Measure (LIM), is based on one-half the median income and was evaluated by Statistics Canada as a

---

* Telephone conversation, February 2, 1999.

replacement for the LICOs. But few now pay much attention to LIM since the formula has been shown to have major drawbacks.

In 1998 Statistics Canada reported that "while the total population increased 6% between 1990 and 1995, the low-income population increased 29%. There were 1.2 million more persons below the low income cut-offs in 1995 than in 1990. . . . One in four children under six lived in low-income families in 1995, compared with one in five in 1990."*

Note that between 1990 and 1995, on average some 1,267,200 families (of a total of 7,784,865 economic families)† were classified by Statistics Canada as low-income. Their average family earnings amounted to only $5,328. Transfer payments provided, on average, another $7,505. So about 16.3 per cent of all economic families in Canada averaged under $13,000 in total annual income! Of much interest is the fact that there has been a large increase in "the working poor. In 1995, more than half (52.7 per cent) of low-income families . . . worked but remained poor because they earned low wages and/or could find only seasonal or part-time work."**

Yet, incredibly, when we come to the chapter *The War Against the Poor*, we'll find people urging that there should be even more low-wage jobs and demanding that minimum wages should be *lowered* in Canada!

In 1997, Statistics Canada estimated the number of persons below the LICOs at 5,222,000, or 17.5 per cent of the population, compared to 3,770,000, or 14.1% in 1989, a huge deterioration.

According to the National Council of Welfare's spring 1998 report, by the end of 1996 the child poverty rate was the highest it had been in seventeen years. For single-parent mothers, the rate was above 65 per cent, and for single-parent mothers with children under the age of seven, 81 per cent lived in poverty.†† Of all of those classified as living in poverty, almost 300,000 families and over 400,000 unattached people had incomes that were *less than half* the LICOs poverty line.

---

* *The Daily*, May 12, 1998.
† "An economic family," a Statistics Canada term, "consists of all persons in a household who are related to each other by blood, marriage, common-law or adoption."
** Caledon Institute of Social Policy, *Precarious Labour Market Fuels Rising Poverty*, December 1996.
†† *Poverty Profile 1996*, Spring 1998.

To Market, to Market,
to Buy a New Measure
(And It Won't Cost
Taxpayers a Dime!)

She's an amazing woman, probably in her mid-fifties, on the job as Institute Director for almost twenty years. There's a daycare down the hall, a food bank and a clothes bank down another hall, a job-search centre at the front of the building. Every day one of the staff rounds up yesterday's leftover buns and muffins and donuts from Second Cup and Tim Hortons for the food bank.

She says anyone who doesn't believe that those who show up every morning really want work should come an hour before the Institute opens and watch the men, and some women, stand in a long line in twenty or thirty below, hoping there might be something for them when the few jobs are posted on the bulletin board.

She works about seventy hours a week. The depth of poverty she faces every day would severely depress most people, but somehow she keeps a big smile on her face. I asked her if she has noticed any change in those who depend on the Institute. She said there were three obvious changes. First, there are many more men and women every day. Second, there are many more who are mentally handicapped since they emptied the hospitals. Third, there are more hungry kids and more kids who are poorly clothed.

"POVERTY RATE WOULD PLUNGE TO 12% FROM 17%," reads one headline. "DEFINITION OF POVERTY MUST REFLECT REALITY, CHRÉTIEN SAYS," reads another.* According to some estimates, adopting the Market Basket Measure (MBM) would lift 1.5 million Canadians out of poverty and "halve the annual cost to Ottawa of attempting to meet Canada's commitment to wipe out child poverty by 2000, to $3.3 billion from $6.6 billion."†

"CANADA REDEFINES POVERTY," reads another headline in *The National Post*. Eric Beauchesne tells us that "the federal, provincial and territorial governments have been quietly working on a scheme to slash the official poverty level in Canada by nearly 30% or 1.5 million people. . . . It won't cost taxpayers a dime and may even save them money. . . ."

Our governments are thinking about replacing the LICOs with a new Market Basket Measure of poverty. According to the proposed measure, a family of two adults and two children that could eat nutritious meals, buy some clothing for work and social occasions, and rent an apartment at a reasonable cost would not be deemed poor, providing they have additional income equal to 60 per cent of the combined cost of food and clothing to cover other expenses such as school supplies, household and personal-care expenses, telephone and transportation costs, as well as some reading, recreation, and entertainment expenses.

Sounds reasonable.

The MBM would produce a national poverty rate of about 12 per cent, a substantial reduction from the LICOs figure of almost 18 per cent. But as David Ross, head of the Canadian Council on Social Development puts it, coming up with "a new measure will not solve our poverty problem. The solution to poverty lies in society caring enough to actually *do* something about it . . . lowering the poverty rate with the stroke of a pen is not going to reverse our decline."**

Ross underlines the important point that all poverty lines are relative. But many people have quite different concepts about what

---

* Southam Newspapers, December 15, 1998.
† *National Post*, December 15, 1998.
** Letter to *Globe and Mail*, December 22, 1998.

should be in the market basket. "For example, is the objective simply to stave off starvation," or are we *really* hoping to provide a nutritious, healthy diet?

As to the validity of the LICOs approach, Ross makes another important point: "Instead of relying on economists at the Fraser Institute or committees of public servants to define what is necessary, why not ask average Canadians? Since 1976 Gallup was doing just that – asking Canadians what they thought was the least amount of money a family of four needs to get along in their community. Over the last 20 years their answer has been almost bang on the LICO measure. . . ."

So, what will be the consequences if we officially adopt the MBM as a new definition of poverty? Will there be fewer people sleeping under bridges? Will there be fewer Canadians dependent on food banks? Will there be more employed in full-time, secure jobs? According to Richard Shillington:

> Many in the political elite consider LICOs just too generous. . . . However, no federal politician has to live on [what] is considered "excessive" for a single mother. . . . The Market Basket Measure limits our obligations to low-income children. . . . It acknowledges that children living on their budget will feel excluded from Canadian society because there will not be funds for things that many Canadian kids take for granted. Children living at the government's new line will, over time, fall progressively further behind the Canadian norm, but will not officially be poor.
>
> The government admits that its Market Basket Measure reduces poverty immediately by about a third – without improving the standard of living of a single child.
>
> The label "poverty" is irrelevant to the lives of children – it's deprivation and their real and perceived life chances that matter.
>
> The poverty line should reflect social goals for Canada. The MBM will be preferred by those who see our obligation to children as a basket – like a Christmas hamper. Those who seek equality of opportunity for children will want a relative measure which compares low-income children to the norm.

The new government measure implies a new, more limited social contract. A country as wealthy as Canada is lowering its expectations not because we can't afford social supports, but to make inequality acceptable.

Is this what the House of Commons had in mind in 1989, when it passed the unanimous resolution to end child poverty by the year 2000?*

The Market Basket Measure, which is still being developed, has already been endorsed in principle by provincial social-services ministers. The final MBM report should be available at about the same time this book is published. It's far too early to determine the impact of officially adopting the MBM, but there is an increasing number of social activists who already strongly oppose it.

Most poor people in Canada live *well* below the LICOs line. In 1997, poor single mothers with children were almost $8,000 below the line; poor couples with children were over $10,000 below the line. Virtually all economists who measure poverty in Canada agree that since 1989 the poverty gap has increased substantially.

I think we should consider the proposed MBM in the context of what you will read in the chapters that follow.

---

* *Toronto Star*, January 29, 1999.

Hunger in Canada:
"Pay the Rent or Feed the Kids"

*Don't worry about LICO. None of the people have been any-
where near the LICO line for a long, long time.*

> – Julia Bass, executive director,
> Canadian Association of Food Banks.

*One mother told me that it takes hours to walk to the food bank.
"Young families are being torn apart for lack of food. The government just isn't listening."*

*I asked some food-bank people if there was enough food.
The answers were always the same: "Never! We're always
juggling, always having to cut back, always appealing for
more help."*

*I asked if people were embarrassed to come to the food
bank. "Many, many are reluctant. It's a last resort. They've
gone through so many unpleasant intermediate stages. Sometimes they don't want their children to know. They disguise the
bags. They don't want their neighbours to know that someone
on the block has to go to the food bank."*

In the words of Graham Riches, director of the School of Social Work
and Family Studies at the University of British Columbia:

Food banks have served to depoliticize the issue of hunger in
Canada by undermining governments' legislated obligations to
guarantee adequate welfare benefits and by obviating the need

35

for responsible public action. . . . Food banks allow us to believe that hunger is being solved. Yet this is not so. . . . continued food bank activity essentially depoliticizes the issue of hunger in society by legitimizing it as a matter for charitable concern rather than social justice.*

And from *Children's Feeding Programs in Atlantic Canada*:

Governments refuse to acknowledge the structural conditions that cause poverty and food insecurity for children in Canada. Children's feeding programs are a band-aid measure to support the nutritional health of poor children. Neither providers nor recipients seem to ask why a significant number of members of society cannot adequately feed or clothe themselves or their children or why their full participation in society is denied. Feeding programs, intended to provide food to hungry children, hide the roots of child poverty and give those who have the power to change it reasons for doing nothing.

Why do feeding programs mushroom? Even in middle-class areas? It may be that governmental cut-backs, designed to force individuals to buy their social needs privately rather than being provided collectively enable other institutions to step in, thus side-stepping governmental plans. Just as food banks depoliticize hunger, children's feeding programs depoliticize child hunger. They have given permission to a charitable response to be institutionalized, a response that privatizes the public concern over children's inequalities in Canada.†

In my interviews for this book, I asked the heads of several food banks in various parts of Canada what if any changes they had observed in the people who must rely on them for emergency assistance. The answers were remarkably similar. They all saw more severe poverty, much greater destitution, a higher percentage of children and youths under eighteen, more working poor, more people who were hesitant about

---

* Hunger in Canada in *First World Hunger*, St. Martin's Press Inc., 1997.
† L. McIntyre, K. Travers, J. Dayle. Final report to Health Canada, NHRDP NO. 6603-1461-201, 1997.

crossing the food-bank threshold, and more formerly middle-class men and women embarrassed about asking for food.

In 1981, Gerard Kennedy (now an Ontario MPP), local church groups, and others established Canada's first food bank, in Edmonton, in the Prince of Wales Armoury. Most of the food was donated by food companies and was edible, but not saleable surplus inventory. Some were opposed to the move. They feared it might give government the opportunity to slough off its social responsibilities. The new food bank was supposed to be temporary. There would be no food hampers. Perhaps a total of some two hundred people would be helped.

By 1998, more than 17,000 people a month relied on Edmonton's food bank. The number had more than doubled from 1993 when Alberta's Conservative government began its drastic social-assistance cutbacks. Ask the staff at the food bank what they now see: "More despair, more human tragedy." About half of those who rely on the food bank are under eighteen.

Eight years after Canada's first food bank opened, in the spring of 1989, over 330,000 Canadians were receiving assistance from food banks across the country.

Six years later, in the words of Loren Fried, executive director of the North York Harvest Food Bank, "In 1995, when Paul Martin replaced the Canada Assistance Plan with the Canada Health and Social Transfer, he unleashed the most destructive chain reaction of government domino downloading and government cost-cutting of welfare and social spending that has ever been inflicted on Canada's poor and marginalized population."[*]

That same year, Toronto's Daily Bread Food Bank reported that 78 per cent of two-parent families on welfare – up from 23 per cent in 1995 – must use food money to help pay the rent, and one in four food-bank users must skip a daily meal, while 5 per cent reported that they frequently had to let their children go without food.[†]

At about the same time, the same food bank reported that "people are now forced to spend more of their basic [welfare] allowance on rent, . . . recipients' ability to pay for food has been diminished in some cases

---

[*] *Globe and Mail*, December 6, 1997.

[†] Michael Valpy, *Globe and Mail*, October 3, 1996.

by as much as 50 percent." As many as 88 per cent of recipients reported they did not have enough money for basic necessities and almost 22 per cent missed meals on a regular basis. Almost half had no telephone. A segment in the Daily Bread Food Bank's report speaks for itself: "The Single Mom's Dilemma: Pay the rent or feed the kids."*

The food bank's conclusion? "Among welfare recipients assisted by food banks in Metropolitan Toronto, single persons, single parents and couples with children now face a shelter crisis precipitated by a reduction in the maximum social assistance shelter allowances. . . ." Most of those assisted by the food bank paid rent in excess of the shelter allowances. As a result, they are forced to pay for their rent by cutting back on food.

The following year, 1997, a *Toronto Star* editorial spelled out what was happening in Toronto:

For the fourth year in a row, the Daily Bread Food Bank has come up short in its spring food drive. More disturbing than the drop in donations is the explanation offered by food bank executive director Sue Cox: "It is no longer a shock that there is hunger in our community."

Sixteen years ago, when the first food bank opened its doors in Edmonton, Canadians reacted with horror. No economic downturn since the Great Depression had forced the poor to turn to charity for food. The recession of the early '80s is long gone. But food banks – hundreds of them – remain. No longer are they a source of shock or shame. They're an accepted, almost commonplace, part of the urban landscape.

But poverty is not on Canada's political agenda. . . . Nor is it a topic of public debate.

Most of the clients at Daily Bread are household heads in their late 30s, with at least a high school education and a strong employment history. They want to work, but there are no jobs.

These people are not victims of a recession; the economy

---

* *Can Welfare Recipients Pay Rent and Eat Too?* September 19, 1996.

is growing, corporate profits are healthy, exports are booming and interest rates are low. They are victims of a society becoming even more polarized between rich and poor. In good times or bad, they remain trapped at the bottom of the economic pyramid.*

In 1997, the Daily Bread Food Bank reported that more and more children were relying on them and the degree of hardship evident was greater than seen before. While the average annual household income in the Greater Toronto Area was almost $66,000, for food-bank users it was $11,000. For 67 per cent of recipients, the cost of their rent was more than their social-assistance shelter limit, so a portion of their food budget went for rent. About one in three food-bank users could not afford a telephone. Many could not afford public transit. A large number missed meals regularly.

In the fall of 1997, the Canadian Association of Food Banks' (CAFB) *Hunger Count* reported that some 670,000 men, women, and children received emergency food assistance in March of that year, and children accounted for around 42 per cent of those assisted. Since the association's annual *Hunger Count* began in 1989, the number of recipients more than doubled. "There is little doubt that hunger is now more widespread in Canada than a decade ago."†

Note that while the members of the CAFB distribute more than one hundred million pounds of food annually across Canada, the association received no financial assistance from any government. Canadians now turn to food banks in 508 communities across the country, compared to 150 in 1989. Meanwhile, as we shall see later in more detail, federal transfer payments to the provinces for social services declined from $556 per capita in 1989 to $312 in 1997 (constant dollars).

The December 1997 report of the Daily Bread Food Bank, *A Common Hunger*, is revealing:

Over the last 15 years it has become increasingly difficult for low-income households to feed themselves on a secure basis.

---

* April 11, 1997.
† *Hunger Count, 1997*: A Report on Economic Food Assistance in Canada.

... The traditional response to the problem of household food insecurity – food bank charity as a substitute for public policy – is untenable.

In Toronto, some thirty percent of food bank recipients say they have no money for food at least two days a week. Thirty-eight percent of welfare recipients had insufficient money for food at least two days a week.

Incredibly, after the Ontario government made severe cuts to welfare assistance, government officials asked for a list of food banks in the province so hungry people could be directed to the nearest one. By the end of 1997, food-bank use in Ontario had increased by another 30 per cent over two years earlier. In the spring of 1999 the Daily Bread Food Bank found itself facing a large shortfall in their food donations from the public.

Some two weeks before Christmas 1997, twenty-year-old Jennifer Whatley wrote about her experience as a food-bank volunteer:

It was a pleasant evening in December. Inside our home, Christmas presents overflowed from under the tree.

My mother and I had come to volunteer at a food bank.

Piled all over the floor, covered in a dusty white flour, were enormous boxes of donated food that had come in by the truck-load from across the city . . . boxes were stacked to the ceiling. They were full of food considered "waste material" by grocery stores. There were hundreds of dented cans and other foods with labels that read "Damaged."

The workers kept replenishing these stocks as people pushed their shopping carts around them. I tried hard not to look at the people shopping. I wondered, "What kind of people are forced to rely on a food bank?"

I felt strange as I sorted through canned and packaged goods. There was every kind of bean you could imagine and dozens of Kraft Dinner boxes. I could not believe that people would actually have to eat this ill-assorted food for Christmas.

I stole a glance at the shoppers close to me. An old man who could have been anyone's grandfather. A woman and her two young children who might have played in the same parks my brother did. A heavyset women accompanied by a teenager who could have gone to my school.

I began to wonder how people wind up at a food bank. I knew there must be a million stories here, in the lined faces of these shoppers with crumpled lists and dusty shoes.[*]

In April 1998, the *Toronto Star* reported that a Health Canada survey indicated that 57 per cent of Toronto-area mothers using food banks continued to suffer from hunger. The study concluded, "Charitable food assistance programs cannot compensate for seriously inadequate social programs." The major impact of the Ontario government's 21.6-percent cut in welfare payments in 1995 fell on poor women and children who were forced "to live at such levels of deprivation." A few days later the *Star* editorialized:

Empty bins [and] stark evidence that the Easter food drive was coming up painfully short. . . . Why the shortfall in these times of growing prosperity? Are we too busy with our own lives to give? Too indifferent to the increasing demands on our time and wallets? Whatever the reason, the sad fact is that people will suffer, turned away empty-handed when they go seeking food. Food banks are the providers of last resort. Turned away here, means people will go hungry. . . . No one goes to a food bank by choice . . . some 50,000 of them are children.[†]

Meanwhile, back in Edmonton, the number of hampers handed out increased to more than 17,000 per month in addition to over 200,000 meals and snacks per month. The indefatigable director of the main food bank in the city, Marjorie Bencz, reported large increases in the number of children, single mothers, and working poor. "As rents go up, they run out of money for food." I asked her if, in conservative Alberta, she ever received negative calls. She said it was very important not to overemphasize these because there were so many wonderful people

[*] December 9, 1997, © Young People's Press.
[†] April 22, 1998.

who helped, but yes, there were calls like "Stop helping those lazy, good-for-nothing people," "Don't feed those Indians," "Why are you promoting those leeches?" and "Why the hell do they keep having all those children?" She said she was disturbed by how many people shift the blame for their own problems to the poor.

By 1998, food-bank needs in Ontario were 31 per cent higher than three years earlier, "despite economic improvements and lower unemployment rates in most communities."*

In March 1998, "at least 330,000 people in Ontario needed food relief," the same number who received assistance all across Canada in 1989. There were "some 123,000 children in Ontario who live in such acute poverty that their families cannot afford sufficient food for them to eat. . . . The number does *not* include those children who receive meals in breakfast programs or family meal programs. Studies in Toronto suggest that at least 30% of food bank children go hungry at least once a week, and often more frequently."

How much food do people get? "Typically, food banks give a three-day supply of food for each person in the household, and limit access to once a month." In some Ontario food banks, the maximum number of visits allowed is only three per year.

In the conclusion of its annual report, the Ontario Association of Food Banks minces no words:

> Hunger . . . exists in Ontario – and exists more frequently than we would like to believe. The rising economic tide has failed to reach many individuals and the combination of lowered income from welfare and part-time work with still-high unemployment has meant little relief for food banks and those they serve. . . . The past year has seen declining donations; those who have been struggling for many years to close the gap left by inadequate government programs are beginning to "burn out" and there are reports of food banks closing in some communities.

For Toronto's Daily Bread Food Bank the situation is similar. With Ontario's "meaner" welfare system and Ottawa's unemployment

* The Ontario Association of Food Banks, *The Ontario Food Bank Report*, 1998.

insurance cutbacks, "Most unemployed people are now on welfare. . . . And the number of people who must survive on part-time, poorly paid and short-term work is increasing. . . . Six out of ten food bank recipients have at least a high school education, and one-third of these are also college or university graduates. . . . Two-thirds of households spend more than half their income on rent. . . . One in five parents experience severe food deprivation (no money for food) at least two days a week."

And in conclusion, "Hunger is a health issue: if people cannot work, we must provide adequate incomes to keep them healthy. To ignore the health issues is to invite higher health-care costs in the future."

Just a few blocks from Premier Ralph Klein's condominium over-looking the North Saskatchewan River Valley in Edmonton, Marjorie Bencz reports that due to government cutbacks to social programs, the situation is bleak. "More and more staff across the province, including some of our best top people, are burned out." The provincial legislature is only six blocks away, but no cabinet minister ever visits the food bank, no government MLAs, no deputy ministers. Certainly not the premier or the minister of social services.

The volume of food available is in no way keeping up with demand. There are now seventy-four communities in Alberta with food banks that provide food for some 53,000 Albertans. Between 1993 and 1996 the demand for food more than doubled in Edmonton, but available resources increased by only 5 per cent. "This has meant substantial hamper cutbacks, both in quantity and quality."

Should the large increases in food-bank usage come as a surprise? Hardly. In fact, they could easily have been predicted. They are a direct result of federal and provincial cutbacks to social assistance programs, and result from poor wages and inadequate or non-existent benefits for part-time workers, tightening welfare and unemployment insurance eli-gibility regulations, inadequate assistance for single mothers and the disabled, and increasing rental costs.

Professor Graham Riches in his paper *Abolishing Food Banks* writes:

We know from our experience and from studies in Canada that food banks have quickly become substitutes for inadequate financial assistance benefits; that they often run out of food and turn people away; that they cannot guarantee nutritious food; that they cannot maintain the level of volunteering that is required; and that despite these facts their continued existence allows the public to believe that the problem of hunger is being solved. But, as we know, this is not the case. What we know is that as the food banks have become institutionalised, they increasingly allow the federal, provincial and municipal governments to look the other way and enable them to avoid addressing the fundamental issues of the breakdown of public welfare in Canada.*

For the National Anti-Poverty Organization (NAPO), there is little doubt about the place of food banks in Canadian society: "Hunger is a political issue. The increased use of food banks is a shocking and barbarous testament to what is happening to Canada's social safety net. Slashing social assistance benefits and eligibility, cutting unemployment insurance, high unemployment, a lack of affordable housing and child care, stagnating and declining real wages are all contributors to the shame that is hunger in Canada."†

Julia Bass, executive director of the CAFB, as always speaks to the point: "Food banks were supposed to be a short-term, emergency response to an acute crisis, not a major social service for a substantial proportion of the population as they are now. . . . We've gone backwards in the last five to ten years; this used to be a society with a sense of community that took care of people. . . . We at food banks are at the end of the food chain; we know this is not working."**

In March 1998, the number of Canadians forced to rely on food banks during the month increased to almost 720,000.

On the West Coast, the effects of poverty can be seen in the food-bank lineups. The Greater Vancouver Food Bank Society was established in 1982 in response to concern about increasing hunger, serving 8,000 in its first year of operation. Since then, the number of people needing food assistance has increased to the point where the food bank now serves, on average, about 8,000 men, women, and children *every*

---

* University of Regina, Faculty of Social Work, *Canadian Review of Social Policy*, 1989.
† NAPO, November 1998.
** Canadian Press, November 14, 1997.

week. Pat Burns, executive director of the food bank, reports that the number of recipients has increased at the rate of 20 per cent per year for the past four years. "We see an ongoing need to help people with food who would otherwise go hungry or put themselves or their children in risk of serious malnutrition," says Burns. "But we always need ever more resources to do a better job."

In Ottawa, about 30,000 people receive assistance from the food bank each month. Almost half of them are children. In our nation's capital, about 20 per cent of all children live below the LICOs poverty lines.

And in booming Calgary, one of the wealthiest cities in the country, Jim Cunningham of the *Calgary Herald* reports: "More than 6,600 Calgary children don't get enough to eat every day. . . . Another 9,500 young people experience hunger on an intermittent basis. . . . The problem of child hunger is so serious in Calgary, it is outstripping the ability of aid groups to counter it."*

---

* April 6, 1999.

From the Hungry to the Homeless

According to one of Ralph Klein's favourite cabinet ministers, former Social Services Minister Lyle Oberg, street people are there by choice. Meanwhile, a Calgary task force reported that the city's homeless population included thousands of working people who could not find affordable accommodation in an overheated economy.* And Al Palladini, Mike Harris's minister of Economic Development, Trade and Tourism, said, "Street beggars are blemishing Toronto's image as a tourist attraction, and the time has come to make them move along. . . . Some of these people are basically doing it because they want to do it. . . . Some of them should be moved out of there."†

Neo-neanderthals in power.

How is it that so many well-to-do Canadian cities now have the terrible tragedy of so many homeless? In city after city the problem is described as "a scandal," "a tragedy," "a disaster." And what has been the response from government? As columnist Jeffrey Simpson noted, "Premier Mike Harris replied, 'To say that government should build more housing and have more boondoggles and ripoffs is not a solution.'"**

---

* *Edmonton Journal*, February 8, 1999.
† *National Post*, January 12, 1999.
** *Globe and Mail*, November 4, 1998.

As the federal and provincial governments cut back on their social allowances and housing programs, the pressure on the voluntary sector has increased well beyond its capacity to provide anywhere near adequate relief. Most major cities now have jam-packed hostels and are forced regularly to turn many people away. The most prominent reaction of government has been indifference. But, as Simpson pointed out, "Presumably few of the homeless vote. . . ."

In 1993 the federal government withdrew from new social housing. The provinces have had, for the most part, mediocre records relating to the housing needs of the poor. As Aron Spector of Carleton University in Ottawa has pointed out:

> The implications of an increasing dependence upon the private rental market as the source of shelter for low-income Canadians have been made abundantly clear in the 1990s. . . .
> In 1995 households in the lowest income quintile renting non-subsidized housing spent an average of 54 percent of their income for shelter . . . and increasingly many low-income households are finding themselves with no option except emergency shelters or the street.
>
> Federal cutbacks in social housing have been justified as part of the effort to restore federal finances. At the same time, the federal and various provincial governments have encouraged middle- and upper-income households to become home owners by increasing access to the mortgage market, by sheltering savings to be used to purchase new housing and by allowing the temporary use of registered retirement savings as down payments. It is less well known that once a middle- or upper-income household owns a home, the existing income tax system shelters the resulting benefits. This presentation shows that tax revenue lost from middle- and upper-income Canadian households far exceeds the modest subsidies to low- and moderate-income households who are fortunate enough to find accommodations in social housing. As a result, the costs of programs that encourage home ownership more than offset the savings purported to have been made by reducing the commitment to low- and moderate-income households through social housing.

Curtailing subsidized social housing programs while continuing to provide tax advantages to home owners is . . . a very
selective way of chanting the mantra of deficit reduction. It
continues an erosion of the social safety-net, while accentuat-
ing regressive income-based inequality. . . . It is clear that the
present governments have chosen political expediency over the
welfare of low- and moderate-income Canadians.*

By October 1997 the increasing numbers of homeless were a highly
visible problem. "Emergency shelters across Canada are bracing for the
chilly blast of winter and realizing that they do not have enough space
to accommodate the hundreds of people now living on the streets. . . .
About 5,350 homeless people now sleep in Toronto's shelters each night
. . . the city is bracing for more. . . . In Vancouver the lack of services for
the homeless has finally caught up with us. . . . There's no place for the
homeless to stay."†

In another succinct analysis of poor people's shelter problems,
NAPO sums it up: "Shelter is the largest single budgetary expenditure of
most Canadian households – especially low income households." NAPO
quotes a 1995 report of the House of Commons Standing Committee on
Human Resources Development:** "If people do not have access to
safe, adequate, and affordable housing, they will have difficulty gaining
control over other aspects of their lives. A good home can provide a
proper study environment for children, the stability and support so critical to adults going back to school, and safety for the elderly."

Moreover, "Canadian Mortgage and Housing Corporation (CMHC)
estimated that in 1991 one in eight Canadian households lived in resi-
dences below acceptable housing standards. Given the dramatic rise in
the need for shelters and hostels for the homeless in the past five years,
NAPO can only assume that current statistics would be much worse."

"Subsidized housing has become a rare commodity in Canada . . .
federal funding for new social housing units, with the exception of
housing on Indian reserves and a series of short-term initiatives, was

* Institute for Research on Public Policy, *Policy Options*, November 1997.
† *Globe and Mail*, October 23, 1997.
** *Canada: Security, Opportunities and Fairness: Canadians renewing their social programs.*

terminated in 1993. The budget for existing social housing was capped in 1994, and subsequently reduced in 1995 and 1996. Homelessness has become a disaster in Canada . . . the visible homeless live on the street, in shelters, in motels on government vouchers and in institutions including hospitals and jails. The invisible homeless inhabit abandoned buildings and vehicles, trade sex for temporary shelter and sleep on the floor of other people's homes. . . . By conservative estimates there are over 200,000 Canadians who are homeless, according to the Toronto Disaster Relief Committee.

"Homelessness in Canada is growing at an alarming rate. As the numbers of homeless people rise, the discrimination against them from middle and upper income earners also increases. This is evidenced by Canadian cities that have introduced or passed anti-panhandling by-laws. In most urban centres homeless people attempt to generate some income by begging for money on downtown streets. Some cities define this begging as a problem and have passed laws to make it illegal to do so. The resources being devoted to developing and enforcing such legislation could be used to address the real problems; poverty and lack of affordable, safe housing."

Winnipeg, Vancouver, Sudbury, Oshawa, Charlottetown, and Kingston are among Canadian communities that have banned or tightly restricted panhandling and loitering. Legislation includes fines of up to $1,000 and jail terms. In the words of Arthur Schafer of the University of Manitoba's Centre of Professional and Applied Ethics,

Sweeping the existence of beggars under a legal carpet is the wrong way to deal with this complex problem. To deny anyone the right to ask another person for help, in a public place, would seem to violate our society's commitment to freedom of expression. We ought to be especially concerned about any law that would curtail debate about social policies affecting the poor, the homeless, the unemployed.*

Here is Cathy Crowe in the *Toronto Star*:

* *Globe and Mail*, February 15, 1999.

Hostels are overcrowded and intolerable. The homeless are forced to stay in temporary emergency shelters such as church basements or school gymnasiums. Each night homeless people follow the path of a forced migration to whichever temporary facility happens to be open that night. Then the spring comes and the programs shut down. Once again alleyways, grates, squats, parks and under bridges become "home."

To be homeless is to risk one's mental health. . . . Severe depression emerges.

The homeless situation is worsening daily at an alarming rate. . . . Any delay in firmly and massively responding will only contribute to compounding the present crisis of suffering and death which is already an epidemic which no civilized society can tolerate.*

According to the Daily Bread Food Bank in Toronto, with the increasingly prevalent combination of very low incomes and high housing costs, "people are caught in a choice between eating and paying rent."† Moreover, very often there is no money to pay a rental deposit, especially a first and last month deposit.

Anne Golden's 291-page task-force report on the homeless in Toronto, released in January 1999, is an outstanding document which has received much praise. The four task-force panelists tell us that "our report demonstrates that the problems are solvable and the solutions are available. On that basis we have a moral obligation to take the actions needed" including increasing shelter benefits for those on welfare and for the working poor, creating a minimum of 5,000 more social housing units over the next five years for people with addictions or mental illness, increasing low-rent housing by some 2,000 units a year. For Golden, "Clearly, solving homelessness with hostel beds and mattresses is not the answer. We must move from a crisis mentality to prevention."** Golden's report tells us: "At the current rate of placement, families would have to wait 17 years for housing. . . ."

---

* October 30, 1998.
† *Shelters: The Price of Hunger*, October 19, 1997.
** *Toronto Star*, January 15, 1999.

An editorial in the *Toronto Star* summed up what has happened in Ontario:

> Since taking office almost three years ago, Premier Mike Harris has turned a troubling housing problem into a public shame. His policies have forced people out of their homes and into the street.
>
> [Harris] scrapped all new public housing programs, including long-planned projects to provide homes to the poor and the mentally ill.
>
> Next, he cut welfare rates by 22 percent – a move that sparked thousands of evictions in Metro alone and is blamed for a huge increase in the number of families now living in hostels.
>
> This year, he dumped Ontario's aging, dilapidated public housing stock on local municipalities without enough money to repair or maintain the apartments, townhouses and co-ops that house more than 100,000 poor seniors, families and people with physical and mental disabilities.
>
> Some think that the unemployed are pampered by getting $520 a month to live in Canada's most expensive city. A welfare cut will increase the number of people without shelter.
>
> If the Tories cared whether children grow up in squalor, whether the disabled can live in dignity, whether our elderly have enough to eat, they would not have launched the massive attack on social programs that created such desperate homelessness in the first place.[*]

Golden's task-force report suggests that GST rebates be given to builders of low-cost housing, that Ottawa provide surplus land, that interest-free loans be provided for construction, and numerous other policies. Clearly, though, the key to the problem lies in more funding from Ottawa and from the provinces across the country. To rely once again on the private sector would be to once again abandon the homeless.

In November 1998, the mayors of Canada's largest cities called homelessness in Canada "a national disaster." The Golden report called it

---

[*] February 2, 1998.

"a national emergency." Bill Gillespie described the situation in a CBC-Radio documentary:

> People are sleeping on grates. . . . We're finding them every-where, in bank-machine nooks, in the ravines, under bridges, in bus shelters. . . . It's amazing where people are. . . . They're of all ages. . . . They've tried to get into shelters with no luck . . . men, women, and children completely stressed, drained out. At first we were dealing mostly with skid-row alcoholics – the same people over and over. Now there's a big variety, more youth, more people turfed out of mental homes, more middle-aged men and women. In the morning they go to soup kitchens wherever they can find one. The next night maybe they'll be lucky enough to get one of the cots in the Armoury. In most of the shelters the air is heavy with sweat, there are foreheads pressed to the table. There are people who have never been in a situation like this before who are barely surviving. Every day their numbers grow while governments point the fingers at one another.*

When the Chrétien government stopped funding low-cost housing, Canada became the only major developed nation without an important national social housing program.

Paul Martin's February 1999 budget totally ignored the homeless. A month later, David Collenette, representing the Chrétien government, gave a pitiful, evasive, patronizing response to impassioned requests for assistance from the Toronto conference on homelessness. As far as the federal government is concerned, the homeless are a low priority. In our nation's capital, "the number of people at risk of becoming homeless is on the rise. . . . Homelessness in Ottawa–Carleton is a problem that is large both in scope and magnitude. . . . There is a five to seven years waiting list for social housing. . . ."†

Today, all across Canada there are thousands of men, women, and children living in bushes, sleeping in abandoned buildings, and hiding in underground parking lots. The national "scandal," "tragedy," and

---

* From Bill Gillespie's CBC-Radio documentary on *The World at Six*, December 26 and 31, 1998.
† Ottawa–Carleton Social Services Development Report, March 29, 1999.

"disaster" are of little interest to most of our federal and provincial politicians. Too bad if the shelters are packed and the hostels are turning people away. Too bad if homelessness across the country is getting worse. Tough luck if more and more poor Canadians are ending up on the street.

PART TWO

Poor People Have Poor Children

We all know the importance of early childhood experience to success in adult life. . . . The fact is, we pay a heavy price for having children in our society grow up in poverty.

– Prime Minister Jean Chrétien
The House of Commons, September 13, 1998

Child Abuse by Politicians

The principal said that about half the kids in his school were aboriginal. Most of them were very poor. He said that he wakes up at three in the morning worrying about how he can put together better fundraising proposals. He says he now needs to spend more time on proposals than on teaching. The entire staff is stressed. The kids mean everything to them. The staff often come to him with tears in their eyes because of what they have seen or what a child has told them. He says, "Can you imagine? We have to go out and raise money for some of the school books we need. The parents don't have the money. We have to beg, borrow, and steal so we can get books, atlases, and other reference material." He also said that he couldn't believe the number of deaths these kids have had to deal with.

I asked him if he was premier of the province, what would be the first thing he would do to help change things. He answered without a moment's hesitation, "We need good head start programs and full-day kindergartens. We need smaller class sizes with maybe fifteen in a class instead of over thirty." Just then a teacher came into his office. She told us about the little girl who wouldn't stop eating again at the school lunch

*program. She always showed up with nothing in her stomach
and she knew there would be nothing to eat after she left school.
A couple of times after school they caught her eating ice cubes.*

On November 24, 1989, when the House of Commons unanimously
passed its now infamous resolution pledging to work towards abolishing
child poverty in Canada by the year 2000, the LICOs child-poverty rate
was 15.3 per cent. Eight years later, it was almost 20 per cent.

The Canadian Institute for Advanced Research and the Centre for
Studies of Children at Risk tell us: "According to the United Nations,
Canada is the best place to live for adults, but for children we are ranked
far down the list among industrialized nations."*

The 1989 Commons resolution read, "This House . . . seek[s] to
achieve the goal of eliminating poverty among children by the year
2000." In their 1998 annual report card, Campaign 2000† wasted few
words: "Nearly a decade later, *one in five* children in Canada lives in
poverty – an increase of 564,000 children since 1989." Since 1989, the
number of poor children is up almost 50 per cent, children in families
with incomes of less than $20,000 (in constant 1996 dollars) are up 65 per
cent, and children in working-poor families are up 45 per cent. Moreover,
children in families needing social assistance are up 51 per cent and
children living in unaffordable rental housing are up 91 per cent. And the
number of poor children in lone-parent families is up 92 per cent.

In their 1993 policy Red Book, the Chrétien Liberals told voters,
"We must give our children the best possible start in life, investing our
resources to help the most vulnerable children overcome some of the
difficulties that limit their life chances from the very beginning."

Now let's hear from the fine journalist Mary Janigan:

The drive to alleviate child poverty has become the intergovern-
mental crusade of the late 1990s – if only because the number of
poor children is growing. In 1989, 934,000 children belonged to
families with incomes below the Statistics Canada low-income

---

* B.C. Campaign 2000, *Child Poverty in BC Report Card*, 1997.
† Campaign 2000 is an umbrella organization made up of about thirty national and forty community, religious,
medical, educational, social, child-care, trade-union, anti-poverty, and other Canadian groups concerned about
poverty in Canada.

cutoff. In 1996 . . . there were 1.49 million – an increase of almost 60 per cent. The trend is evident – and worrisome.*

Some crusade!

Later in 1996, in a pastoral letter, the Canadian Conference of Catholic Bishops severely criticized the Chrétien government, likening its social spending cuts and its failure to take proper steps to eradicate child poverty (in the words of press reports) to "child abuse." The level of child poverty in Canada "in one of the richest societies in world history is nothing less than a damning indictment of the present socioeconomic order."† In 1997, an Angus Reid poll showed that about 70 per cent of Canadians believed the federal government was not doing enough to combat child poverty.

FIGURE 9

Child Poverty Rates Since the House of Commons Resolution

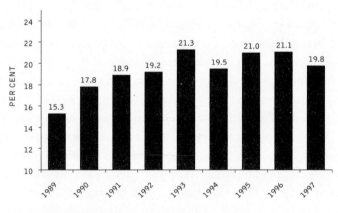

SOURCE: Statistics Canada, *Low income persons*, Cat. #13-569-XIB.

Of all the figures in this book, this one demonstrates government hypocrisy at its worst. Note the growth in child poverty since 1989, the year the House of Commons voted unanimously to work towards abolishing child poverty by 2000.

* *Maclean's*, July 6, 1996.
† The Social Affairs Commission, Canadian Conference of Catholic Bishops, *The Struggle Against Poverty*, October 17, 1996).

Figure 9 demonstrates just how seriously we can take the 1989 House of Commons resolution.

Here's a look at the number of children under the age of eighteen living in poverty during the same years:

1989	1,016,000	1994	1,362,000
1990	1,195,000	1995	1,472,000
1991	1,281,000	1996	1,498,000
1992	1,316,000	1997	1,397,000
1993	1,484,000		

From 1989 to 1997 the number of poor children in Canada increased by over 37 per cent while the total number of children in Canada increased by only 6 per cent! The figure for 1996 was the highest since 1979, when such numbers were first calculated. In 1996, the rate of poor children of single-parent mothers was a shocking 65 per cent. It's worth noting that there is a long-standing myth that *most* poor children live in single-parent households. Not so. In 1996 there were 730,000 poor children in two-parent families, compared to 673,000 poor children in single-parent families headed by women.

Using the LICO measurement, in 1989 about one in seven Canadian children was poor. By 1996, one in five was poor. In wealthy Ontario, child poverty was up 85 per cent. No doubt skeptics will say that these figures must be exaggerated. What about tax concessions and transfer payments for poor families, the elements in Ottawa's "War Against Poverty"? Didn't the lot of poor children in Canada improve? It's true that social programs have helped, but not nearly enough. Campaign 2000 calculates that the GST credit, the Child Tax Benefit, and Employment Insurance have helped pull some 600,000 Canadian children up over the poverty line. But Statistics Canada numbers show how inadequate government programs have been.

Let's now look at the percentage of children living below the LICO line in comparison to the unemployment rate. It's a comparison to ponder.*

* Statistics Canada, *Low Income Persons*, Cat. #13-569-XIB.

	Child Poverty Rate	Unemployment Rate
1989	15.3%	7.5%
1990	17.8	8.1
1991	18.9	10.4
1992	19.2	11.3
1993	21.3	11.2
1994	19.5	10.4
1995	21.0	9.5
1996	21.1	9.7
1997	19.8	9.2

Quite a difference! As the unemployment rate has come down in recent years, the rate of child poverty has remained persistently high. One explanation is that Canada's official unemployment rate, as many have argued, is vastly understated. But another explanation has to do with "the working poor." Of course, child poverty is essentially family poverty. According to Campaign 2000, "Fully one third of poor children lived in families where the parents had the equivalent of full year employment. They were still poor." "Left poor by the market," as the CCSD terms them. As well, since the House of Commons resolution to eliminate child poverty in Canada by the year 2000, the number of children living in families experiencing long-term unemployment went up 44 per cent.

All in all, that's some remarkable "crusade"!

The bishops' condemnation of politicians involved in "child abuse" is a much more accurate description.

On the Same Page in the Dictionary: Poverty and Power

I talked to the father for almost an hour. He said that soon after the accident in which his wife was killed – he was only mildly injured – the company that he worked for for over twenty years went bankrupt. He and his wife had been married late; now he was in his mid-fifties with the two boys, ten and seven, and he was having a terrible time finding a job, mostly because of his age. His wife had had a part-time job at the supermarket, but between the two of them they were just getting by. Now it was a different story.

He said that the boys usually walked with him to the food bank. He said he had to be careful not to walk by places like the museum or the Science Centre because the boys always wanted to go in, and since they started charging admission he couldn't afford to take them any more.

He said one night last week his younger boy came to him in the kitchen and asked him, "Dad, why do you always have to say no?"

What does it really mean to be a poor child? I thought I had a pretty good idea before I started writing this book, but I was mistaken. I knew very little.

The average income of poor families in Canada is *well* below the LICO and LIM poverty lines. The impact on most poor children is devastating.

Many poor children frequently arrive at school with nothing in their stomachs. Many schools across the county are on waiting lists for lunch programs. The people who staff the volunteer programs are invariably heroic, but the programs are almost always underfunded and the funding that is received is often uncertain month to month or year to year.

One full-time school counsellor told me she can't believe the number of families living in condemned properties: "Third-world accommodations, fire hazards full of cockroaches, silverfish, broken windows, no heat." She estimates that 20 to 30 per cent of the kids in her district show up in September with no school supplies. She constantly sees children "crying out for help," but there's no money to help. She also sees teachers sneaking kids into their empty classrooms at noon-hour so they can share their lunch with a poor little boy or girl.

Here's a partial list of what it means to be a poor child:

- Poor families have much higher than average infant mortality rates (the poorest quintile about twice the national average).
- Poor children have higher rates of disability. Poor families have many more low birth-weight children, a frequent result being chronic health problems.
- Poor children tend to perform more poorly in school, have higher rates of conduct disorders, more frequent and more severe emotional disorders, more hyperactivity, and higher dropout rates.
- Poor children have higher rates of smoking, alcohol consumption, and pregnancy.
- Poor families frequently suffer a great deal of emotional distress.
- Poor children have little or no opportunity to participate in organized extracurricular activities such as sports and field trips. They can't afford Boy Scouts or Girl Guides, or music, art, or dance lessons. Many can't afford sleds or skates. They rarely get to play video or computer games.

- Mothers of poor children often must rummage through bags full of donated second-hand clothing. The children are often made fun of at school because of their clothes.
- Most poor children rarely get to buy books or toys. Nor can they usually afford any extra school fees.
- Deprived infants and toddlers frequently experience behavioural problems that prevent success in school.
- Poor children have chronic health problems at roughly twice the rate of other children.

In the words of the CCSD, based on material from the Canadian Institute of Child Health,

> the presence of children with disabilities in a household can lead to financial hardship for the families. Many families must struggle to meet the high costs associated with caring for children with disabilities both in terms of time and money. In the absence of appropriate child care, it is not unusual for one parent to have to leave the paid labour force to care for their child at home. Reduced income and often high levels of stress, coupled with shrinking public supports and services, create a cycle of disadvantage. In a poor family, the impact of a disability is heightened because the family may not have the resources to meet their child's needs.

- Poor children frequently or invariably lack nutritious food. The result can be lifelong health problems.
- Poor children make fewer visits to the dentist, optometrist, or family doctor than other children, even though their health needs are likely greater.
- Studies have shown that poor children often suffer stunted physical growth and curtailed mental development and as adults have a shorter life expectancy.
- According to the Canadian School Boards Association in a 1997 report, poor children are "more likely [to face] feelings of deprivation that may lead to despair, social impairment, psychological problems, injury and early death. . . ."

- According to Campaign 2000, poor children are twice as likely to repeat a grade before the age of eleven, face poor employment prospects, and are twice as likely to have delayed vocabulary scores and more likely to have low math scores.
- Poor children more frequently face physical, mental, and sexual abuse, witness domestic violence, are frightened and often terrified by family conflict.
- Poor children frequently have low resistance to infection and higher rates of communicable diseases.
- Poor children are frequently lonely and are poor at developing relationships.
- Poor children living in poor neighbourhoods and dilapidated housing frequently encounter environmental hazards such as toxic chemicals, pesticides, lead, benzene, poor air quality, and insect infestations.
- Poor teenagers are much more likely to be both not in school and not employed.
- Poor children are more than three times as likely as well-to-do children to require special remedial education classes.
- While about 65 per cent of high-income families have a computer in their homes, only about 12 per cent of low-income families can afford to buy or rent one.
- Poor preschool children are much more likely to be "academically delayed." Many poor first-graders don't know the alphabet, know no nursery rhymes, and have little experience with one-on-one relationships.
- One of the most common results of poverty in children is low self-esteem.

Let's look at the above in the context of federal and provincial cutbacks. Over and over I have heard social workers say: "I've never worked so hard, for so many long hours in my life"; "We're terribly short-staffed. The cutbacks are killing us"; "We used to have a cap on the number of cases we could properly handle. Now we're seeing twice as many. There's no way we can do these kids justice. Remember, we're dealing with kids who live in jeopardy"; "We simply don't have the money. We're forced to hire staff who aren't properly qualified."

The social workers also speak of the success stories, the kids who have been saved from abuse, who've been turned around, who now have reduced aggression, improved attitudes, a greater interest in school, and kids who become volunteers themselves. Quite often in my interviews I saw tears in the eyes of the professionals or volunteers I met when I asked them to talk about the impact of the government cutbacks and the kids who could be saved but who aren't being saved.

It's difficult to do justice to the importance and the value of the long list of programs that have faced substantial cutbacks across the country. Among them are programs

- to provide hot lunches for children in impoverished areas.
- to encourage poor children to stay in school.
- to establish peer and parental support groups.
- to help improve children's health.
- to help provide tutoring and to teach job-preparation skills.
- to provide parental counselling for parents with at-risk school-children and parenting skills for parents with at-risk infants and toddlers.
- to provide services for deaf and disabled children.
- to provide parent drop-in and parent-teacher liaison.
- to provide recreational opportunities for poor children.
- to provide mentors to work with poor families with children.
- to advocate alternative sentencing and rehabilitation for young first-time offenders.
- to assist new immigrant families with children.
- to provide after-school and school-holiday food assistance for children in need.
- to provide guidance and support for those experiencing family violence.

This is but a small sample of valuable programs which have been badly hurt by government cutbacks.

Some of the key programs that have been curtailed are those that help protect children who are being sexually, physically, or emotionally abused, kids who are beaten up and mentally battered. As one social worker put it to me, the kids in these programs who do receive proper attention "build up their confidence, their skills, their health. There's often a *huge* change in attitude; they've got new vitality and energy, new self-esteem. They often become volunteers to help other children."

Among other programs suffering cutbacks across Canada are programs to assist children with fetal alcohol syndrome, programs to train and support foster parents, to help rehabilitate young offenders, to help intervene in families facing crisis, to help refugees, to provide safe-house counselling and family and premarital counselling, adoption programs, and programs to help street kids.

Let's contrast all of this with the 1997 words of Anne McLellan, Canada's minister of justice: "Working province by province, year by year, we will build a program to ensure no child in this country has to live in poverty."*

Tom Kent, long-time respected public policy advocate, reminds us that "human learning begins at once. The 'wiring' of the brain is governed by the stimuli it receives. The critical period is early. The development of the brain is pretty well determined by the age of six. The learning that takes place by then relates not only to cognitive skills but also to confidence and emotional development, to social knowledge and competence. In large measure, early learning sets the personality."

Studies show that poor children quickly fall behind in school and far more poor children drop out early. They also show that most welfare recipients have a poorer education than those who are employed. Yet, more and more, things have become more difficult for poor children. According to NAPO:

In many cases it is now expected that parents will pay for mandatory workbooks and school supplies! 'Extras,' such as art supplies and computer accessories are often only available if parents can afford to pay for them. For low income Canadians with school-age children, these costs are often the difference between paying rent and having enough food to eat. Many of these parents have to go through the degrading process of

___

* *Edmonton Journal*, February 22, 1997.

asking school principals for charity or alternatively depriving their children of educational opportunities.

. . .

When combined with cuts to unemployment insurance, welfare and falling wages, the rise of user fees for health care has resulted in erecting a huge barrier for individuals with low incomes. This barrier means that poor people are forced to choose between paying for basic necessities like food and shelter or paying for medically necessary drugs and services.

Increasingly, those with a poor education face dim job prospects. At the same time, those poor kids who do make it through high school then face the huge increases in the costs of post-secondary education.

In 1997, the *Toronto Star* reported: "A Statistics Canada study shows that young people from disadvantaged backgrounds in Ontario lag far behind the rest of the student population in basic literacy. Indeed, kids at the bottom of the socio-economic pyramid score so poorly that they drag down the province's rating to well below the national average. . . . From kindergarten to university, we see a disturbing bifurcation of the education system. Rich parents send their kids to private schools and hire tutors, while less advantaged students are left behind to cope with bigger classes and fewer programs." It didn't used to be that way: "Children from low-income families were treated like other kids, they were encouraged to stay in school, they could afford to go to college or university without incurring massive debts." But today "kids from disadvantaged backgrounds face the prospects of running up a $20,000-to-$40,000 debt for an undergraduate degree that might not lead to a job."*

According to Alanna Mitchell, writing in the *Globe and Mail*, "The findings speak of what has become almost an unmentionable in Canadian society: an entrenched class system . . . [with] the possibility that Canada's growing proportion of poverty-stricken children could create an underclass, with all the social chaos that suggests. . . . The figures are stark."†

---

* September 11, 1997.
† *Globe and Mail*, April 18, 1997.

In an excellent column in the *Calgary Herald*, columnist Robert Bragg wrote about the meaning of poverty:

> Poverty means absence, a lack of choices, restrictions. By definition poverty equates to "indigence, want, scarcity, deficiency." Homelessness is a euphemism for poverty.
>
> Poverty slides into the dictionary on the same page as Power. . . . They are opposites. Poverty is the absence of the "ability to do or act" which is the primary definition of power. . . . Power and wealth have been the guiding stars of our society for several decades.*

Unfortunately it's true that power and wealth in Canada care very little about poor children. As columnist Michael Valpy observed, "Finance Minister Paul Martin showed no lack of boldness in setting targets for deficit reduction. Why not for child poverty?"†

And what can be said of our prime minister? In a pre–Canada Day interview published July 1, 1999, Jean Chrétien discounted the urgency to do more to help poor Canadian children. When asked if child poverty would be a future Liberal priority, Chrétien replied, "We debated that. . . . There were statistics that were given to us that the level of poverty is much less in Canada as in the United States even though they are richer than us."**

Rabbi Arthur Blefeld of the Campaign Against Child Poverty wrote to the *Globe and Mail*:

> I was astonished to read Prime Minister Jean Chrétien's remarks on child poverty. What could he have been thinking? Does he really intend to minimize the tragedy of a million and a half Canadian children [living in poverty] by saying we are doing better than the United States? The United States has the worst record on child poverty among the industrialized nations of the Western world.††

---

* August 31, 1997.
† *Globe and Mail*, February 20, 1997.
** *Globe and Mail*, July 1, 1999.
†† *Globe and Mail*, July 5, 1999.

In an editorial, the *Toronto Star* asked, "When did the United States become Canada's benchmark for creating a fair, progressive society?"*

Contrast Chrétien's above comments with his 1997 quote at the beginning of the next chapter.

---

* *Toronto Star*, July 3, 1999.

Single Parents, Child Care, and Child Tax Benefits

Children must remain at the top of our national agenda. . . . Our government will not evade its own responsibilities and opportunities.

– Prime Minister Jean Chrétien,
September 1997

The woman in the church food bank said that in lots of cases the mother is out of the house waiting at the bus stop, heading for some low-wage job before the kids are even awake. But there are lots of other cases where the kids leave for school long before the mother gets out of bed. Some of the kids pour themselves some cereal, if there is any. But towards the end of the month the fridge and cupboards are usually empty.

In most cases (well over 90 per cent) when parents separate or divorce, the children stay with their mother. Just under half of all poor children live with single mothers. In 1973, fewer than 5 per cent of young children lived in one-parent households. By the mid-1990s this proportion rose to 13 per cent.

Given the great attention that the plight of female, lone-parent, no-earner families has received over the years, has their situation improved in relation to their ability to earn income or receive adequate family child support? On the contrary, their tiny average market income has actually decreased, peaking at $2,378 (constant 1996 dollars) in 1986, and falling to only $1,256 in 1996.* Meanwhile, their government transfer payments, which were $13,907 in 1993, fell to $12,470 in 1996, and their average total net income fell from $15,408 in 1993 to $13,373 in 1997, back to about the level of ten years earlier. So, after a decade of pious pronouncements from federal politicians, single non-working mothers were worse off than they were before.

For female lone-parent families where the mother was employed, total after-tax and after-transfer income, on average, again in constant 1996 dollars, also dropped from $24,525 in 1992 to $23,962, in 1997 and remained at a level only a few dollars higher than it was in 1989.

How do lone-parent mothers with children escape poverty, especially those with low educational qualifications and modest work experience? Many of these women cannot afford a telephone, or the transportation costs connected with seeking employment. And what's to happen to the child or the children if their mother goes off to work or to job training?

The availability of reliable, quality, low-cost, publicly subsidized, not-for-profit child care is essential to the welfare of all poor families, especially single-parent families. In the Nordic countries, a publicly subsidized child-care system for young children up to primary-school age provides excellent facilities, including nurseries and kindergarten. In most of Western Europe, child care is a top social priority, a given. In 1998, the Quebec provincial government introduced a very popular five-dollars-a-day program so parents pay a total of only about a hundred dollars a month. By the fall of 2001, care for all infants and children under the age of twelve will be included.

But daycare or child care in most of Canada is far from a priority. On the contrary, across the country there is a severe shortage of spaces. Many provincial governments have cut back or even eliminated support, and staff wages are frequently pathetic, despite long, often stress-filled, hours. Standards are lax; in the words of one child-care organization executive, "We're often looking at what amounts to only babysitting." According to the National Council of Welfare, "The absence of a national system that guarantees quality, affordability and accessibility is nothing short of outrageous."†

---

* Statistics Canada, *Income after tax, distribution by size in Canada, 1996*, Cat. #13-210-XPB.
† *Preschool Children: Promises to Keep*, Spring 1999.

During the 1993 federal election campaign, the Liberals promised an additional 150,000 "quality child care spaces." Instead, they are spending two billion dollars on British submarines.

In 1997, Canadian governments promised to work quickly to develop a national children's agenda to improve the well-being of our country's children. To date, little has been accomplished, but talks continue. A modest "children's agenda" may be part of the next federal budget.

A 1998 Human Resources Canada report showed that the average annual salary of a caregiver employed in child-care centres was less than $19,000. Many child-care workers have university degrees or at least a two-year college certificate. Benefits and pension plans are mostly modest, if not non-existent. Frequently I have heard from staff that they can't even afford to send their own children to the centre where they work. Overall, the profession is very poorly paid. In some cases, high-quality staff receive seven dollars an hour.

What are the choices for a lone-parent mother? If she must work for low wages and has to face costly child care, she is much better off on welfare. If she is faced with paying for child care and not being able to pay for food, clothing, rent, and utilities, there is no choice.

There is another factor to consider. As the OECD indicates, "More extensive systems of subsidized child-care can also facilitate second earners in households with children. . . . Such factors may partly explain why women's labour-market participation is so high, and low-income rates so low, in certain Nordic countries."* According to economists Gordon Cleveland and Michael Krashinsky of the University of Toronto, while the costs for a good national child-care program would be high, the net benefits would be much higher. "The economists calculate that the rewards of good child care on children's development would be worth $4.31 billion a year – the result of low dropout rates, higher future incomes, and fatter tax revenues."† When they add the benefits received by working mothers, Cleveland and Krashinsky show total benefits of about $10 billion a year, or about twice the costs of the child-care program.

But has Ottawa done nothing? The Chrétien government has widely

---

* "Low-income dynamics in four OECD countries," *OECD Observer*, January 1999.
† *Globe and Mail*, March 5, 1998.

trumpeted the Canada Child Tax Benefit, the program providing financial assistance for low-income families with children and the National
Child Benefit Supplement. And many journalists have jumped on the
bandwagon with great enthusiasm. But the National Council of Welfare
has a different perspective. In an autumn 1998 document, *Child
Benefits: Kids Are Still Hungry*, the council shows that the impact of
Ottawa's programs to help poor children is far less than anticipated.

> Families headed by single-parent mothers face the highest risk
> of poverty of any family type year after year, yet most of these
> families are effectively cut off from the extra money provided
> by the federal government. . . . We find it totally unacceptable
> that a country as prosperous as Canada cannot guarantee all of
> its children the basic necessities of life.

The council's study of the federal government's programs to assist
poor children is a harsh analysis. The government has allowed provincial and territorial governments to claw back the full amount of new
supplements granted welfare families.* "Single-parent families are particularly disadvantaged because of the high percentage of these families
on welfare. And because 90 percent of poor single-parent families are
headed by mothers rather than fathers, the Canada Child Tax Benefit
winds up discriminating against women. Single-parent mothers and
their children are the family type most in need of help from governments. *Yet they are the family type that gets little or no additional
support from the Canada Child Tax Benefit* [my emphasis]."

The council's research shows that, in 1997, of a total of 798,000
poor families with children under eighteen, 412,000 were single-parent
families and only 17 per cent of these were net beneficiaries under the
Canada Tax Benefit! "Overall, only 36 percent of all poor families with
children would get to keep the additional money provided by the federal
government." The rest would be clawed back.

"The inevitable result," the council concludes, "is that many poor
families and most poor single-parent families will not get to keep any of
the additional $1.7 billion a year committed by the federal government.

---

* Newfoundland and New Brunswick do not claw back benefits.

. . . Here is a program where substantial sums of new federal money are being spent, but, the additional money benefits barely one-third of the poor families with children and bypasses the other two-thirds. Many of the families being bypassed are single-parent families in desperate circumstances." These families have average incomes about $10,000 below the LICOs line. Moreover, the number of such families doubled between 1980 and 1996.

It is true that the Child Tax Benefit helps many poor families. But, as it is presently designed, is it not a striking example of government blind to human suffering? Of all family types, single-parent mothers who live on incomes of less than half the LICOs line are the most in need, yet most receive little or no assistance from hundreds of millions of dollars in new government-program spending.

Moreover, for those who are trying to re-establish themselves by seeking employment, even a token amount of wages may result in dollar-for-dollar decreases in welfare assistance. And once the poor are no longer on welfare, there is usually no subsidized child care, nor any subsidized dental care, prescription drugs, and medical benefits. The council puts it well: "Families with children would find it easier to work their way off welfare if they knew they would not lose these benefits once the parents entered the workforce. . . . The lack of guarantees is a major blunder. . . . The new system penalizes welfare families [trying to work] their way off welfare."

For many Canadians, indexation is not a problem. But for a poor family, the fact that the Child Tax Benefit is not indexed to inflation is a major blow. Try asking a family that has trouble buying food for their children if an income drop of hundreds of dollars will make a difference to them.

Somehow, Jean Chrétien and Paul Martin decided that children aren't as important as seniors. While senior benefits are protected from inflation by indexation, the Liberal government in March 1998 opposed a House of Commons amendment that suggested full indexation for child benefits. Fourteen Liberal backbenchers supported the motion, which went down to defeat 114-113. In 1997, the Canadian Labour Congress (CLC) calculated that the real value of an unindexed Child Tax Benefit would decline by 27 per cent over a ten-year period. In the words of the CLC, "Total income from social assistance and related allowances and tax credits still leaves families on social assistance with incomes anywhere between 25% and 69% below Statistics Canada's Low Income Cut Offs. They are still poor."*

Of great concern to the National Council of Welfare is "Too Much Rhetoric" used by the Child Tax Benefit program's supporters, who trumpet "fair treatment for low-wage families with children" and programs that "get kids off welfare." In the council's words, "Both those arguments are misleading."

Of further concern is the lack of accountability relating to the provincial and territorial spending of the additional clawed-back federal funds. How much of their spending "is actually new money and how much offsets cuts" in their own programs? As well, "there are no national standards to speak of in the way the money is being spent."

Summing up, for the council "the rhetoric about children as our future has become increasingly hollow . . . Kids Are Still Hungry."

After Paul Martin's February 1998 budget added more funding to the Child Tax Benefit, NAPO's view was almost identical to that of the National Council of Welfare. While the enriched tax benefit

> will provide some additional income support and in kind benefits to working poor families . . . there are several reasons to be skeptical with respect to the extent to which these initiatives will reduce the rate of child poverty which has increased rapidly in the 1990s. First, the enriched CTB will do nothing to reduce child poverty amongst the nearly two-thirds of poor children in welfare families (an estimated 1 million poor children live in welfare families, compared with about one-half million children in low-income working families). This is true because . . . provinces intend to clawback the enriched CTB from welfare recipients through reducing social assistance benefits by an equivalent amount.

"Second, even in the case of working poor families, the impact of the enriched CTB in reducing poverty may be minimal. The amount of the new funding is relatively small" and will be eroded by inflation.

---

* Canadian Labour Congress, *The Canada Child Tax Benefit*, December 10, 1997.

"Over the 1984-1997 period the real value of the CTB declined by about $1 billion.

"The enriched CTB, coupled with previous cuts in social assistance benefits, may increase the supply of low-wage labour (by forcing some of the welfare poor into the ranks of the working poor), thereby lowering the price of labour."

NAPO goes on to point out that the real value of provincial minimum wages eroded by 26 per cent from 1976 to 1995. At the same time, the real value of social-assistance payments has also fallen in most provinces, due to inflation, while several provinces have made drastic cuts to benefits. Moreover, there has been significant tightening of eligibility requirements, "partly as a result of the virtual disappearance of national standards for social assistance since the introduction of the Canada Health and Social Transfer." For NAPO, "the dominant ideology of our time seems to put more and more emphasis on the market place, with minimal government intervention to protect the interests of the poor. . . ."*

Before I leave the subject of poor children and go on to the question of the distribution of income and wealth in Canada, I want to briefly return to the topic of hungry kids. In an outstanding piece of research,† Lynn McIntyre, Sarah Connor, and James Warren looked at child hunger in Canada. Among the many important conclusions in their paper's executive summary:

> . . . about 57,000 Canadian families with children experience hunger. Single parent families, families on social assistance and Aboriginal families are over-represented. One third of the families experiencing hunger are often dual wage-earner families, the working poor. Hunger was a problem that co-occurred with the mother's poor health and activity limitation. The difference in annual income between those who experience frequent hunger and those who experience occasional hunger is $5,000.
>
> Parents realize that food deprivation can affect the development of young children, and therefore, deprive themselves of food first.

---

* NAPO, *Poverty and the Canadian Welfare State*, June 1998.
† *A Glimpse of Child Hunger in Canada*, Applied Research Branch, Human Resources Development Canada, August 1998.

Children experiencing hunger in their formative years can be subject to developmental delays or more permanent developmental problems. Such consequences of malnutrition and hunger can result in greater health and social costs later in life.

The interplay between health and family food insecurity is distressing and it is unclear which comes first. . . . For children, the relationship is clearer as they are probably born into conditions of disadvantage that subsequently affect their health and well-being.

In terms of equity, it is reassuring to note that immigrants and racially visible persons are not over-represented in hungry families. In fact, almost half of the hungry are those who call themselves Canadians or claim to be of British descent.

Those who reported frequent hunger are most likely to be single mothers on social assistance who are also likely to suffer from chronic ill-health. Over two-thirds of mothers reporting hunger had completed high school and over 50% had some post-secondary education. Education is clearly insufficient to ward off hunger or extreme poverty in women with children. In fact, few women are immune to poverty. Many are just a job loss, a male parent loss, or an illness or disability away from poverty and the possible experience of hunger.

Poverty is strongly associated with lower health status in children. The prevalence of poorer health status in children in this study, while expected, is nonetheless a disturbing finding. . . . One could . . . surmise that the indirect costs associated with having a child with a chronic illness, such as transportation to health appointments, or indirect expenses associated with hospitalization, could deplete family resources necessary to purchase food.

In Edmonton, in the Boyle/McCauley inner-city area, children miss on average six meals per month. In Toronto, about thirty thousand children use breakfast, lunch, and snack programs. Today, all across Canada, hungry children depend on volunteer food programs. More and more the volunteer sector is being forced to try to provide essential services, including food, clothing, and shelter. Food banks and shelters are keeping people alive. While the entire concept of food banks should be deplorable, they have become fixed institutions in hundreds of communities across the country. In Lynn McIntyre's words, "Food banks are clearly not an adequate public policy response to hunger, neither in terms of accessibility, availability, desirability, nor in terms of nutritional support."*

The CCSD reported a 1998 University of Toronto study: "It provides strong evidence that food banks cannot replace the social safety net for families. Although these women were using food banks, more than half reported experiencing hunger and 27 per cent said that their children had gone hungry."†

Not for a single moment would I dream of ever being critical of food banks, school lunch programs, community snack programs, or other assistance for hungry kids. The hard-working, dedicated staff and volunteers all across the country who help out each deserve the Order of Canada in my opinion. I am, however, highly critical of the politicians and bureaucrats who through indifference and ineptitude allow children to go hungry. These politicians and civil servants deserve our scorn and contempt.

Recently, two United Nations committees have criticized the federal government for discriminating against the poor and for allowing the clawbacks of child tax benefits by the provinces.** Is there good reason to believe that Ottawa's "children's agenda" will be much of an improvement? Or will one million welfare children continue to be ignored?

In Maude Barlow's book *Straight Through the Heart*, she quotes Paul Martin when he was in opposition:

> The fact is that 25 per cent of the people on social assistance in this country are mothers under the age of 28 with one or two or more children and less than grade 8 education. How are these mothers going to get off social assistance? How are they going to be trained? How are they going to get jobs if we don't have an adequate daycare system?††

---

* Workshop paper for *Investing in Children*, National Research Conference, 1998.
† *Nutritional Vulnerability and Food Insecurity Among Women in Families Using Food Banks.*
** The Committee on Economic, Social and Cultural Rights, December 4, 1998, and the Human Rights Committee, April 7, 1999.
†† Toronto, HarperCollins, 1995.

Darn good questions.

But an even better question is why, after six years as one of the two most powerful people in the country, Mr. Martin has done virtually nothing about child care? Meanwhile, as we have seen, there are many more poor mothers and even more poor children in Canada since he was elected to power.

PART THREE

The Distribution of Income and Wealth

Since the Reagan and Thatcher years, the ideal of a more equitable economy – one that spreads wealth more evenly throughout society – has lost its popularity. We live in an age of economic Darwinism, where the survival of the financially fittest is the religion.

– John Kettle,
Globe and Mail,
November 9, 1998

Rising Yachts and Sinking Rafts

It is impossible to understand poverty in Canada without examining the distribution of income and wealth in our country. John Strick of the University of Windsor has put it well:

> One of the goals generally attributed to society is a fair distribution of income and wealth among its members. Opinions vary on what is fair, but it is generally agreed that severe inequalities in income levels are not acceptable. History has shown that the market system usually produces a distribution of severe inequality.
>
> Statistics on Canadian income distribution reveal considerable inequality.*

In his book *The Good Society*, economist John Kenneth Galbraith writes:

> The good society does not seek equality in the distribution of income. Equality is not consistent with either human nature or

---

* *Canadian Public Finance*, Toronto, Holt, Rinehart and Winston of Canada, 1992.

the character and motivation of the modern economic system. As all know, people differ radically in their commitment to making money and also in their competence in doing so. . . . However, this does not lessen the need for a clear view of the forces controlling the distribution of income and of factors forming attitudes thereon.*

The 1997 edition of the U.N.'s *Human Development Report* looked at the richest 20 per cent and the poorest 20 per cent in developed nations around the world. In terms of the gap between the two, Canada has a worse record in distribution of income than, among others, France, Norway, Netherlands, Japan, Finland, New Zealand, Sweden, Spain, Belgium, Australia, United Kingdom, Germany, Denmark, Italy, and Israel. Only in the United States and Switzerland was there a wider gap.

The report said, "A rising tide of wealth is supposed to lift all boats. The yachts and ocean liners are indeed rising . . . but the rafts and row-boats are taking on water and some are sinking fast."

We've all read many stories about how the wealthy few in the United States have more riches than scores of countries put together, how Bill Gates's net worth is greater than the combined net worth of the poorest 40 per cent of Americans, how the world's top 450 billionaires have assets of greater value than all the inhabitants in countries with some 45 per cent of the world's population, and so on. Before we turn our attention to Canada, let's look more closely at what has been happening in the OECD country with the very worst income distribution record.

In September 1997, *The Economist* looked at "the great divide" of growing income inequities in the United States:

In 1995, the OECD reported that the gap between the lowest and highest-paid workers in America was the widest among its 25 member-countries; last year, the Census Bureau reported that the gap was the widest recorded in America since the Second World War, with the top 20% of households swallowing 47% of income.†

* Boston, Houghton Mifflin, 1996.
† September 6, 1997.

The Economist produced a chart (Figure 10) under the title "Class war in the making?" that could hardly have been more clear.

FIGURE 10

Share of Aggregate Income, U.S.A.

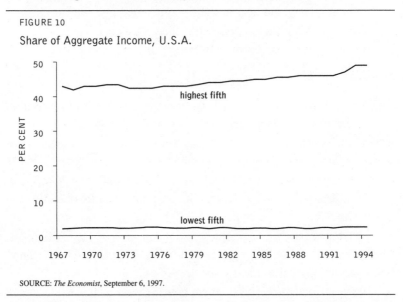

SOURCE: *The Economist*, September 6, 1997.

While this figure of total income says a great deal, as we shall see later the rich are getting much richer in the U.S. while the world's wealthiest country has by far the highest poverty rates.

At the end of 1997, a new study from the Center of Budget and Policy Priorities in Washington, D.C., showed that in real terms the income of the richest fifth of American families with children grew by 16 per cent since the mid-1980s, but that of the poorest fifth fell by 3 per cent. According to *The Economist*, "Take the comparison . . . back to the late 1970s and the gap is wider still: the income of the richest has grown by 30% and that of the poorest has fallen by 21%."[*] Figure 11 is adapted from the magazine.

In April 1998, Fred Brock wrote about "The Richer Rich . . .":

The income of the top 1 percent of Americans, or about 2.6 million people, now equals that of the bottom one-third of the

---

[*] December 20, 1997.

FIGURE 11

Family Income, Late 1970s to Mid 1990s, U.S.A.

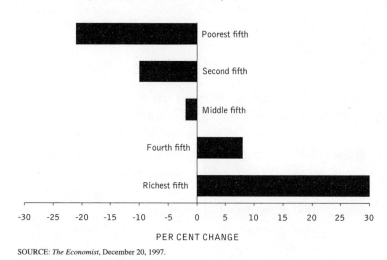

SOURCE: *The Economist*, December 20, 1997.

The top 20 per cent of American families had big increases in their incomes while the poorest 20 per cent suffered big declines.

population – or 88 million people. . . . By the early 1980's, when the [income] gap started to widen, the poorest 20 percent of Americans had 4.3 percent of all incomes; by 1996, that share dropped to 3.7 percent.*

A month later *The Economist* told us:

In the United States where the number of billionaires increased from about ten in 1980 to almost 200 in 1999 . . . inequality has increased sharply over the past 30 years. . . . Barely a week passes without some executive hauling home a planet-sized pay packet, often for merely keeping his company's performance in line with the stock market. As well, by one count, eight in ten

---

* The *New York Times*, April 19, 1998, quoting from the May 1998 *Smart Money* article by A.R. Hunt and Alan Murray.

Americans earning more than [$1 million] a year leave nothing
to charity in their wills.*

In constant dollar terms, between 1979 and 1996 the average earnings
of the bottom fifth of male earners in the United States fell by a shocking 44 per cent† and average real hourly wages were lower than thirty
years earlier.

Robert Reich reviewed Andrew Hacker's *Money, Who Has How
Much and Why*** in the *New York Times Book Review*:

If $30,000 is set as a middle-class income, fewer than a third of
all employed Americans can be considered middle class.

At the very top, with yearly incomes over $1 million, sit
some 68,000 of the nation's highest rollers (from whose ranks
Hacker tells us, came one-quarter of all the delegates to the
most recent Republican National Convention).

The bottom 80 percent of the population, meanwhile
receives a smaller share of the nation's total income than it did
20 years ago. . . . At the same time, the poor have become
poorer. . . . For all its riches, the United States now has a greater
percentage of its citizens in prison or on the street, and more
neglected children than any other advanced nation.

Hacker suggests that a number of American states have intentionally
curtailed welfare payments so as to create "a ready pool of women to
work at minimum wage as household servants, motel maids and in
food processing plants," while at the same time rich Americans who
paid an average tax of 47 per cent in 1979 paid some 32 per cent
in 1994.

Why is all this happening? American economist Mark Levinson
reviewed Frank Levy's book *The New Dollars and Dreams*†† in the *New
York Times Book Review*:

---

* May 30, 1998.
† *The Economist*, January 16, 1999.
** New York, Scribners, 1997.
†† New York, Russell Sage Foundation.

At the end of his book Levy hints at another explanation for growing inequality. There has been, he states, a "shift of power away from the average worker and towards a firm's shareholders. Deregulation, globalization and technology have reduced the typical employee's bargaining power, and no countervailing institution has risen to exert an opposite force." Levy's failure to pursue the implications of this statement – that the problem is not that workers lack skills, but that they lack power – is the main flaw in an otherwise thoughtful and meticulously researched book.*

Well, enough about the United States. Their income distribution record, like their poverty record, is the worst among all the OECD nations. Let's turn our attention to our own country.

FIGURE 12

Gross Domestic Product at Market Prices

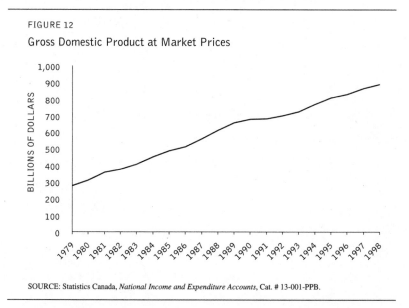

SOURCE: Statistics Canada, *National Income and Expenditure Accounts*, Cat. # 13-001-PPB.

Over the past two decades, Canada's GDP has tripled. Despite this growth, during the same period, child, individual and family poverty increased substantially.

---

* January 10, 1999.

Figure 12 indicates how GDP has risen in Canada. Given the steady increase in GDP, one might suppose that in an egalitarian, benevolent society, our political leaders would produce policies intended to close the gap between rich and poor. In the next chapter we'll see what actually happened.

The Rich Getting Richer,
the Poor Getting Poorer

We must promote equal opportunity among Canadians.

– Prime Minister Jean Chrétien,
Edmonton,
December 8, 1998

I walked with the single mother around the sea wall for almost two hours. She had moved to the coast eight years ago hoping for a better life. It didn't turn out that way; now she has two young children and she has AIDS. She says poverty is such a shame; it's so destructive. There's so much success on television. For the kids the mirror image of society is a buffet: designer clothes, nice shoes, wonderful vacations. Inevitably you blame yourself, it's your own fault. You're always trying to find ways to hide your poverty from others; you feel you can't tell people of your needs, what your struggles are at home.

She says she tries to pay the bills at the beginning of the month; the cheque from Ottawa comes around the twentieth of the month. She says, "You want to know how hard it is? I'll tell you. I was sick in bed. My daughter comes home from school and makes herself a piece of toast. When I got out of bed and saw what she had done I blew up. That toast was supposed to be lunch for the next day! I just blew up with my daughter over a slice of bread for God's sake! I never, never ever thought I would have to raise my kids in poverty. I am so ashamed."

89

According to former Conservative cabinet minister Garth Turner, writing in *Canadian Business* magazine, it's a myth that the rich are getting richer and the poor poorer, as well as a myth that poverty is on the rise.* According to Christopher Sarlo, writing in the Fraser Institute's *Fraser Forum*, "The old saw that 'the poor are getting poorer' is complete nonsense, at least for Canada."[†]

Before we look at the facts of the matter, let's see how the Canadian public feels. *Maclean's*, in their 1998 year-end poll, asked Canadians, "Do you think that generally in Canadian society the gap between richer and poorer people is increasing, staying about the same or decreasing?" Seventy-one per cent said it was increasing, while only 5 per cent said that it was decreasing.**

Are the rich getting richer and the poor getting poorer? Michael C. Wolfson, director-general of Statistics Canada, examined "Earnings inequality and polarization indicators for effective labour force participants."[††] Following is a look at the shares of labour income:

	1974	1995
1st quintile	4.8%	3.5%
2nd quintile	12.6	10.5
3rd quintile	18.4	17.6
4th quintile	24.0	25.2
5th quintile	40.2	43.2

So, in the period from 1974 to 1995 the lower 60 per cent of the Canadian labour force had lost ground, the upper 40 per cent had gained. Note that this analysis does *not* include large sums earned in the form of stock options, nor does it include most large executive bonuses. Without question the share of the top quintile would be *considerably* higher if such income were included. Moreover, in the words of one of Canada's leading tax experts, "huge sums of money are transported unreported out of the country every year to the Cayman Islands, the Bahamas, Monaco, etc." Needless to say, these dollars do not show up in income-distribution calculations.

---

* September 1996.
† November 1998.
** December 28, 1998.
†† *Monthly Labor Review*, Washington D.C., April 1998.

Commenting on the figures in Statistics Canada's income-distribution report for 1995, the *Globe and Mail*'s Bruce Little summed up the report nicely: "The numbers . . . go a long way to explaining why the purveyors of high-priced toys can enjoy rising sales, while their customers pass panhandlers on the street while out shopping. There are a lot of people who are very poor by any measure and a lot who are very well off."*

In its report for 1995 on income distribution after tax, Statistics Canada reported that income for the poorest fifth of Canadian families fell by about 20 per cent between 1989 and 1995. Meanwhile, the real income of the richest fifth continued to increase.†

In its 1997 income distribution report, Statistics Canada advised that 1997 was the fourth straight year that the proportion of family income from transfers decreased, to 11.3 per cent of total income from 12.9 per cent in 1993. The decline in government transfer payments was of particular significance for lower-income families since over half of their income comes from this source.

By spring 1996, the Centre for International Statistics at the CCSD was reporting

the labour market is producing greater inequality among families with children than it did a decade ago, with especially severe income losses among lower-middle-income earners and the poor. . . . The average after tax income of a middle and lower-middle-income family is roughly $1,400 less today than that of a similar family 10 years ago.

Families in the poorest quintile had an average market income of $7,814 in 1984. A decade later, these families brought home an average income of just $5,325, representing a shocking decline of 31.9%.

This loss is in stark contrast to families in the top quintile, whose average market income increased by 5.2% (from $97,733 to $102,792).**

---

* January 13, 1997.
† *Income after tax, distributions by size in Canada*, 1995, Cat. #13-210-XPB.
** Clarence Lochhead and Vivian Shalla, *Perception*, Spring 1996.

The CCSD produced a chart (Figure 13) looking at market income for families with children over a ten-year period.

FIGURE 13

Change in Average Market Income for Families with Children, 1984 to 1994

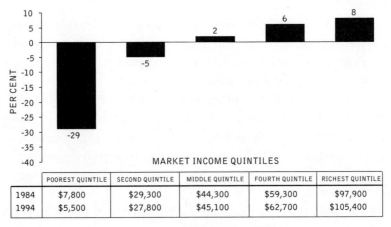

	POOREST QUINTILE	SECOND QUINTILE	MIDDLE QUINTILE	FOURTH QUINTILE	RICHEST QUINTILE
1984	$7,800	$29,300	$44,300	$59,300	$97,900
1994	$5,500	$27,800	$45,100	$62,700	$105,400

AVERAGE MARKET INCOME

Over the decade shown, the poorest 20 per cent of Canadian families suffered a huge drop – almost 30 per cent – in their total income (in constant 1984 dollars) from employment.

The CCSD reported, "[In 1984] the median market income of families with children in the wealthiest quintile was 12 times higher than the median market income of families in the poorest quintile. By 1994, the wealthiest families with children enjoyed an income that was nearly 24 times higher than that of the poorest families with children."[*]

In their publication about income distribution for 1996, Statistics Canada drives home the point: "The result of these income shifts is that income *inequality grew in 1996 as it has during most of the 1990s, whether calculated on income before transfers or on total income* [my emphasis]."[†]

---

[*] *The Progress of Canada's Children*, 1996.
[†] *The Daily*, April 13, 1997.

Economist Ross Finnie of Queen's University School of Policy Studies is a respected expert on the subject of income distribution. In July 1997 he completed an update on the subject for Human Resources Development Canada.

There is now substantial empirical evidence that suggests that there has been an increase in earnings inequality in Canada. . . . Those at the upper end of the earnings distribution [are] doing relatively better than before, those at the bottom faring more poorly, and [there has been] a general "hollowing out" of the middle.

Furthermore, the widening of the distribution of earnings has occurred as average earnings levels have remained effectively stagnant, meaning that those in the lowest reaches of the distribution appear not only to be doing *relatively* worse than previously, but have in some cases experienced *absolute* declines as well. . . .*

Former Conservative finance minister Michael Wilson once said that what Canada needed was more millionaires. By November 1997, Ernst & Young reported that there were more than three times the number of millionaires in Canada than there were eight years previously and that the number is expected to triple once more within the next eight years. Michael Wilson got his wish.

Late in 1997, under a front-page headline "GAP GROWS BETWEEN RICH AND POOR: Booming Canadian economy does little for bottom fifth of families, study shows," the *Globe and Mail* reported: "The gap between Canada's haves and have-nots has widened dramatically, becoming by some measures the starkest in about a generation, Statistics Canada says." The percentage of Canada's total income from 1993 to 1996 going to lower-income Canadians fell by over 6 per cent, "lower than at any time in the 1980s and 1990s," while "the richest fifth captured 40.6 per cent of total income, the highest recorded over two decades."†

---

* *Earning Dynamics in Canada: The Distribution of Earnings in a Dynamic Context, 1982-1992.*
† December 23, 1997.

Clarence Lochhead and the Centre for International Statistics at the CCSD have done excellent work on the subject of the impact of government transfers on income distribution.

> The poorest 20 percent of Canada's households, who earned less than one per cent of [1995] pre-transfer income, received nearly 40 per cent of all government income security benefits. After receiving government transfer payments this group of Canadians was still left with less than six per cent of all household income.
>
> By comparison, the richest 20 per cent of Canada's households in 1995 earned nearly half of all pre-transfer income; they received eight per cent of all government income security transfers, and they ended up with 44 per cent of all household income.*

After transfers, the lowest two quintiles of income had 15.7 per cent of total income (8.3 per cent before transfers) while the top two quintiles had 68.2 per cent (compared to 75.7 per cent before transfers).

A *Toronto Star* editorial put the situation well: "With each fresh batch of statistics, it becomes more apparent that we have a growing underclass in this country. . . . Although the economy is enjoying healthy growth, and the stock market is booming and business is in fine shape, we are becoming a nation of 'haves' and 'have-nots.'"† In 1998, economist Charles Beach of Queen's University, another expert on income distribution, advised, "I've been more concerned in the past couple of years because the economy is shifting out of recession, but so far we have not seen a reversal of the trend in polarization. . . . If anything, it appears to be becoming more widespread."**

Later in the year, Beach, along with his colleague Ross Finnie, wrote of

> quite strong evidence (for both men and women) of a long-run polarization of earnings in almost all age/sex groups (excepting perhaps older women). . . . As the buffer of government trans-

---

* *Perception* 21.4.
† April 28, 1998.
** *Maclean's*, April 27, 1998.

fers is reduced in the name of deficit reduction, this suggests the distribution of family incomes will start showing quite marked increases in polarization, inequality and household poverty rates even as unemployment rates may further decline and the current economic growth continues.*

So despite the fact that in 1997, in the words of Statistics Canada, "income inequality was held in check . . . in contrast with the trend to increased inequality seen since the early 1990s,"† it looks probable that the already large gap between rich and poor in Canada may widen even further.

The Growing Gap, published in the fall of 1998, was the first major document by the Centre for Social Justice's new research group. Among its major conclusions was that in 1973 the top 10 per cent of Canadian families with children under eighteen took twenty-one times the market income of the poorest 10 per cent of families. By 1996, the top 10 per cent made 314 times the market income of the poorest 10 per cent. As Naomi Klein wrote in the *Toronto Star*: "The gulf between rich and poor is on its way to becoming the economic indicator that speaks to people most directly, usurping all of the traditional measures. . . . Average annual income once offered some solid hints about our standard of living, until we realized that by averaging the inflated salaries of executives with the eroding pay of workers, we were glossing over the widening gulf."**

In early winter 1998, Statistics Canada once again confirmed the growing inequality:

Over 25 years . . . these changes resulted in a greater proportion of families at the lower rungs of the income ladder and, therefore, greater overall inequality. . . . Income inequality among families increased between 1970 to 1995. . . . It increased significantly among dual-earner families, young families and families in Ontario and British Columbia.††

---

* *Canadian Business Economics*, November 1998.
† *The Daily*, April 14, 1999.
** November 12, 1998.
†† *Perspectives*, Cat. #75-001-XPE.

Figure 14 looks at income shares in 1996. And what about poor families? In 1980 about 12.3 per cent of all families earned less than $20,000. Sixteen years later it was 12.9 per cent.

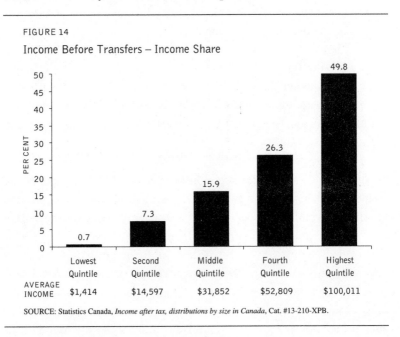

FIGURE 14

Income Before Transfers – Income Share

SOURCE: Statistics Canada, *Income after tax, distributions by size in Canada*, Cat. #13-210-XPB.

In 1996, the top 20 per cent of income earners received over seventy-one times the market income of the lowest 20 per cent.

Perhaps as good an indicator as any is a look at what has happened to average family market income during this period (see Figure 15).

In 1991 mutual-fund investment in Canada amounted to some $34.6 billion. By 1998 it had topped $286 billion. Adding term deposits, GICs, annuities, and mutual funds together, the total approached $500 billion in 1998. One thing is for sure, poor people had few such assets.

While it is true that taxes and transfers reduce the degree of inequality in Canada, the sobering fact is that, even after these adjustments, income distribution by quintiles has deteriorated in recent decades. Tax policy and social programs have kept the distribution from getting much worse, but market income distribution has become even more unequal than in the past.

In May 1999, the Federation of Canadian Municipalities reported

FIGURE 15

Average Total Change in Family Market Income, 1980 to 1996

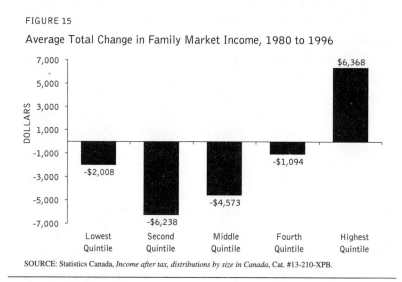

SOURCE: Statistics Canada, *Income after tax, distributions by size in Canada*, Cat. #13-210-XPB.

Over the sixteen-year-period shown, 80 per cent of Canadian families lost market income (in constant 1996 dollars), while the top 20 per cent gained.

that the poorest 10 per cent of Canadians suffered a drop of almost 19 per cent in their income from 1992 to 1996, while the top 10 per cent saw their total incomes increase by almost 7 per cent.[*]

A word of caution about measuriing income distribution inequality. Careful attention needs to be paid to the definitions and measurements employed. For example, the right wing in Canada loves the Statistics Canada annual publication *Income after tax, distributions by size in Canada* (#13-210-XPB) because it shows the after-tax and after-transfer income gap as relatively stable instead of increasing. But drawing such a conclusion is erroneous ("bizarre" in the words of one noted income distribution economist) for a number of reasons. First, press reports tend to focus on family income while ignoring a number of groups with disproportionately high levels of poverty such as unattached seniors, other single men and women, and people who live on reserves – a total of 1.6 million Canadians. Second, taking all family income and dividing

[*] *Quality of Life Reporting System*, May 19, 1999.

it by the number of families is just as misleading as measuring standard of living by taking GDP and dividing it by the population. A growing number of very high income families disproportionately affects average income figures for families. A much better measurement for finding a "typical family" would be to look at median income (counting halfway), a method that shows a growing income polarization and more Canadian families falling below the low-income line. One last point: measuring inequality by looking at quintiles does not produce the same degree of polarization that measuring deciles does.

Trickle Down Has Fizzled Out

We met for coffee a block north of the Eaton Centre. They said they had just had their rent raised again to way beyond what they could afford. They would have to move within ninety days and come up with first and last month's rent, plus the moving costs. But the biggest problem would be uprooting the kids yet again. The three kids liked the school they were going to and had made good friends. The mayor, somehow without anyone seeming to notice, had sold off much of the city's subsidized housing for low-income families. The developers came in, fixed the houses up, and now poor families had no place to go but back to the dilapidated houses or apartments in the inner city. The family had had some stability; the kids don't want to leave. But now they'd be back to the bad streets with hookers, druggies, gang violence, and lots of stress. "I won't feel safe," she said. "I won't feel safe for my kids. We were fighting our way out, but now we're going to be leaving from what was a caring adult community to an area of bad poverty, dysfunctional homes, alcoholism and plenty of violence. Oh, sure, there's lots of good people in the inner city, but boy it's tough to raise kids there." Her husband looked grim, shaking his head throughout the interview.

In the fall of 1998, *The New Yorker* published an article about Augusto Pinochet, in which the writer deplored income disparity in Latin America: "The wealthiest twenty per cent of Chileans earn fourteen times as much as the poorest – and the gap appears to be widening. For the twenty-five per cent of Chileans still living below the official poverty line, the trickle down benefits of the free market miracle remain elusive."* In Canada, we Canadians have come up with our own "free market miracle," defying the laws of gravity. It's called fizzle-up economics. Clearly, free-market policies have enriched many, but far more are poor or with stagnant or declining real incomes.

The OECD analysed changes in the distribution of market income in Canada over a twenty-year period. The result is shown in Figure 16. Over twenty years, the bottom 70 per cent of Canadian workers and families lost ground, while the top 30 per cent gained. And, as we have already seen, more recently the gap has widened further.

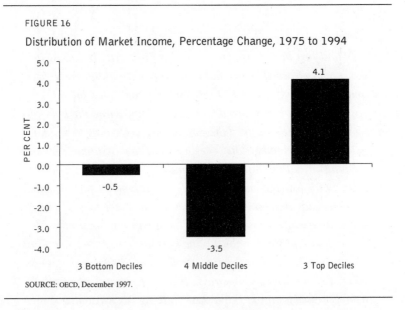

FIGURE 16

Distribution of Market Income, Percentage Change, 1975 to 1994

SOURCE: OECD, December 1997.

This figure shows changes in income distribution after dividing Canadians into deciles (10-per-cent groups). The bottom 70 per cent lost ground over twenty years.

* October 19, 1998.

Between 1980 and 1996, Canada's GDP at market prices increased from $310 billion to $829 billion, a $619 billion increase. Let's look again at how low-income Canadians fared during this substantial growth. Figure 17 shows the percentage distribution of families and individuals with income of less than $20,000. Despite the huge growth in the Canadian economy from 1980 to 1996, the share of low-income earners in Canada actually increased. So much for trickle-down.

FIGURE 17

Income Under $20,000

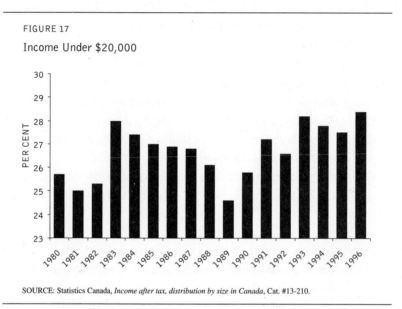

SOURCE: Statistics Canada, *Income after tax, distribution by size in Canada*, Cat. #13-210.

While Canada's GDP continued to grow, so did the percentage of Canadians with low incomes, reaching levels well above those of the early 1980s. (Calculations are in constant 1996 dollars.)

The next year, 1997, Statistics Canada advised that

an improving economy helps reduce the proportion of low-income families in the population, primarily by raising their labour market earnings. In addition, the unemployed may have a better chance of finding employment; workers may have a better chance of finding better paying jobs; and people not in the labour force may decide to look for and, in fact find a job.

Sounds most reasonable, doesn't it? But,

> on the other hand, a recent study found that the effectiveness of
> economic growth in reducing low income among Canadian fam-
> ilies . . . appeared to be fizzling out. The impact of economic
> growth weakened for all types of families since the early 1980s
> *because of increasing inequality* [my emphasis]. In other words,
> families located at the bottom of the income distribution shared
> less in the employment and earnings gains of more recent eco-
> nomic expansions.*

Precisely.

And what of the future? Economists Andrew Sharpe, executive
director of the Ottawa-based Centre for the Study of Living Standards,
and Myles Zyblock reported that, "in light of recent fiscal retrenchment
seen at many levels of government such as the scaling back of welfare
and unemployment insurance, it is expected that the incomes of those
located in the bottom quintiles will be adversely and disproportionately
affected"†

In *The Growing Gap*, economist Armine Yalnizyan has a telling table
that compares the market-income ratios for the poorest 10 per cent of
Canadian families with children under eighteen, with the richest 10 per
cent. Here is the ratio of the income of the richest to poorest. (In 1981 the
top 10 per cent earned 23.7 times the income of the bottom 10 per cent.)

1981	23.7	1992	101.4
1984	60.0	1993	221.0
1986	44.3	1994	195.0
1989	35.3	1995	114.3
1990	48.7	1996	314.3
1991	77.3		

The political and economic right in Canada, ardent followers of the
Ronald Reagan, Margaret Thatcher theories that free-market forces

---

* *The Daily*, December 10, 1997.
† *Macroeconomic Performance and Income Distribution in Canada*, Human Resources Development
Canada, 1997.

would benefit all, promised great benefits from privatization, deregulation, and free trade. It's clear there were indeed benefits for some, but unfortunately the vast majority of Canadians didn't get to share in them.

Tom Kent summed up an important aspect of what has been happening to the poor:

> When white-collar and unionized blue-collar jobs were plentiful, a good many disadvantaged children could make their way at least to the lower-middle class. The walls are higher now. The prospect for more of our children is uncertain, unsatisfying, poorly-paid work, or none. We are generating a new underclass of resentful youth, alienated from the society of comfort and order.[*]

Before we leave the question of distribution of income, let's look at how the different quintiles fared from 1980 to 1996, but this time after

FIGURE 18

Average After-Tax Income

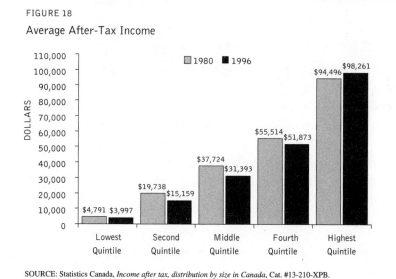

SOURCE: Statistics Canada, *Income after tax, distribution by size in Canada*, Cat. #13-210-XPB.

Note the large income decreases for the three middle quintiles from 1980 to 1996 (in constant 1996 dollars).

[*] *Social Policy 2000*, The Caledon Institute, January 1999.

tax. Figure 18 shows that the four lower quintiles dropped in average income. Only the highest quintile gained.

Now we must consider individual transfer payments (social program benefits) from government. What is remarkable is that average real transfers for the lowest-income quintile increased by only $1,579 over the sixteen-year period, while transfers for the highest quintile increased by almost as much, $1,398. Figure 19 gives the results after transfer payments have been added in.

FIGURE 19

Average Total Money Income

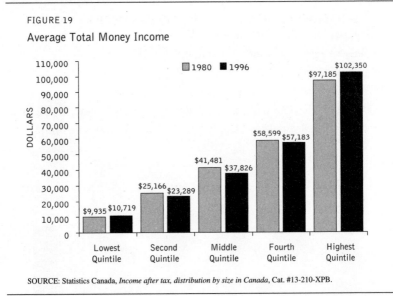

SOURCE: Statistics Canada, *Income after tax, distribution by size in Canada*, Cat. #13-210-XPB.

After government transfers are included, the poorest Canadians had tiny income gains while the top 20 per cent continued to increase their incomes and the middle 60 per cent lost ground (in constant 1996 dollars).

You can see that the lowest quintile, over sixteen years, ended up with a tiny gain of $784, while the highest quintile gained $5,165, and the other three quintiles all ended up with lower incomes.

For those whose automatic reaction to such information is that it's meaningless because, after all, the wealthy or high-income earners pay marginal tax rates of over 50 per cent, it's worth noting that in 1996 those in the highest income quintile, with average earnings of $102,350, paid total income tax at the effective rate of 25.1 per cent, while those in the second-highest quintile paid income tax at the effective rate of 20.5 per cent.

Now let's look at the final results for the five quintiles, after both government transfers and income tax, again in constant 1996 dollars. For the second and middle quintiles, the income drop was substantial, but most of the net loss was not in income taxes. For the highest quintile, most of the income decline was in higher income taxes. So, after tax and after transfers, what are we left with? Figure 20 tells it all.

FIGURE 20

Average Income After Transfers and Income Tax, 1996

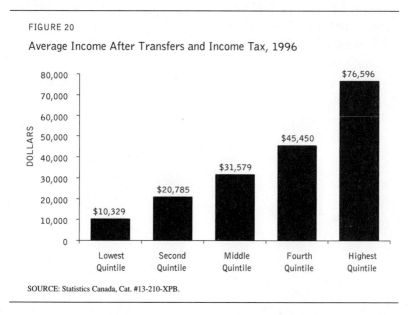

SOURCE: Statistics Canada, Cat. #13-210-XPB.

Imagine how you would fare if you had to manage on a total income of $10,329 – a figure that includes *government assistance.*

It should be pointed out that in recent years transfer payments to individuals in the highest quintile amounted to an average of $4,088, compared to $6,722 for the lowest quintile. In a country with so much poverty, do we really need to provide individuals and families earning on average over $100,000 a year such a large amount in government transfers? I think not.

A Statistics Canada survey of average household expenditures for 1996 showed the average household spent about $49,100 on everything from taxes and shelter to clothing and reading materials. The poorest families averaged 62 per cent of all their spending on food, clothing, and shelter, while the richest averaged 35 per cent.*

John Kenneth Galbraith makes an important point. For the less privileged, there is little choice: "They are under the pressure of more urgent need; that they will spend the money they receive is thus certain. Accordingly, income that is widely distributed . . . helps to ensure a steady flow of aggregate [total] demand. There is a strong chance that the more unequal the distribution of income, the more dysfunctional the economy becomes. . . . The basic need . . . is to accept the principle that a more equitable distribution of income must be a fundamental tenet of modern public policy in the good society, and to this end progressive taxation is central."†

We will come to the question of our not-so-progressive taxation system shortly.

---

* *Globe and Mail*, February 13, 1998.
† *The Socially Concerned Today*, University of Toronto Press, 1998.

Wealth: The Numbers That Really Count

He's a United Church minister who for years has been doing whatever he can to help the poor. Once a month there's a free dinner for about 150 men, women, and children. They have a small food bank in the church basement where people are allowed to pick up a modest hamper once or twice a month. There's been a big increase in recent years in the number of people asking for help. He says that somehow we've developed an expendable class that doesn't know one day to the next where their food is coming from; for many, "Love your neighbour" has been forgotten.

We met later for lunch with an Anglican minister. That morning a social worker had told him of a woman who had been forced to live in a car for two weeks. Another single mother had her telephone cut off and then her utilities. When she and her kids moved they ended up living next to loud drunks who partied through the night. None of them could sleep. The United Church minister told of a family of six sleeping on the floor, a baby in a cardboard box, and having to make a litre of milk last for days.

They went on like this for an hour and a half. It was very *depressing.*

As the rich get richer their wealth, unless squandered, accumulates. Accumulated wealth earns additional income, often with little effort or significant productivity. The remarkable stock-market boom in recent years, stock options, and inflated corporate salaries and bonuses have enriched a great many, with the top 10 per cent reaping the biggest gains. The wealth gap between rich and poor in Canada is far greater than the income gap.

The last Statistics Canada survey of wealth in Canada was done fifteen years ago, so our wealth statistics are well out of date. A new "Survey of Financial Security" should be released soon. In my 1991 book *The Betrayal of Canada*,* I showed that in 1988 the top 1/100 of 1 per cent of all enterprises in Canada controlled over 56 per cent of all corporate assets in the country, the top 1/10 of 1 per cent controlled 75 per cent and the top 1 per cent controlled over 85 per cent. "Put another way, 99% of Canada's half a million corporations own only 14.6% of corporate assets."

When these shocking numbers were published by Statistics Canada in 1991, there were no front-page headlines even in the business sections of newspapers. In fact, most Canadian newspapers failed to carry even a small paragraph on the subject. There was no debate in Parliament. There was hardly a stir in the nation. Yet these are the numbers that really count in any discussion of tax policy . . . the workings of the political process, or public policy of any kind – and especially in discussions about the future of our country.

By any standards of fairness and competition . . . by any measurements employed to determine how a free enterprise economy should function, these numbers are unacceptable and appalling. Our tax system and our hopelessly inadequate anti-combines laws have resulted in a situation in which a small number of huge corporations and powerful conglomerates (both foreign and Canadian) and a small number of families own and control Canada.

---

* Stoddart Publishing.

According to former Conservative cabinet minister James Gillies, writing in the magazine *Inside Guide*, "The degree of concentration, or in other words the lack of competition, in many markets in Canada is the greatest in the world and the concentration of economic power is enormous."[*]

Hal Jackman, former chairman of National Trust Company and former lieutenant-governor of Ontario, added his own comments in the same magazine:

> Greed and cupidity are, of course, not unique to the 1980s. They have been with us throughout history. However, what made the 1980s different from the years that preceded our most recent gilded age has been the unseemly worship or toleration of standards of conduct which in previous ages would not have been considered acceptable.

I concluded my chapters on corporate concentration in *The Betrayal of Canada* with these words:

> Finally, is it any wonder that time after time, when public opinion polls clearly show how Canadians strongly feel about various issues, the Mulroney government does exactly the opposite? For Mulroney, the polls from Bay Street, Rosedale, Forest Hill, Westmount, and Mount Royal are the polls that count.

Anyone who reads the papers knows that during the 1990s new records in mergers and acquisitions were broken almost every year. In 1997, the colossal $101 billion in takeovers and mergers in Canada astounded all observers. In 1998 the figure jumped to over $148 billion.

In Canada, the rich are getting much richer, the corporations are getting much bigger, and both have become far more powerful.

In the first volume of *The Canadian Establishment*, Peter C. Newman calculated that in the mid-1970s a tiny handful of about a dozen families and interrelated conglomerates controlled about 80 per

---

[*] *Inside Guide*, June 1991.

cent of the Toronto Stock Exchange's three hundred corporations. Given the recent record-breaking years of corporate concentration, Newman has "no doubt that the degree of concentration of wealth has increased considerably."*

By the mid-1980s, the wealthiest 10 per cent of Canadian families owned almost half of total wealth in Canada. Using statistics for 1995 in the *Financial Post Magazine*, NAPO calculated that the net worth of the fifty wealthiest Canadians was more than the *combined* government revenues of Newfoundland, Nova Scotia, New Brunswick, Prince Edward Island, Manitoba, Saskatchewan, and Alberta.

In 1996, economist Sylvia Ostry, as reported in the *Financial Post*, "deplores the growing disparity between rich and poor, with 2% of the population owning 70% of the wealth. I think it's very dangerous. . . ."†
The same year, Saskatchewan Premier Roy Romanow told an Ottawa conference that "one per cent of Canadians have 40 per cent of the wealth."** However unfair all these statistics may seem, we know that the situation today is much worse. However unfair income-distribution statistics may seem, they pale in comparison to wealth statistics.

It should be noted that each year Statistics Canada used to publish excellent, comprehensive statistics on corporate concentration in its annual CALURA report.†† They no longer do so.

If in the past the wealthy and the economic elite heavily influenced the decision-making process in Ottawa, today they run the show. Those in doubt should read Peter C. Newman's excellent chapter on the Business Council on National Issues in his book *Titans*.*** The chapter's title says it all: "Taking Over the National Agenda":

> The members of Canada's business establishment have good reason to believe they are running the country's economy. . . .
> They declared war on governments and battled out each outstanding public policy issue. Without ordinary citizens becoming aware of it, Ottawa capitulated. The regimes of Brian

* Conversation with the author, January 10, 1999.
† March 23, 1996.
** *Globe and Mail*, November 28, 1996.
†† *Corporations and Labour Unions Returns Act*, Cat. #61-220-XPB.
*** Toronto, Viking, 1998.

Mulroney and Jean Chrétien came to agree that what was good for the BCNI was good for Canada.

The big, wealthy corporations, in Newman's words, now have "unprecedented political power." And poverty and power are still on the same page in the dictionary, though in reality millions and millions of miles apart.

PART FOUR

Why Are People Poor?

The Bottom Line Has
Replaced the Golden Rule

The social counsellor told me about the man, but he made me promise to change the story so no one would know who it was or which city he lived in. He had been a moderately successful executive who over thirty years had worked his way up to a good management position. He always got along well with people, was a conscientious worker, and was devoted to the company.

One day just over eight years ago, the firm was sold to a big corporation from Chicago. The American firm promised to keep production in Canada and that there would be no layoffs. Eighteen months later, the man was out of a job, "downsized." He was given a modest goodbye package and a nice gold company pin.

He still had a big mortgage on his home. Two of his married kids had needed money, so he had given them a large chunk of his savings. Now he had little income, and try as he might, day after day and month after month, he couldn't find another job. Nobody came right out and said so, but at fifty-six he was too old.

He had to quit his golf club and his wife started looking for work, eventually ending up as a clerk at Eaton's. The man kept looking for work without success. Last year they had to sell the house and move into a walk-up apartment. He took his own life two months later.

What causes poverty?

There are lots of different reasons, but these are three main reasons. I will come back to the three main reasons in a moment, but first some of the other reasons.

All of the following can contribute to poverty: sustained illness, death of the chief family breadwinner, physical or mental handicap or disability, family breakup, inadequate education, substance abuse, entrapment in the cycle of poverty, being an aboriginal in a country that has treated terribly its aboriginal population, being a poor immigrant with poor education and inadequate language skills . . . the list goes on. This is not to say that all people with any of these problems must be poor or must become poor or must stay poor. It is to say that there is abundant evidence that these factors are common contributors to poverty.

All of these conditions and situations may be an immediate cause of poverty, but in addition there are three major reasons why we have so many poor people in Canada.

The first is uncaring and inept politicians and bureaucrats. Other countries, as we shall see, have adopted economic policies which have produced much lower unemployment and poverty rates. In Canada, we have allowed Bank of Canada governors, finance ministers, and deputy finance ministers to put their own dogmatic, anti-inflation theories ahead of the welfare of millions of Canadians. And we have had prime ministers who, despite all their rhetoric to the contrary, have cared little about the welfare of those who directly suffer from their governments' myopic, doctrinaire policies.

The second major reason for so much poverty in Canada is the direct result of the first: high unemployment and low job creation.

The third major reason is an abundance of poor-paying part-time jobs with few or no benefits, jobs that create "the working poor," men and women who don't show up in unemployment statistics, but do show up in Statistics Canada's low-income counts.

In 1993, when Canada's Catholic bishops criticized the federal government for failing to hear the "cries of anguish" from the unemployed, they said, "Unemployment of such magnitude is evidence of real moral disorder. . . . The working person is being sacrificed to the political ideology of the day. . . . There is a war declared in this country on the working person causing a rising rate of suicides, homicides, violence against women and children, and broken families. . . ." But, somehow, public attitudes towards high unemployment rates have changed. In the 1972 federal election, Pierre Trudeau and his Liberal government came within two seats of being tossed out of office and were forced into minority government with the NDP. One of the principal reasons for voter dissatisfaction was an unemployment rate just above 6 per cent. In 1962, John Diefenbaker similarly saw his government reduced to a minority position, with a 5.9-per-cent unemployment rate a significant factor in the election campaign.

In the preface to this book I warned readers not to celebrate unduly the recent decline in unemployment rates. Let's look at Canada's unemployment rates by decade, for the past fifty years (see Figure 21). Canada's unemployment rate in the 1990s has been the highest since the

FIGURE 21

Average Annual Unemployment Rates by Decade

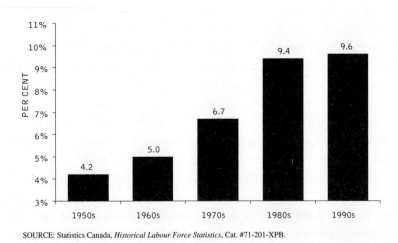

SOURCE: Statistics Canada, *Historical Labour Force Statistics*, Cat. #71-201-XPB.

Canada's high average unemployment rates in the 1980s and 1990s – more than double the 1950s rate – have been a major contributor to our high levels of poverty. (1999 figure estimated and forecast.)

terrible years of the 1930s, the decade of the Great Depression. Next, here are the Statistics Canada figures for the number of *officially* unemployed persons from 1979 to 1998 (see Figure 22). By 1998, despite some recent improvement, there were still about 435,000 more unemployed in Canada than there were almost two decades earlier.

FIGURE 22

Unemployed Persons in Canada

SOURCE: Statistics Canada, *Historical Labour Force Statistics*: Cat. #71-201-XPB.

Even though the number of officially unemployed persons in Canada has declined recently, it is still well above the level of twenty years ago.

But wait: it's really *much* worse than that.

Over the years there has been a great deal of criticism of Canada's official unemployment rate. The critics have contended it is too low, much too low. In December 1996, the Caledon Institute of Social Policy advised: "The official unemployment statistics greatly underestimate the problem. In 1995, the real unemployment rate – which includes people who have given up actively searching for work and part-time workers who want full-time jobs – was 15.2 percent or 60 percent higher than the 9.5 percent official rate."* Moreover, Caledon reported that the average duration of unemployment rose from fourteen weeks in 1976 to

---

* "Precarious Labour Market Fuels Rising Poverty."

twenty-four weeks in 1995. In the decade before the FTA came into effect (1979 to 1989), long-term unemployment in Canada (as defined by Statistics Canada) averaged 21.2 per cent of total unemployment. During the first ten years of the FTA (1989 to 1998), it increased to an annual rate of 25.2 per cent. Those four percentage points may not seem like a lot, but they translate into a considerable increase in the number of people pushed into poverty.

How reliable are official unemployment figures and rates? They're quite reliable, but they depend on the definitions used. There has been much discussion on the subject of "discouraged workers," people who want to work but who have looked so long for a job that they have simply given up. The percentage is particularly high in Newfoundland, but discouraged workers exist in every province; they are not counted as unemployed or as part of the labour force by Statistics Canada. In 1997, discouraged workers numbered about 108,000; most lived in Quebec and the Atlantic provinces.

Were we to also factor in labour force participation rates (the percentage of the population, fifteen years of age and older, who have jobs or who are looking for jobs) and involuntary part-time work (which increased from 20 per cent in 1990 to 29.4 per cent in 1998) there would be further increases in the official unemployment rates.

How do Canada's unemployment rates compare with those of other countries? Despite the recent improvements in Canada, our rates have remained higher than the average of the Group of Seven developed nations (G-7) and the OECD average (1999 figures are OECD forecasts) as shown in Figure 23. It's interesting to compare Canada's unemployment rate with Norway's. According to OECD and International Labor Organization standardized unemployment rates for the past twenty years, Canada's average annual unemployment rate was 9.5 per cent; Norway's was 3.7 per cent. I use Norway as an example because right-wing critics perpetually blame Canada's high unemployment rate on our "high" taxes and "high" government spending and social-program spending in particular (compared to GDP). Yet Norway, whose unemployment rate is less than half of our own, has higher taxes, higher government spending, and higher social-program spending rates than Canada. I could have used several other European countries to make the same comparisons.

FIGURE 23

Unemployment as a Percentage of the Labour Force

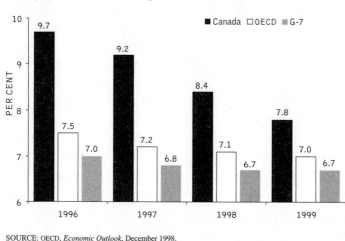

SOURCE: OECD, *Economic Outlook*, December 1998.

When we compare Canada's unemployment rate with rates in other developed nations, we have little to be proud of.

Here are some other countries with low unemployment rates at the time this book went to press: Luxembourg, 2.8 per cent; Austria, 4.4 per cent; Czech Republic, 3.8 per cent; Sweden, 4.9 per cent; Switzerland, 2.6 per cent; Netherlands, 3.6 per cent; Denmark, 5.4 per cent; Iceland, 2.6 per cent. Japan, whose economy has been a mess in recent years, has still managed to keep its unemployment down to, under, or around 5 per cent.

We're frequently bombarded by politicians and the press with comparisons to U.S. unemployment rates. Fair enough; U.S. rates have been lower than Canada's, beginning in the 1980s. But it's important to understand that Canada and the United States measure unemployment differently. If Canada had the same system of measuring unemployment as the U.S., our rate would be significantly lower. In the U.S. it's much more difficult to be officially classified as unemployed for a variety of reasons, among them the highest rate of imprisonment of all the OECD nations. (Prisoners are not counted as unemployed.) Mind you, it's true that a large prison population does create a great many jobs building and staffing prisons.

So why are Canada's unemployment figures so bad compared to many other countries and to the G-7 average (9.6 per cent for Canada compared to 6.6 per cent for the G-7 during the past ten years) and the OECD average (7.2 per cent)? After all, as indicated earlier, we've had more than a decade of free trade, relatively low nominal interest rates, and booming exports. There are several reasons. First, our monetary policy has kept unemployment artificially high during much of the past two decades. Second, downsizing has had a serious impact on middle-aged and older workers. As the *Globe and Mail* put it, "Many job hunters 45 and older have to give up their search in the face of discrimination by employers."* Dalton Camp also put it well:

> Worry about the rate of unemployment is becoming generational; the contemporary and truly sophisticated no longer think about it. Shareholders of the great corporations have reaped the profits of employee downsizing, as have financial institutions. At the same time, the public is being urged to downsize its expectations of government, to see its role reduced and thus its responsibilities for economic management.
>
> But in a world in which the Bottom Line had replaced the Golden Rule, it has also been established that unemployment can be a good thing. We know from observation, for example, that nothing panics the markets more than the threat of full employment.†

Let's for a moment turn our attention to Paul Tellier, *The Financial Post Magazine*'s CEO of the year for 1998. It's difficult to look at Tellier's performance without dismay, especially his downsizing of the Canadian National Railway (CN) workforce, chopping it almost in half. In Prince George, B.C., a woman, who with her husband worked for CN, a woman with teenagers and with mortgage payments to make, burst into tears when Tellier visited the city. "Why do you do this to me?" she cried. "Why do you do this to my family?"** For Tellier, "You're standing there and all the employees are watching you. The challenge is to be

---

* April 15, 1997.
† *Toronto Star*, July 16, 1997.
** *Financial Post Magazine*, 1998 annual edition.

very sincere, to be very honest, not to use jargon, and to say 'Listen, we are not in the business of protecting 36,000 jobs in CN.'"

Under Tellier, CN has become about 70-per-cent foreign-owned, mostly by Americans. The focus of the railway is no longer east-west, it's north-south. For the CEO of the year, John A. Macdonald's "policies were a mistake." Macdonald warned that unless we were careful "we should fall helpless, powerless and aimless into the hands of the neighboring republic."

However, have no fear: another great Canadian institution, *Time* magazine, tells us that "Paul Tellier and CN are changing the nature of the Canadian Dream," and "the irony of harnessing a railway that once symbolized national sovereignty to a continentalist vision is not lost on Tellier. . . ."* As to criticism about what has happened to CN under his direction, Tellier advises, "I find this argument that you're no longer 100% Canadian, this is horseshit."†

Tellier, by the way, received a total pay package of $1.55 million in 1998, a 23-per-cent increase over 1997, plus a special pension arrangement that added twenty-five years to his CN seniority. No doubt the family in Prince George and thousands of other laid-off CN workers were pleased at this news.

I won't spend much time on the infamous NAIRU (the non-accelerating inflation rate of unemployment), a so-called natural rate of unemployment, which has been a long-time fundamental economic policy measurement of the Bank of Canada and the Department of Finance and the benchmark which for so long guided our monetary strategy. (Linda McQuaig's book *The Cult of Impotence* is a fine review of this topic). Carol Goar, commenting on the NAIRU, summed it up well:

> Economists have been propagating this argument for years. . . .
> It is demonstrably wrong. . . . Tell (this theory) to the nurses
> who have been laid off because of hospital cutbacks or the
> aspiring teachers shut out of the school system by educational
> cutbacks. The private sector is not going to create the jobs these

---

* January 18, 1999.
† *National Post*, April 14, 1999.

people want, no matter how low interest rates go or how good the business climate is.

How does a nation that has accepted the logic that budgets must be balanced, governments must be lean and inflation must be squelched, deal with the human casualties of the marketplace?*

Among the millions of human casualties in Canada are the poor.

Incredibly, David Dodge, former deputy minister of finance, warned the minister, Paul Martin, that Canada's social programs were responsible for keeping our unemployment rates high.† That's like saying food is responsible for hunger.

Lack of education is another major cause of unemployment. During the 1990s, a pattern clearer than ever before has emerged. The increase in new jobs for those with university degrees and college diplomas far exceeded the employment increase for those with only a high-school diploma. For those who didn't complete high school, there was a sharp decline in the number of jobs. In today's world, employers want workers with an adequate education. As I pointed out earlier, poor youths have a much higher school dropout rate than those who aren't poor. The cycle of poverty.

At the post-secondary level, declining government support has had a major impact on Canadian universities. Real spending on post-secondary education has fallen by almost 35 per cent since 1977. A June 1999 study by the Association of Universities and Colleges of Canada** says serious underfunding is resulting in an erosion in the quality of education and rapidly rising tuition fees which become "a daunting prospect"†† for poorer students.

The higher the rate of unemployment and underemployment, the lower are government tax receipts and the higher the cost of social-support payments. You would think it only natural for government to strive for low unemployment rates as the basis of economic policy.

---

* *Toronto Star*, March 1, 1997.
† *Globe and Mail*, October 14, 1997.
** *Trends: The Canadian University in Profile*.
†† The words of James Turk, executive director of the Canadian Association of University Teachers, quoted in the *National Post*, June 11, 1999.

Unfortunately, in Canada crushing inflation has long been our fundamental economic policy. Montreal economist Pierre Fortin blames first "extremely tight" monetary policy, and then "tight fiscal policy has taken over. . . ."* Canada's "job-creation performance under both the Conservatives and the Liberals has been disastrous" because of poor government economic strategy.

The highly regarded U.S. economist Paul Krugman said, "I cannot understand why Canada is not pursuing a more expansionist monetary policy when your unemployment levels are so high." Good question. In an interview with the *Toronto Star* from his Sloan School of Management office in Cambridge, Massachusetts, Krugman said, "Canada's decision to pursue anti-inflationary targets that are more ambitious than those in the United States makes no sense given your unemployment rate." According to the *Star*, "Krugman returned to how baffled he is that the majority of Canada's mainstream economists appear so wedded to inflation fighting when jobs are clearly the order of the day."†

The Bank of Canada finally saw the light and began to reduce interest rates. But horrendous damage had been done. Even today, real interest rates in Canada – about 4 per cent – are far too high by historical standards. Businesses paying prime plus one in 1998 were paying real interest at an average rate of 6.6 per cent, almost double the historical average rate.

Some people have suggested that the official unemployment rate is lower now because many Canadians have "opted" to retire earlier and are no longer in the labour force. This is no doubt true; mandatory retirement, downsizing, and government layoffs are important factors in reducing the labour force. In the mid-1970s, the average retirement age was around 65; today it's closer to 60. Many "voluntary" retirements represent people who have been pushed into accepting early-retirement packages (many of them quite inadequate), people who would much rather be working, but have dim prospects for employment because of their age. Moreover, permanent layoffs of workers aged 55 to 65 have increased markedly in recent years.

---

* *Globe and Mail*, May 29, 1997.
† March 23, 1997.

At the other end of the labour force, youth unemployment has been horrendous, with rates running considerably higher than in the 1970s. While Canada's total unemployment rate in the 1990s averaged an annual rate of about 9.6 per cent, for youths aged 15 to 24 it averaged a disgraceful 15.6 per cent, and the youth participation rate plummeted from over 70 per cent in 1988 and 1989 to a dismal 62 per cent in 1998.

The consequences are ominous, according to Miles Corak:

> The well being of children is increasingly a concern for at least two reasons. The first has to do with the fact that labour markets have changed dramatically over the last two decades in ways detrimental to the young, resulting in the coming of age of a group that many expect not to reach the standard of living of their parents. The second has to do with a concern for the children of this generation since it is often assumed that experiencing low income as a child may lead to a lifetime of low income.
>
> Labour market conditions have deteriorated for the young, particularly men, with the result that a much higher proportion are now part of the "contingent" work-force. Their earnings capacity seems to have permanently deteriorated during the 1980s, raising the risk that they and their children will fall into a state of low-income.*

By the summer of 1997, there were more than 430,000 Canadian youths actively seeking work, and the teen labour-participation rate was the lowest in a quarter-century. By Christmas 1998, the official unemployment rate among young Canadians 15 to 24 stood at 15.8 per cent. In reality it was much more likely in the range of 20 per cent. Meanwhile, Canada's first ministers sombrely declared that youth unemployment was a "national priority."

Deborah Sunter, chief of Statistics Canada's labour-force survey, has shown that the youth employment rate fell more than eleven percentage points since 1989, and that almost half the young people with jobs were working part-time, compared with only 21 per cent in 1989.

---

* *Social Institutions and the Future of Canada's Children*, Statistics Canada, *Labour Markets*, Cat. #89-553-XPB.

Meanwhile, fewer students were able to find summer jobs.* Both the employment rates and participation rates began a dramatic decline in 1989. Sunter shows that the proportion of youths with no work experience stood at 9.7 per cent in 1989, 15.8 per cent in 1993, and 19.9 per cent in 1996. By December 1997, it reached almost 25 per cent. Another ominous trend.

Of all the OECD countries, Canada's youth unemployment rate was higher than that of twenty-one other countries. Meanwhile, as youth unemployment rates skyrocketed, so did university tuition fees. A great combination.

In the Liberals' notorious 1993 Red Book of election promises, we find, "No group faces bleaker economic prospects than Canadians under 25. A Liberal government will help return hope to young Canadians." Some hope. The Liberals' much-touted Youth Service Canada program, launched in 1994, had affected only 13,000 young people by the spring of 1998. Paul Martin's 1998 budget doubled the program's funds, but a program that assists only a tiny percentage of the over 400,000 young people who are officially unemployed is hardly a cause for celebration. Again, there's many more than the official number of unemployed youth. *Not* included in the official rates are about 225,000 youths who are not in school, do not have jobs, but have not sought unemployment-insurance benefits. Canadian Imperial Bank of Commerce (CIBC) economist Benny Tal says, "This is a very dynamic segment of the population that's not being utilized. Mostly they're not looking for work because many believe that either jobs are not available or they do not have the necessary skills."†

Some conservatives suggest that job-creation policies are beyond government. Columnist Andrew Coyne, for instance, writes, "By now, most politicians know there is nothing they can do about unemployment in the short-term and that they are likely to do more harm than good by trying. . . . None of [the policies politicians will offer] will make the slightest difference in the number of jobless. . . . No party, whatever half-hearted charade it may put on, has any idea how to promote economic growth. . . ."**

---

* *Canadian Economic Observer*, May 1997, Cat. #11-010-XPB.
† Southam Newspapers, March 20, 1998.
** Southam News, April 10, 1997.

So, these conservatives conclude, let's leave it all to the private sector and the market. Al Flood, former chairman of CIBC, "is on a mission to persuade corporate leaders they have a duty to hire more young people. . . . More than 100 companies have signed up for Career Edge, a program which provides internships for unemployed gradu-ates."* After three years, with more than three hundred big corporations involved, Career Edge managed to average only about 1,700 part-time jobs a year.

Conservatives who say government can't do anything to produce economic conditions that will help reduce unemployment lead a blink-ered, doctrinaire existence. The evidence from many other countries is abundant and clear that a well-thought-out package of basic economic policies can result in sustained low rates of unemployment.

After inept politicians, unemployment is the number-one cause of poverty in Canada. We'll look at the third major cause, poor-paying jobs, shortly. But let's close this chapter with a quote showing the troglodyte mentality that poor Canadians face. What we need to do, our "national newspaper" tells us on its editorial page, is to "lower the minimum wage in order to help many members of our target population price them-selves back into work." Moreover, "we need more low-skill, low-wage jobs, not fewer."†

So, it's not the war against poverty we're to be engaged in, it's the war against the poor.

---

* *Toronto Star*, August 12, 1997.
† *Globe and Mail*, September 12, 1997.

The Great Free Trade Hoax

He said that one thing about working at a low-pay job is that you're always just one unexpected event away from big trouble. If a water pipe freezes and breaks, or if the old car you use to get back and forth into the city for your job breaks down, or if one of the kids needs some special medicine, there's big, big plenty serious problems. Only one of the three kids is in school and the wife stays home to look after the two young ones. He said that with his grade-ten education, getting a decent-paying secure job was next to impossible. He knows he should have tried to stay in school longer, but his dad had just lost the farm and the family needed any money he could bring in. He knows that he should try to get some job training, but none of the programs would give him and his wife enough to look after the kids properly. He couldn't go to his family for help and his wife didn't have any family she could turn to. They live as cheaply as they can; they wash clothes at the laundromat and hung them to dry on the fence, until the landlord complained. Sometimes they don't even have the money for soap or deodorant.

The flip side of unemployment is employment.

In 1988, the year before the Free Trade Agreement came into effect, the ratio of those employed as a percentage of the population fifteen years and over stood at 62 per cent.* During the first ten years of the FTA the employment rate averaged only 59.5 per cent. Once again, the 2.5 per cent difference may seem small, but it translates into a difference of some 350,000 jobs a year.

In the decade before the FTA, employment in Canada increased by 2,498,600 jobs. During the first decade of the FTA, employment in Canada increased by only 1,507,500 jobs, a huge difference of almost one million jobs.

In the decade before the FTA, full-time employment in Canada increased by 1,719,200 jobs. During the first decade of the FTA, full-time employment increased by a dismal 975,500 jobs.

During the decade before the FTA, part-time employment averaged 16 per cent of all jobs. In the first decade of the FTA, part-time employment averaged 18.3 per cent of all jobs.

In the decade before the FTA, the number of payroll employees in Canada increased by 2,037,900. During the first FTA decade, the number of payroll employees increased by a paltry 803,200.

Even these awful statistics are overly generous to the Mulroney and Chrétien governments. More than half of all jobs created in Canada during the 1990s have been in the category of the "self-employed." In the words of the OECD, "The fact that many own-account workers list themselves as self-employed because they have no other job opportunities suggests that a substantial part of the rise in the 1990s may be in the form of 'hidden' unemployment."†

Self-employed workers in Canada on average earn between 50 and 65 per cent of the earnings of paid workers and usually work longer hours and have poor benefits. About half of the self-employed earn less than $20,000 a year and about 25 per cent earn less than $10,000.

Many of those who are self-employed are there for one of two reasons. First, they can't find a payroll job. Or, second, they have been let go from a payroll job. Sometimes the reason they have been let go

---

* Statistics Canada, *Historical Labour Force Statistics*, Cat. #71-201-XPB.
† *OECD Economic Surveys, Canada*, 1998.

reflects a growing trend of corporations escaping the cost of payroll benefits by increasingly hiring part-time, irregular, temporary, or contract casual labour, or by farming out parts of their operations.

Only about 10 per cent of those classified as self-employed hire employees. This also is a big change from the previous decade, when about two-thirds of those newly self-employed hired others. Bruce Little notes, "From 1989 to 1996, the number of self-employed people increased by 450,000, but only 10 per cent started a business. The other 90 per cent were working on their own, which suggests that the overwhelming majority chose self-employment as a last (or only) resort."[*]

For those who might think that the large increases in the numbers of the self-employed can be attributed to a surge of entrepreneurial enthusiasm, the evidence is clear that this is not the case: when the labour market improves there is a rush of self-employed job-seekers back to available paid employment.

As indicated previously, during the first decade of the FTA only 1,507,500 jobs were created. But of those, 704,300 were self-employed "jobs," while 581,100 constituted an increase in part-time jobs. That leaves a pathetic remaining average of only 22,210 new jobs a year.

These numbers go a long way to explaining why we have so much poverty in Canada. Is it any wonder there are so many more insecure Canadians in all parts of the county, even if they're not now below any poverty line? And is it any wonder, as we shall see, that we have such high personal bankruptcy rates and escalating household debt, and such low personal savings rates?

An important measure of the state of the economy is the labour-force participation rate – the percentage of the population fifteen years of age and over who are employed or who are looking for jobs. Warren Jestin and Adrienne Warren of the Bank of Nova Scotia estimated that had our participation rate remained constant in the mid-1990s, the unemployment rate would have been between 13 and 14 per cent, considerably higher than the official rate. Economist Arthur Donner calculated the real rate of unemployment in 1997 at 14 per cent, instead of the official rate of 9.2 per cent.

---

[*] *Globe and Mail*, August 3, 1998.

For the past ten years, had the participation rate remained at historical levels, the unemployment rate would be about 2.5-per-cent higher for the decade and would have measured over 10.7 per cent in 1998 instead of the official rate of 8.4 per cent.

In January 1999, economist Marie-Josée Kravin put into perspective Ottawa's jubilation about the falling official unemployment rate:

Canada's unemployment rate has finally dropped to 8% and Ottawa is just elated. More women are working and more full-time jobs have been created, but it is too early to uncork the champagne. Last week's jubilation blithely obscured the fact that the proportion of working-age Canadians participating in the labour force has declined substantially during this past decade. Proportionately fewer workers are seeking jobs, which embellishes the unemployment record. In 1990, for example, total participation rates in Canada were 68%, but in 1998 they had sunk to 65.6%. If participation rates had held steady, 650,000 more Canadians would have been searching for work and this would have propelled the unemployment rate up by roughly three percentage points. By 1990 standards, therefore, we are well into double-digit unemployment.*

Before leaving the question of the participation rate, let's look at Figure 24, showing what has happened to it since the FTA came into effect. Figure 25 shows what has happened to part-time work in Canada during the past two decades.

Many part-time workers are involuntarily part-time: they want and need full-time jobs. The percentage of involuntary part-time workers has increased steadily since the FTA was implemented. Most part-time jobs offer lower pay, few benefits, and less job security. Many of these workers are paid at or near the minimum wage, which comes nowhere near to providing income that approaches the poverty lines. The *Report on Business Magazine*† compared part-time employment in the first year of the FTA with the results seven years later:

---

* *National Post*, January 15, 1999.
† February 1997. Original source Dun and Bradstreet Canada.

FIGURE 24

The Labour Force Participation Rate

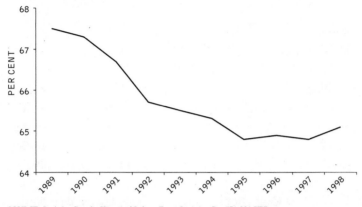

SOURCE: Statistics Canada, *Historical Labour Force Statistics*, Cat. #71-201-XPB.

Because of poor job prospects, fewer Canadians have sought employment in recent years. If the participation rate had remained at historic levels, the unemployment rate would be much higher.

FIGURE 25

Part-Time Employment as a Percentage of Total Employment

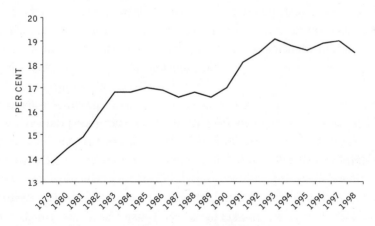

SOURCE: Statistics Canada, *Historical Labour Force Statistics*: Cat. #71-201-XPB.

More and more involuntary part-time work with low pay and fewer hours and benefits has been another major contributor to poverty in Canada.

Part-time employees as a percentage of the total workforce

	1989	1994	1996
Construction	8.7%	9.5%	34.7%
Retailing	16.3	19.8	34.2
Services	11.3	13.0	32.3
Manufacturing	6.0	6.4	27.7
Wholesaling	4.9	6.2	23.4
Transportation	6.3	7.7	22.3
Agriculture	18.3	24.8	21.1
Mining	8.5	8.4	16.5
Finance	2.4	3.1	16.3
Total	9.5	11.1	29.3

In 1997, the Centre for the Study of Living Standards reported that, if involuntary part-time workers were taken into consideration, the unemployment rate in 1995 would have been 12.7 per cent instead of 9.7 per cent. In 1995, 801,000 part-time workers wanted full-time jobs.

Why is all of this happening? The centre's Andrew Sharpe is clear about its significance. "Part-time workers are more attractive to employers than full-time workers for at least two reasons – they provide greater flexibility in scheduling and receive lower wages and fewer benefits."[*] Exactly. Of course, people at work in poor-paying, low benefit jobs don't show up in the unemployment figures, nor for the most part in the welfare rolls. So governments can claim success: the unemployment rate falls, the welfare payouts drop, and the unemployment-insurance surplus is burgeoning. When they should be ashamed of what has been happening, governments are proud of their social cutbacks. All one has to do is listen to the boasts of Jean Chrétien, Paul Martin, Mike Harris, and Ralph Klein.

All things considered, then, is it any wonder that even as the official unemployment rate has fallen, the number of low-income Canadians has increased?

As indicated earlier, among those who have suffered the most from Canada's poor labour market have been young Canadians. The drop in youth (15 to 24) employment in Canada during the past two decades has been dramatic as Figure 26 demonstrates.

---

[*] *CSLS News*, September 1997.

FIGURE 26

Youth Employment

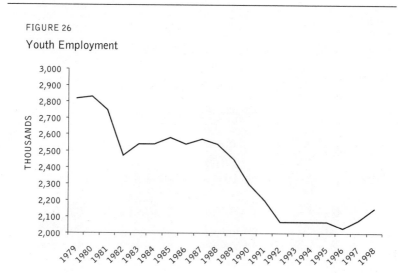

SOURCE: Statistics Canada, *Historical Labour Force Statistics*: Cat. #71-201-XPB.

Young Canadians were hit hard by the poor labour-market conditions of the 1990s. The number employed now compared to twenty years ago has actually dropped by more than half a million.

Remember now, our first ministers declared youth unemployment "a national priority." Some priority.

Many of the large corporations that so enthusiastically backed the FTA are the same corporations that have chopped jobs in Canada. A headline in the *Globe and Mail* in 1996 says it all: "JOBS CUT DESPITE HEFTY PROFITS:" "A parade of Canadian blue-chip companies are proudly reporting hefty – and sometimes record – profits to their share-holders, but many of the companies continue to slash jobs as if the recession never ended."[*]

Before we sum up on the question of what has happened to employ-ment since the FTA, look at the depressing picture shown in Figure 27 (overleaf). Now for another very revealing comparison. Figure 28 shows increases in exports from Canada, compared to employment increases – employment changes essentially remained flat.

---

[*] February 6, 1996.

FIGURE 27

Employment Growth

Average Annual

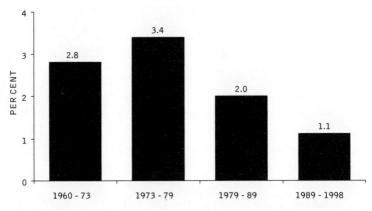

SOURCE: OECD, *Historical Statistics* and Statistics Canada, *Historical Labour Force Statistics*, Cat. #71-201 XPB.

Since the Free Trade Agreement came into effect in 1989, the growth in employment has been dismal.

FIGURE 28

Exports and Jobs Since the Free Trade Agreement

SOURCE: Statistics Canada, *Historical Labour Force Statistics*, Cat. #71-201 XPB; and
Statistics Canada, *Canada's Balance of International Payments*, Cat. #67-001-XPB.

While both the Mulroney and Chrétien governments have trumpeted increased exports, job creation has been flat.

Through much of 1999, Canadians were bombarded with laudatory tenth-anniversary comments in the media about how successful the FTA had been for Canada. The comments came mostly from the same big-business sources that helped buy the 1988 free trade election for Brian Mulroney but also from the former prime minister himself and his closest political colleagues. Surely, they said, it was self-evident; the FTA has been such a great success because there has been a huge increase in exports to the United States and now about 40 per cent of our GDP (and by inference our jobs and our standard of living) depends on that trade. (Actually, 1998 exports to the U.S. amounted to 30.3 per cent of GDP.) But we can see from the previous disastrous employment figures (as we shall also see in pages to come) that the impact on Canadians has been devastating.

There are several points to be made. First, counting exports without considering imports is like measuring your financial status on the basis of the paycheques you receive without considering all your bills. It's the *net* trade balance that should be measured in terms of the GDP, not just exports; the FTA was not a one-way deal. In 1998 our total exports of goods and services exceeded imports by only 1.3 per cent of GDP. Second, when measuring the net trade balance, it should be calculated in constant dollar terms, and it must include both merchandise and non-merchandise balances. Third, the nature of our exports must be considered. A very large percentage of what we export to the U.S. is merchandise that foreign subsidiaries have already imported from the U.S. and then exported from their Canadian "screwdriver" assembly plants. This process involves importing labour-intensive products and then exporting merchandise that has a comparatively low Canadian labour content. Fourth, under the provisions of the FTA, U.S. ownership of Canada has increased substantially. The year 1998 set an all-time record for American takeovers of businesses in Canada. U.S. corporations in this country tend to buy parts and components and business services from their parent corporations, even if such items are competitively available here in Canada. Far too often the jobs end up in the U.S., and because of transfer pricing between the parent and the subsidiary, much of the profits (and tax revenue) also end up in the U.S., not in Canada. Moreover, U.S. direct investment in Canada is overwhelmingly for takeovers, not for the establishment of new businesses. Takeovers usually result in fewer jobs, not more jobs. The terrible employment figures you have seen in this chapter are a devastating indictment of the poor performance of the Canadian economy under both the Mulroney and Chrétien governments. Monetary policy, tax policy, and other government policies have been a factor. But anyone who believes that the FTA and NAFTA have helped the Canadian economy is dreaming. The poorly thought-out trade agreements have had a major negative impact on the lives of average Canadians. We'll see more of the results in the chapter titled "The Big Disconnect."

One final point. In Appendix Two at the back of this book you will find a table that will come as a huge surprise to anyone who has followed the decade-long debate about the FTA and NAFTA. Next time you hear Brian Mulroney or Tom d'Aquino or your morning paper's editor spouting off about our booming exports that came from free trade, you might want to remind them about the employment figures in this chapter and about the remarkable bottom line of Appendix Two.

UI, EI, Oh!

I asked the retired archbishop why most people don't seem to care very much about poverty, about hunger, about suffering. He said they don't believe it; they don't believe we have so much poverty. They just don't see the degree of poverty out there. I mentioned a wealthy friend who was very generous in his efforts to help the poor. The archbishop said the problem is far too big to try to rely on wealthy volunteer contributors. The solution must be political; the country must do it. I asked him if he had witnessed an increase in poverty in recent years. He said yes, a big increase. So many children so deprived, children unable to cope, totally unable to compete with children in other parts of the city. I asked if he thought the church was doing enough. He answered immediately, no, not nearly enough. I asked why that was. He said most of the people who go to the cathedral never go to the poor parts of town, even the priests. The priests are too far away. They don't want to see it. There's not much poverty at the cathedral. I asked if he had often gone to see the premier and government ministers and the MPPs about the poor. He said, Yes! To Death! Nothing ever gets done.

They listen and nod their heads. Nothing happens. There's not
many votes in feeding the hungry.

An October 20, 1998, news item suggests, "Human Resources Minister
Pierre Pettigrew has endorsed a study by his department that says the
unemployment insurance system is meeting its main objective, even
though just 42 per cent of the country's jobless qualified for benefits last
year." According to Mr. Pettigrew, "The system is sound and it's
working."* Working for whom? Paul Martin, no doubt.

Unemployment-insurance was designed to be a program which was
to provide help for workers who were laid off, couldn't find a job, faced
illness or disability, or had to leave their jobs for just cause, including
personal reasons. These workers would have a cushion until they could
get back into the labour force. They would be able to meet some but not
all of their normal basic personal and financial needs without resorting
to meagre welfare assistance.

No one should believe for a moment that UI was an overly generous program. It wasn't, but it mostly served its intended purpose in
keeping landlords from serving eviction notices and giving families
enough money to buy proper, nutritious food. All working Canadians
contributed to providing the insurance that they themselves might
someday need.

The Mulroney and the Chrétien governments changed all that. All
working Canadians still contribute, but the "insurance" has disappeared
for most of the unemployed. The ridiculously renamed Employment
Insurance (EI) program in most cases now provides neither a guarantee
of employment or a guarantee of insurance. Thanks to federal government "reforms," hundreds of thousands of unemployed men and women
are now left out in the cold, and, as we have seen, many of them are *lit-*
erally out in the cold.

Before the Mulroney government took over, between 68 and 87 per
cent of the unemployed received benefits. By 1998, that number was
down to under 39 per cent.† The result, in human terms, is the type of

---

* *Globe and Mail.*
† In the United States only about one-third of the unemployed qualify for benefits; in Germany it's about 90
per cent and in France about 98 per cent. *New York Times*, March 9, 1999.

deprivation described on the previous pages. The result, in fiscal terms, is an annual surplus of billions of dollars from the EI account, money from workers and from business that Paul Martin has diverted elsewhere. Forget the fact that the UI program was designed to protect the unemployed. It's now clearly designed to protect the Liberal government. Much, or most, *or all* recent federal surpluses have come straight from the EI fund.

The Mulroney and Chrétien government cutbacks have been truly draconian: much tougher eligibility requirements, lower benefits, shortened periods of compensation. Among those harmed the most have been young Canadians, women, part-time workers, seasonal workers, mothers on maternity leave, contract workers, and those seeking job training. Many of these people must pay EI premiums even though they are most unlikely to receive benefits. Moreover, even if a person has paid into a UI or EI fund for, say, thirty years, once they have been unemployed for a year and have received benefits for forty-five weeks, they are no longer entitled to receive further compensation. Yet according to Pierre Pettigrew, "We can see the system really does work for those it was intended for."[*] By the fall of 1998, almost 40 per cent of the unemployed had been without work for more than one year.

Too bad. There's always welfare.

Remember that these huge benefit cutbacks took place during the decade with the worst levels of unemployment since the Great Depression. Makes sense, doesn't it? If there's high unemployment, cut people off and reduce benefits, but keep charging those premiums.

Figure 29 (overleaf) shows the percentage of unemployed receiving EI benefits. The figure for 1998 was down to 38.8 per cent.

In 1998, Ottawa took in almost $19.6 billion in employment-insurance premiums, but paid out only $11.8 billion in benefits. From 1994 to 1998 inclusive, Paul Martin's surplus on the EI account amounted to an enormous $31 billion dollars.

The February 1999 budget forecasted an additional surplus of almost $10 billion over two years. In 1998, about 925,000 unemployed Canadians received no benefits. *Toronto Star* columnist Rosemary Speirs hit the nail on the head:

---

[*] *Toronto Star*, October 22, 1998.

FIGURE 29

Percentage of Unemployed Receiving EI Benefits

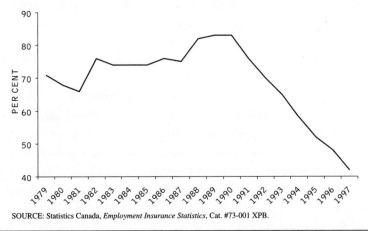

SOURCE: Statistics Canada, *Employment Insurance Statistics*, Cat. #73-001 XPB.

Up until about ten years ago 70 to 80 per cent of unemployed workers received UI benefits. Now – disgracefully – fewer than 40 per cent do.

Once, Liberal cabinet ministers argued a more generous regime benefited the whole economy by maintaining the purchasing power of those who lost their jobs. Today, the government reflects the attitude that Chrétien occasionally lets slip – that EI recipients lie around watching TV and drinking beer. Cutting them off, his ministers have argued, would force the jobless to get to work.

Unfortunately, as we have seen, for a great many people the jobs are simply not there. As Speirs indicates, the "problem isn't laziness . . . the problem is finding a job in an era of government cuts, corporate downsizing and layoffs like those just announced by Canadian National Railways. . . ."

But matching American meanness has failed in its purported goal of reducing unemployment here. We now have a huge pool of long-term unemployed without prospects. A third are on social assistance, but the rest are making shift somehow with no help from the public purse. They sure aren't lazing around on benefits, because they haven't had any for a long time.*

We've already noted the growing number of involuntary self-employed men and women. They already have below average incomes. If their businesses fail and they must close shop and look for work then too bad; no EI benefits.

One direct result of what you've seen in Figure 29 is a huge increase in the burden on provincial social-assistance spending, an increase estimated by Pierre Fortin at some $2.5 billion a year. But with reduced federal transfers, the provinces, particularly Ontario and Alberta, have substantially cut back their own social-benefits payouts.

What causes poverty? Inept and callous politicians must head any list. For Paul Martin to reduce taxes for high-income earners while continuing to collect premiums from low-income and middle-income Canadians is unconscionable. To do so while denying the unemployed benefits, while so many poor Canadians suffer, is beyond contempt. Labour leader Bob White had it right: "It was remarkable last year to watch the government discover the growing child poverty problem in Canada. You don't think cutting mom and dad's UI benefits has anything to do with it?"†

---

* *Toronto Star*, October 22, 1998.
† *Globe and Mail*, June 1, 1998.

PART FIVE

Work, Wages, Profits, and Hypocrisy

Canada is performing better than it has in a generation.

– Gordon Thiessen,
Governor of the Bank of Canada,
Globe and Mail,
March 26, 1998

The Working Poor and
the Big Bonus Bankers

*Do I eat that orange or leave it to kids? She says she some-
times debates that sort of question for an hour. The kids are
always coming home from school asking for money. We need
the money for this and that and the other thing at school they
say. Kids are always losing stuff like mitts and scarves.
Sometimes other kids take them. When it happens to us it's a
real crisis. She says the government doesn't understand or
doesn't care. What's the difference? Too often, mostly when I
haven't eaten, I get stressed out. Then the kids get stressed out.
The kids are always asking why they have to go to school in
the same clothes every day. I tell them to tell the kids who stick
their nose in that you wear the clothes because you like them.
It drives me insane when I see the kids suffering. It's just so
goddamn bloody unfair.*

One of the main reasons people are poor is poor wages. The working
poor want work, but when they do get work they usually stay poor.

Columnist Richard Gwyn calls our persistent high unemployment
rates "our [unadmitted] policy of keeping unemployment high [which]
does far more to curb inflation by discouraging wage demands and by

encouraging all those with jobs to work ferociously hard to keep them."

In recent years, about a quarter of all jobs in Canada paid less than ten dollars an hour. Last year, over half a million poor children lived in families where parents had a full year of employment. Almost 40 per cent of working single-parent mothers receive less than ten dollars an hour in wages. One recent estimate put the number of working-poor households in Canada at close to 900,000. Many of these families would be better off on welfare, although the drastic cuts to welfare in Ontario and Alberta must be considered.

As more and more corporations have adopted a strategy of increasing part-time and contract work and cutting back on full-time jobs with their obligatory benefits, more and more families are finding it impossible to earn a decent income from employment. According to Ross Finnie, "Workers in the lower reaches of the distribution have fallen behind in both relative and absolute terms, a sharp reversal from the previous decades of steady increases across the entire distribution."[*]

Between 1989 and 1997 the average low-income family slipped about a thousand dollars further below the LICOs line. As the Caledon Institute of Social Policy said in December 1997, rising inequality in market incomes

is taxing the poverty-reduction power of economic growth, employment creation and income transfers. . . . Canada and the U.S. appear to be entering a new phase of all bets are off when it comes to counting on traditional forces to reduce poverty. . . . The culprit is the labour market, which is increasingly insecure and unequal. The economy of the 1990s is creating an abundance of "nonstandard" jobs which pay low wages, offer few if any benefits and are often part-time or unstable. A job simply cannot provide a living wage for many thousands of Canadians, particularly families with children to support. In 1996, the heads of half (50.3 per cent) of low-income families worked but remained poor because they earned low wages and/or could find only seasonal part-time work.[†]

---

[*] Statistics Canada, *Perspectives*, Summer 1999, Cat. #75-001-XPE.
[†] *Persistent Poverty*.

In a fine paper, Grant Schellenberg and David P. Ross of the CCSD wrote, "The evidence is clear and unequivocal. In the absence of government income support, many Canadian families would be left poor by the marketplace."* Without government assistance, poverty rates would be much, much higher and the depth of poverty much, much deeper. Ross and Schellenberg showed that in 1994 some two-thirds of all husbands in market-poor families, representing about 600,000 households, were in the labour force all year. And many of the rest could not find jobs. In their conclusion, the two authors wrote:

> Quite simply, many jobs do not pay high enough wages to provide even full-time workers with sufficient income to adequately support their families. . . . About 100,000 families were market poor despite having had two supporting adults work all year. . . . The primary contributors to their market poverty was not the number of hours being worked, but rather the hourly wages being earned.
>
> Over the past twenty years, minimum-wage rates across the county have not kept pace with inflation. . . . Between 1976 and 1995, the annual earnings received by full-time, full-year workers employed at minimum wage declined by 25 to 30 per cent in almost every province.

In wealthy Alberta, the drop was 34 per cent.

Poor people depend heavily on government assistance. For example, about 90 per cent of total income for unattached women sixty-five and older comes from government transfers. For single mothers with children under eighteen, it's close to 70 per cent. Even a small reduction in government assistance invariably represents large percentage reductions in total income for the poor.

Yet, contrary to some right-wing propaganda, a large percentage of poor Canadian adults receive most of their income from their jobs. The National Council of Welfare shows that 50 per cent of poor unattached men under sixty-five, 57 per cent of poor unattached women, 45 per cent

---

* Ottawa, 1997.

of poor couples without children, and 60 per cent of poor couples with children were working poor, men and women whose employment fails to lift them out of poverty. Dr. Fraser Mustard, founding president of the Canadian Institute for Advanced Research, has pointed out that employment income for the poorest 20 per cent of Canadians dropped by one-third between 1984 and 1994.*

It doesn't take much math to figure out that in 1999, someone working for seven dollars an hour in a thirty-hour week makes less than $950 a month, before deductions. Those neo-neanderthals who advocate dropping or abandoning the minimum wage should try living on that amount.

In 1997, chairman of the U.S. Federal Reserve Alan Greenspan indicated that he suspected that it was job insecurity that kept the pressure for wage increases low. In Canada as *The Growing Gap* has demonstrated

almost every day we hear stories of how people at the top are rewarded with record-breaking compensation packages. At the same time there is evidence all around us of people doing the same work for less, or worrying about how much more work they have to do to hang on to their jobs. Workers at factories are told to accept wage roll backs or watch their jobs go to another country. Pieceworkers, assembly line workers, cashiers and caseworkers are all pressured to do more in less time. Low-level public employees are laid off, all too often finding themselves doing the same job in the private sector for less, while senior civil servants are generously rewarded for abandoning the public sector.

Garnett Picot, director of business and labour market analysis for Statistics Canada, wrote, in a 1997 article, "The real earnings of lower-paid males fell by 13 per cent over the 1980s and by 9 per cent between the mid-1980s and mid-1990s, while the earnings of higher-paid males rose over the same period."† A year later, he wrote:

---

* *Financial Post*, May 9, 1998.
† *Canadian Business Economics*, Fall 1997.

[There have been] dramatic changes in the labour market which have been observed for some time. There have been significant changes in the earnings of various groups. . . . The real earnings of men with low pay and skill levels have fallen dramatically, as have those of younger workers (under age 35) particularly men.

. . .

From a welfare perspective, one might be more interested in market earnings on a family basis, since it is family income that determines well-being for most Canadians. Inequality in family market income (mainly employment earnings) has increased in Canada during the recent past.*

In the summer of 1998, Statistics Canada reported that one of every twenty employees worked for minimum wage or less in the first quarter of the year. This amounted to about 545,000 employees. Of these, 58 per cent were youths aged 15 to 24 and 138,000 were adult women workers.

It wasn't that long ago that most advanced nations introduced minimum wages to protect workers from being exploited during periods of high unemployment. That Canada still has such low minimum wages and still has so many men and women working at or near those levels leaves much to consider, as does the trend of large corporations letting full-time workers go so they can switch to contract workers. Also to be considered is the behaviour of companies like McCain's Maple Leaf Foods in their brutal guillotining of employee wages and benefits.

The CCSD measured the annual minimum wage in 1995 in all ten provinces, and compared the result to LICOs. The result was an average minimum wage that was 42 per cent below the LICOs line, which, remember, already represents those "substantially worse off than the average, people in the most straitened circumstances." In early 1998, 76,000 minimum-wage workers were the sole adult providers in the family.†

Given the precipitous decline in unemployment payouts and the axing of social benefits, it's astonishing that on the eve of the new

---

* Statistics Canada, "What Is Happening to Earnings Inequality and Youth Wages in the 1990s?" *Canadian Economic Observer*, September 1998.
† Statistics Canada, *The Daily*, August 25, 1998.

millennium there are those in Canada who are now lobbying for the abandonment of minimum wages.

Let's turn from the minimum wage to other wage measurements. In 1975, the average salary of men working full-time, full-year (in constant 1996 dollars) was $41,957. By 1996, over twenty years later, it had dropped to $41,484.*

Statistics Canada measures changes in annual labour income in Canada. Figure 30 shows these changes over the last twenty years. The average earnings have been exaggerated by large earnings increases and bonuses to well-paid executives and professionals, while the earnings of non-unionized workers were at a standstill.

FIGURE 30
Changes in Annual Labour Income in Canada

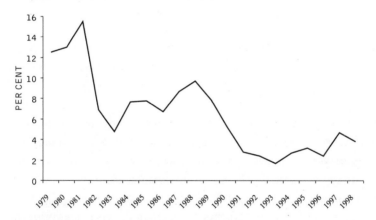

SOURCE: Statistics Canada: *Canadian Economic Observer*. Cat. #11-210-XPB, and *National Income and Expenditures Accounts*, Cat. #13-001-PPB.

Canadian workers have fared poorly since 1989. Average wages have increased only 2.7 per cent, barely above the inflation rate.

Figure 31 (overleaf), provided by the Bank of Canada, presents another clear indication of what has happened to wage settlements in Canada in the FTA era.

---

* Statistics Canada, *Canada Year Book*, 1999, Cat. 13-217-XPB.

FIGURE 31

Wage Settlements

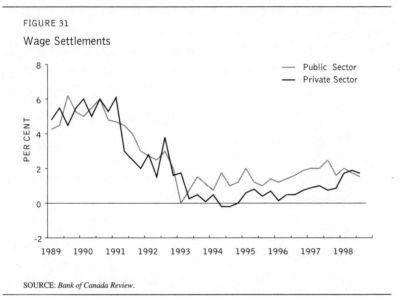

SOURCE: *Bank of Canada Review.*

*The figure shows the annual increase in base wage rates for newly nego-
tiated settlements in the 1990s – these workers have been steadily losing
ground to inflation.*

The following comparison, which looks at the decade before the
FTA and the first FTA decade speaks for itself. In the decade before the FTA
(1979 to 1988), the average annual increase in base wage rates in the
private sector was 6.9 per cent. In the first decade of the FTA (1989 to
1998), the wage rate increase dropped all the way down to 2.7 per cent.[*]

From 1989 to 1998 the annual change in the consumer price index
averaged 2.5 per cent. So for the past decade increases in real earnings
have been almost non-existent.

But some have been doing well while wage settlements tumbled.
Garnett Picot studied the percentage changes in real annual earnings of
paid workers for the period from 1981 to 1995. The numbers in Figure
32 are a remarkable demonstration of one of the key reasons why
there has been growing poverty and a growing gap in income distribution in Canada.[†]

---

[*] Statistics Canada, *Perspectives*, Winter 1998, Cat. #75-001-XPE.

[†] *Canadian Business Economics*, Fall 1997, and Statistics Canada, *Canadian Economic Observer*, Cat. #11-
210-XPB.

FIGURE 32

Changes in Real Annual Earnings by Decile, 1981 to 1995

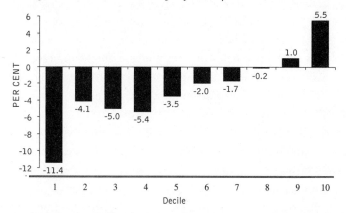

Decile

SOURCE: Statistics Canada, *Canadian Economic Observer*, Cat. #11-010-XPB, September, 1998.

By now a familiar pattern – the poorest of the poor (represented by 1, the lowest decile on the figure) lost the most, while the top earners gained the most.

FIGURE 33

Changes in Hourly Earnings, 1989 to 1998

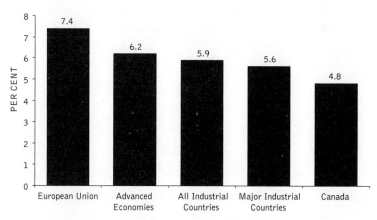

SOURCE: International Monetary Fund, *World Economic Outlook.*

When hourly earnings are measured, Canadians lost ground compared to workers in other developed countries.

It's hard to look at this chart without feeling angry. Whatever happened to social justice?

Well, then, how have workers in Canada done in hourly compensation during the past decade compared to those in other countries? The International Monetary Fund measures things a bit differently than we do, but the results nonetheless are revealing as shown in Figure 33.

In recent years, among the major OECD countries, only Japan had a higher percentage of women in low-pay jobs, and only the United States had a higher percentage of low-pay male workers.

In his September 1998 paper, *What's Happening to Earnings Inequality and Youth Wages in the 1990s,*[*] Garnett Picot probes "the increasing inequality of employment earnings, particularly among men during the 1980s," and the "rising polarization of earnings," both of which have "been well documented." There is no question that "the earnings gap between low and high wage workers has increased in

FIGURE 34

Indexed Real Annual Earnings of Paid Male Workers, Aged 18 to 24, 1979 to 1995

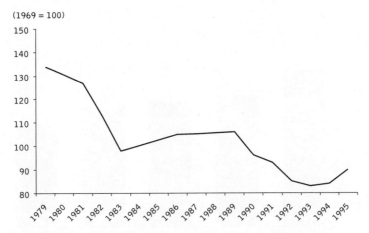

(1969 = 100)

SOURCE: Statistics Canada, Analytical Studies Branch, Research Paper Series # 11F0019MPE No. 116.

Young Canadian workers saw a sharp decline in their real earnings, back to levels of over thirty years ago.

* Statistics Canada, *Canadian Economic Observer*, Cat. #11-210-XPB.

Canada through the 1980s." Moreover, between the mid-1980s and mid-1990s, "there was an increase in earnings inequality among male workers over the period. The real earnings of lower paid males fell 13% over the 1980s, and 9% between the mid-1980s and mid-1990s." Meanwhile, "earnings of higher paid males rose over the same period."

It might reasonably have been expected that as the economic climate improved so would the pay of low-income workers; instead earnings in the bottom decile and earnings for most other Canadians continued to fall. In the case of young men, Picot shows a "36% drop in earnings between 1979 and the early 1990s." Picot's analysis of the real earnings of young Canadians (Figure 34) is both dramatic and sad.

Eighty-Seven Dollars for Me,
One Dollar for You

Well-known author Walter Stewart told me that he wrote a column in the Sun *all about the inflated salaries and bonuses and options of bank CEOs and bank presidents and other bank executives, comparing their big bucks to the poor pay of bank tellers. In his column he explained how the banks fought unionization and how bank staff (about 70 per cent women) were terrified that if they rocked the boat they would lose their jobs. The very next day Stewart visited his bank. The male bank manager turned his back on Stewart, went into his office, and closed the door. The rest of the employees were all women; to a one they stood and applauded.*

According to the Canadian Bankers Association, the average starting annual wage for a bank teller is somewhere between $20,000 and $22,500. But, in at least some locations, banks are no longer hiring new full-time "customer service representatives" the way they used to. In Ottawa, for example, CIBC is now hiring mostly casual, part-time help at an average hourly rate of $9.62. In Edmonton, the banks are hiring more and more help of a casual nature and are paying reduced benefits. Meanwhile, Halifax economist Jim Stanford reports that of four hundred different industries in Canada, stockbrokers, mutual-fund company employees and other financial investment specialists, "in other words, the money managers," had by far the highest average earnings.

Throughout the 1980s and 1990s, the average CEO of a large Canadian company made increasingly more money than the average Canadian worker. As the *Toronto Star* pointed out, "for the average Canadian to match the CEOs' 1996 average earnings ($1.12 million) it would take more than 36 years. . . . (The CEOs) ought to put themselves in their employees' shoes, and consider the message they send when they declare: $87 for me, $1 for you."[*]

According to Jim Stanford,

> The average 1997 total compensation for the 100 CEOs was $3.45 million. CEO compensation grew by a weighted average of 56 per cent during the year. For comparison purposes, Statistics Canada reports that the average Canadian worker earned $31,100 during 1997 (less than one-hundredth of the CEOs average), 2.1 per cent higher than in 1996.[†]

And by the way, while CEOs' compensation skyrocketed, during the year the total profits for the same one hundred companies *fell* by $300 million.

In 1997, Robert Gratton, CEO of Power Financial Corporation, took home $27.4 million in compensation. This topped Frank Stronach of Magna, who had to make do with $26.5 million for the year, and Gerald Schwartz of Onex, who made only $18.8 million, while Jean Monty of BCE Inc. had to get by on a mere $17.2 million.

In January 1998, it was reported that Tony Fell, chairman and CEO of RBC Dominion Securities (owned by the Royal Bank of Canada), received a $6-million bonus for 1997 and had stock options worth about $16 million.

On March 27, 1998, the *Globe and Mail* reported that compensation to the president of Shell Canada increased 27 per cent in 1997, and that of the head of BioChem Pharma increased by 66 per cent. Abitibi-

---

[*] September 20, 1997.

[†] *Globe and Mail*, May 7, 1998, and "Pay vs. Profits: Are CEOs Worth What They Are Paid?" C.C.P.A. newsletter, Volume 1, #2, Ottawa, May 1998.

Consolidated's boss doubled his compensation from $1.6 million to $3.2 million. Sun Media's CEO Paul Godfrey's *bonus* was $755,400, compared to a paltry $281,500 the previous year, while Talisman Energy's CEO package increased a slim 155 per cent to $2.32 million. The very same day, the *Globe* reported that employee wages for 1997 increased by 1.4%.

The next day, the same paper told us that the president of Loblaw collected $6.8 million and a few days earlier had exercised stock options to the tune of $21.6 million. Magna chief Frank Stronach received another $26.6 million in 1998. By 1998 the president of Loblaw had received a small increase to $34.1 million.

Meanwhile, Maple Leaf Foods was cutting employee wages at its plant near Burlington by about 40 per cent.

Late in 1998, Ernst & Young's annual report on executive pay packages showed that Canada's top TSE 300 executives took in an average of $792,700 in salary and bonuses in 1997. In addition, average stock options amounted to $818,000.

By early 1999, the papers were reporting more and more inflated pay packages. Bank of Montreal's then-chairman Matthew Barrett, who had to get by with a mere $3.98 million in 1996, got a boost to $4.27 million in 1997 and received $4.56 million in 1998. Four of Barrett's Bank of Montreal associates collected between $2.1 million and $2.8 million in salaries and bonuses.

Late in 1997, the *Financial Post* reported that CIBC's John Hunkin earned $10.2 million in salary, bonuses, and CIBC shares.[*] In January 1999 the *Globe and Mail* reported that CIBC was trying to stop the bleeding from "one of its worse quarters in decades. . . . The problem child was Mr. Hunkin's World Markets division which lost $186 million in the last quarter."[†] Yes, that's the same John Hunkin who in April 1999 was named chairman and CEO of the CIBC.

In the early part of every year, hardly a day goes by without headlines like "POTASH BOSS PULLED IN $10.6 MILLION" or "IMPERIAL OIL PRESIDENT PAID ALMOST $4 MILLION." In most years, the package increases have been huge. In 1997, for example, top CEOs in

---

[*] December 19, 1997.
[†] January 22, 1999.

Canada had remuneration increases averaging a mere 112 per cent increase over the previous year.

Poor Bank of Canada governor Gordon Thiessen. In 1998 he managed only a 17-per-cent increase to $262,000. (By comparison, Prime Minister Jean Chrétien makes about $150,000, President Bill Clinton $200,000 U.S., and Alan Greenspan of the U.S. Federal Reserve about $200,000 U.S., while the *average* salary for a National Hockey League player jumped to $1.3 million in 1999.) Meanwhile, a letter to *Sports Illustrated* magazine pointed out that pitcher Randy Johnson makes the same amount of money pitching for a single inning as the writer, a special education teacher with twenty years' experience, earns for a full year's work.

Why are workers doing so poorly in Canada while the top brass are hauling away millions? Is it simply corporate and personal greed, as appears to be the case? Could it somehow be related to output? The Bank of Canada compiles a table of worker wage and salary increases per unit of output (Figure 35). How's that for worker incentive?

FIGURE 35

Wage and Salary Increases Per Unit of Output

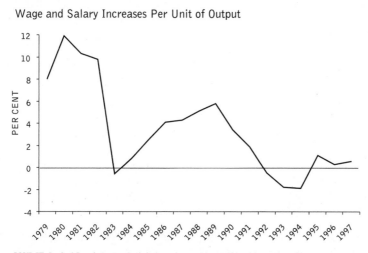

SOURCE: *Bank of Canada Review*, Statistical Supplement, March 1989 and December 1998.

While GDP and productivity increased, most employees have not shared in the rewards of greater economic output. The big declines are a reflection of the recessions at the beginning of the 1980s and 1990s, but note the poor wage and salary increases despite the 1990s recovery.

Depressing, to say the least. We can see quite clearly what happened to wages and salaries during the recessions at the beginning of the 1980s and the 1990s, but why the pathetic showing during the recovery commencing in 1993?

	GDP Increase	Wage and Salaries Per Unit of Output
1993	2.3%	−1.7%
1994	4.7	−2.0
1995	2.6	0.9
1996	1.2	1.9
1997	3.8	1.3
1998	3.0	1.9

It's hard to come to any other conclusion but that the corporate bosses are screwing the workers. It's certainly clear that the bosses aren't suffering.

Laughing All the Way to the Bank

The family had been on the farm for four generations. Their great-grandfather had come out from Dornoch, then up from Minnesota. Every generation they went through the same cycle: drought, hail, grasshoppers, prices that plunged into the root cellar, you name it. But they plugged along pretty darn good. They were never wealthy by any stretch, but over the years they managed and even sent some kids to university in Winnipeg and Saskatoon. One of the boys was quite a hockey player and played for the Wheat Kings for a couple of years. They made their big mistake in 1986 when interest rates weren't that bad and they had a few dollars. It's hard to say whether they talked themselves into buying the new truck and the new machinery or if it was the bank's pushing that did it. Anyway, four years later interest rates jumped. Suddenly they were paying much of their income to the bank in a lousy crop year. The next year the crop was not bad, but prices sank again. Now they couldn't make the payments. For a while the bank didn't press, but that didn't last more than a few months. The bank took the farm away in the fall. The next year interest rates fell and crop prices were back up. They all cried – the mother, the father, the two boys, and their sister – when the bailiff showed up. If only the bank had waited a bit.

Quite often in the business press we'll see a chart like Figure 36 under a headline "BUSINESS PROFITS POST ANOTHER DROP."* But a drop from what? So what if there was a small drop from a previous year of record-breaking profits? In 1997, corporations in Canada recorded an all-time-record operating profit of $110 billion, well above the 1996 record of $95.7 billion.†

FIGURE 36

Corporate Operating Profits

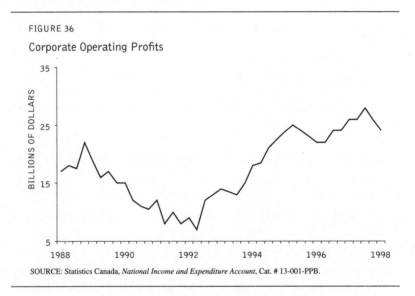

SOURCE: Statistics Canada, *National Income and Expenditure Account*, Cat. # 13-001-PPB.

While most Canadians lost ground or were at a standstill since the early-1990s recession, corporate operating profits reached record highs.

In April 1998, Statistics Canada reported: "Corporate profits rose a sizzling 17% (for 1997) having doubled their share of domestic income . . . in just five years. Conversely, disposable income per person fell slightly. . . . This was the sixth drop in seven years and brought the total decreases to 6.7%."** Sound like a familiar pattern?

According to business-press reports, Canadian companies in 1998

---

* *Financial Post*, August 21, 1998.
† Statistics Canada, *The Daily*, February 19, 1998.
** Statistics Canada, *Canadian Economic Observer*, April 1998, Cat. #11-010-XPB.

were predicting "a profit recession," an "earnings slump," "negative profit growth," and an "expected downturn" which will lead to "sagging profits." We should all be so lucky. A few days after these warnings appeared, the Royal Bank of Canada reported an annual profit of $1.82 billion, "the largest reported pure profit in Canadian history."* In October 1998, Statistics Canada reported that the rate of return for large businesses (those with revenues of over $75 million) in Canada was the highest since the record years of 1988 and 1989. Some recession. Total corporate net profits in 1998 were the second-highest in Canadian history.

How does corporate Canada compare with other countries? Let's turn to Andrew Coyne, now with the *National Post*, when he was still with the *Globe and Mail*: "For most of the postwar period, our companies have also enjoyed higher rates of profitability than their American cousins."† That's certainly not what we hear from most of our editorial

FIGURE 37

Average Percentage Return on Capital
1970 to 1979

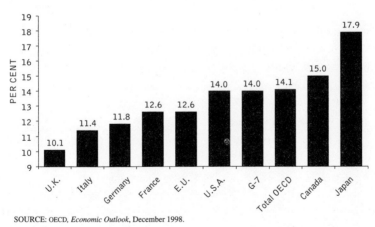

SOURCE: OECD, *Economic Outlook*, December 1998.

This figure shows how misleading the complaints about doing business in Canada have been: the rate of return here is exceeded only by Japan among developed nations.

* *Globe and Mail*, November 25, 1998.
† January 8, 1995.

pages and business columnists. So let's look at some comparative international rates of return on capital in the business sector (Figure 37).

During these years, 1970 to 1979, business in Canada also had a better return on capital than Australia, Austria, Belgium, Denmark, Finland, Ireland, Netherlands, Norway, Sweden, and Switzerland.

Now let's look at the rates of return on capital for the period 1980 to 1998 (1996 to 1998 are OECD estimates and projections).[*] First, here are the 1980s.

	1980	1981	1982	1983	1984	1985	1986	1987	1988	1989
United States	13.7	13.7	12.6	14.2	15.6	15.9	16.0	16.0	16.3	17.3
G-7	12.9	12.7	12.1	13.0	13.9	14.3	14.6	14.7	15.2	15.7
Total OECD	12.9	12.6	12.1	12.9	13.8	14.2	14.5	14.6	15.0	15.5
European Union	11.3	10.7	10.9	11.2	11.8	12.1	12.8	12.9	13.4	13.7
Canada	18.7	18.0	15.7	17.7	19.2	19.2	18.9	19.5	19.9	19.3

So, contrary to the plaintive cry so often presented on the business pages of our newspapers and in our business magazines, corporate Canada has been doing very well indeed. For every single year of the 1980s, Canadian business had a better return on capital than the average of the G-7, the OECD, the European Union, and – surprise, surprise – the United States!

Now, the 1990s.

	1990	1991	1992	1993	1994	1995	1996	1997	1998
United States	17.1	16.6	17.4	17.8	18.3	18.3	18.4	18.5	18.5
G-7	15.5	15.1	15.4	15.5	16.0	16.1	16.3	16.3	16.4
Total OECD	15.3	15.0	15.2	15.3	15.8	15.9	16.0	16.1	16.2
European Union	13.6	13.3	13.4	13.4	14.3	14.7	14.7	15.0	15.2
Canada	17.8	17.3	17.1	17.5	18.3	19.3	19.2	19.2	19.2

Once again, the comparisons are clear. Year after year after year, Canadians have been told just how very tough it is for business to make a buck in this country. Too-high taxes, too much red tape, and so on. Year after year after year, Canadians have not been told the truth.

---

[*] *OECD Economic Outlook*, December 1998.

In July 1997, *Report on Business* magazine listed Canada's ten top "profit leaders." Five of the ten were the big five banks; the top three were banks. Figure 38 looks at bank operating profits for the past twenty years.

FIGURE 38

Bank Operating Profits

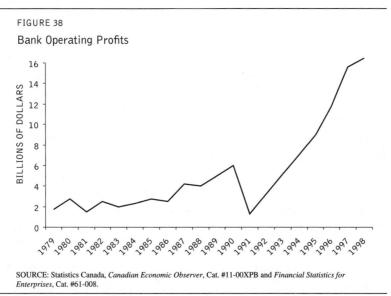

SOURCE: Statistics Canada, *Canadian Economic Observer*, Cat. #11-00XPB and *Financial Statistics for Enterprises*, Cat. #61-008.

Canadian banks are among the most profitable in the world, ranking in the top three of the sixteen major developed countries.

Poor banks! Denied an even greater oligopoly (at least temporarily) by Paul Martin, but nevertheless laughing all the way to the – uh – bank! Mind you, the banks have already been allowed to take over most of the big brokerages and most of the major trust companies, including Dominion Securities, Richardson Greenshields, McLeod Young and Weir, Montreal Trust, Nesbitt Thomson, Wood Gundy, Burns Fry, Lévesque Beaubien, and First Marathon. In the words of economist Arthur Donner and former bank vice-president Doug Peters, "It seems that mergers are to Bay Street like crack cocaine is to an addict."[*] By 1995, the top five Canadian banks already owned over 58 per cent of total bank assets in Canada. By comparison, in the United States, the top five banks owned less than 10 per cent.

---

[*] *Public Policy Challenge of Bank Mergers and the MacKay Task Force Report*, November 6, 1998.

In 1990, bank assets in Canada totalled $473.5 billion. By February 9, 1999, the big six banks in Canada had assets of $1.276 trillion dollars. How's that for growth? In 1997, the Bank of Nova Scotia had a 19.7-per-cent return on equity, the Royal Bank a 19-per-cent return, and the Bank of Montreal a 17-per-cent return. On November 24, 1998, the Bank of Montreal announced that it had just recorded its ninth straight year of record profits. Not bad considering the bank's strident complaints to Ottawa.

Of course, the banks will protest that the operating profits shown in Figure 38 are not net profits; they must pay income and other taxes. In fact, the banks constantly tell us how much tax they pay. But don't we all have to pay income taxes and the GST and indirect taxes, and don't most of us have to pay property taxes, too? Instead of paying taxes, would the banks like to provide their own water supply, their own roads, their own garbage collection, and their own fire department? In the words of one widely respected tax expert, the banks' complaints are "a smelly red herring." In 1995, 1996, 1997, and 1998, the banks' operating *and* net profits in Canada broke all previous records.

In 1987 Pierre Trudeau said, "You know, the worst bitchers are the bankers."*

Perhaps one of the most hilarious moments in modern Canadian bank history came in early November 1998 when "the head of the Canadian Imperial Bank of Commerce slammed consumers for being lousy patriots in their apparent resistance to the creation of two Canadian bank giants. . . . 'We [Canadians] have a little nationalism in this county. Quite frankly, I think we're losing that,' an emotional Al Flood told a hearing of the Senate banking committee in Toronto. . . . 'Why don't we look after Canadians?' he asked." † Readers of this book may wish to write to Mr. Flood, or to his successor, or to their own favourite bank CEO, and ask the following questions:

• How much of Canadian depositors' money have you sent out of Canada for loans to non-Canadians?

---

* *Colombo's New Canadian Quotations*, Hurtig, 1987.
† Bertrand Marotte, Southam Newspapers, *Edmonton Journal*, November 4, 1998.

- What percentage of commercial loans that your bank makes are made to foreign-controlled corporations to help them buy up Canadian companies?
- What percentage of Canadian depositors' money have you used to buy up financial corporations outside of Canada?

And last:

- What percentage of the loans you make in Canada are loans to people with incomes under $20,000 a year?

If anyone wants to bet that they will get the answers to those questions, feel free to call me collect. My number is in the telephone book.

"Ripping the Heart Out of Democracy"

She says there's one girl of twelve and another of thirteen who are prostitutes. When they come to school they're half-asleep. How do you ask them to pay attention? They weren't doing all that bad until the cutbacks. In fact both were doing fairly well in school. You could tell they were from a very poor family, but we had lots of reason to believe that with the right help the potential was there. But after the cutbacks, everything just disintegrated. They had very little to eat, no clothes – for girls that age it was difficult. Moreover, they were dealing with a badly dysfunctional home and it was in a bad part of town to begin with. Anyway, the pimps got hold of the girls. Next came drugs. When the police picked them up on the street and took them to the safe house, they discovered one of the girls hoarding a bag of frozen peas under her bed.

They say in Calgary they've got a ten-year old in one of the safe houses, but the police won't confirm it.

What do you think could have been going through the minds of Jean Chrétien, Paul Martin, Mike Harris, and Ralph Klein when they decided to slash social spending by such large amounts? Do you think any of them or any of their cabinet ministers gave a moment's thought to the millions of poor men, women, and children in Canada who would be so directly affected? Did it ever occur to them that some 40 per cent of welfare recipients are children? Certainly, there's no sign of it. Didn't Paul Martin always say he would never betray his father's long legacy of building and supporting Canada's social programs to help those who need help?

Isn't the evidence clear that the truth is that these men simply don't really give a damn about the poor?

In his February 1998 budget, Paul Martin promised that the federal government's program spending would be at its lowest level in fifty years, going all the way back to 1949.* He was very proud about it.

Program spending includes government transfers to persons, and transfers to other levels of government, which have represented the largest share of total program spending. During the 1992-93 federal fiscal year, Ottawa's program spending amounted to about $122.6 billion. By 1999-2000 it will fall to $111.2 billion, a drop of $11.4 billion. In constant dollars and taking population increases into account, the drop will be much greater.†

Measured as a percentage of GDP, federal program spending in the 1980s averaged about 18 per cent annually. By 2000-2001 it is scheduled to drop to 12 per cent. If you include provincial program spending, the total has fallen from about 35 per cent of GDP in the mid-1990s down to about 26 per cent. Analysts quickly figured out that Paul Martin's February 1999 budget contained some misleading accounting. For example, anticipated 1998-99 program spending was overstated by at least $3.5 billion in money that wouldn't be spent for years. But no matter how you juggled the numbers, program spending has sunk like a stone.

In October 1998, Paul Martin's Department of Finance bragged about its cuts in program spending:

In fact, Canada's program spending has fallen much faster than in other G-7 countries. Between 1992 and 1997, Canada's total

---

* Linda McQuaig points out that in 1949 "we didn't have medicare then, nor much in the way of public pensions or unemployment insurance. Furthermore, the unemployment rate was much lower."
† Federal government program spending as a percentage of GDP was budgeted at 12.6 per cent for 1998-99, 12.2 per cent for 1999-00, and 12.0 per cent for 2000-01.

government spending was reduced from 41.7 per cent to 33.8 per cent of GDP, a reduction of 8 percentage points. Over the same period, government spending in the G-7 countries declined by only 1 percentage point on average, from 35.8 per cent to 34.8 per cent of GDP. As a result, Canada's program spending in relation to the size of its economy is now lower than the G-7 average.

No doubt. I suppose we were supposed to say bravo!

Suppose that, based on the above, Ottawa's program spending in 1998 was simply the same as the average of the G-7 nations, no more, no less. One per cent of our nominal GDP in 1998 amounted to $8.9 billion. So, if we had been only average, neither better nor worse than average, we would have had almost $9 billion which could have gone to help Canada's poor.

No doubt the neo-cons and neo-neanderthals will argue that we had to reduce program spending because we had to reduce the debt. And they're right about the need to reduce the debt. Under the Trudeau and Mulroney governments (most during the nine Mulroney–Michael Wilson years), Canada built up such an enormous debt that increasingly large percentages of federal tax revenue were being gobbled up for interest payments instead of going to help Canadians in need. Each year there was less money for people and more money for the holders of government debt, both inside and outside of Canada. That had to stop. By 1995-96 public debt charges were taking 36 per cent of all federal government revenues.

But social spending was never responsible for the debt buildup. Others have already done an excellent job of showing that high interest rates and loose tax policies were responsible for most of the accumulated debt.[*]

Now let's look more closely at government transfers. As Maude Barlow has written about Paul Martin when he was in opposition:

Paul Martin attacked Mulroney's obsession with the deficit. ("I believe the way you reduce the deficit is by increasing

---

[*] See, for example, Linda McQuaig, *The Cult of Impotence*, Toronto, Viking, 1998.

revenues.") and Mulroney's budget cuts, which he said were "ripping the heart out of democracy." He said the cuts to . . . unemployment insurance were "theft" and called for increased spending to deal with poverty. "We need a new social contract in this nation, one that recognizes that a dollar spent today reduces poverty and despair and gives us much more in the future."*

Right. Too bad Martin has such a poor memory.

Paul Martin became finance minister in 1993. According to NAPO, "in real per-capita terms, federal cash transfers for social programs fell by more than 40% between 1993 and 1997."† If Mulroney was "ripping the heart out of democracy," what can we say about Paul Martin's even deeper social-spending cuts?

Government transfer payments include funding for social payments such as Old Age Security, Guaranteed Income Supplements, pensions, Spouse's Allowances, Employment Insurance benefits, workers' compensation, allowances for training programs, social assistance, aboriginal programs, veteran's pensions, plus pensions for the disabled and the blind. Soon after he became finance minister, Paul Martin and the Chrétien government cut billions of dollars from transfer payments both to individuals and to other levels of government. Not only were the social cuts huge, but, as Gayle Gilchrist James of the University of Calgary puts it, "Up until the last four or five years, it was very clear that assistance was a right, not a privilege. . . . Now that the Canada Assistance Plan has ended, there isn't a right to assistance any more."** In short, the federal government's attitude to the needy changed completely.

Figure 39 shows Ottawa's transfers both to persons and to other levels of government. Of course, the federal government's cutbacks in transfers to the provinces led directly to provincial cutbacks. Ottawa's total transfers to other levels of government dropped from 20.3 per cent of budgetary expenditure in 1976-77 to 13.7 per cent in 1997-98.††

---

* *The Fight of My Life: Confessions of an Unrepentant Canadian*, Toronto, HarperCollins, 1998.
† Press release, January 27, 1998.
** *Alberta Views*, Winter 1999.
†† Department of Finance, *Fiscal Reference Tables*, Table 9.

FIGURE 39

Major Transfers as a Percentage of GDP

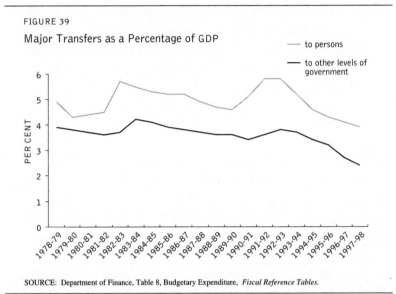

SOURCE: Department of Finance, Table 8, Budgetary Expenditure, *Fiscal Reference Tables.*

Federal government payments for social programs, including health and post-secondary education, have declined sharply, especially over the last decade.

Columnist Dalton Camp described the impact well:

The minister of finance, a hero in corporate circles, a media darling in the financial papers, won the war on the deficit, in large part by cutting transfer payments to the provinces for education, health and welfare services.

The public, blandly taking Paul Martin's word for it, has no idea of the human cost of the minister's victory. The fact that the poor have paid for the balanced budget has become a truism. . . . The poor [have been made] poorer through a public policy of abandoning the needs of the neediest.

There is evidence – appalling evidence – that the stinting and starving of public welfare budgets has put more innocent children at risk just as it inflicts needless pain and suffering upon the rest of society's disadvantaged.*

---

* *Toronto Star*, February 1, 1998.

Allow me to repeat: "The poor [have been made] poorer through a public policy of abandoning the needs of the neediest."

Exactly. Political hypocrites. Child abuse by politicians.

I referred earlier to Paul Martin's pledge to increase spending on reducing poverty and to make a new social contract in Canada. A social contract with whom? Perhaps the following table will tell us. Here is what has happened to government transfers from 1992, the year before Paul Martin became finance minister, to 1996 (the latest year for which such figures are available at this writing).

Average Transfers
Constant 1996 Dollars

	lowest quintile	second quintile	middle quintile	fourth quintile	highest quintile
1992	$10,293	$9,013	$6,625	$5,253	$4,139
1993	10,270	8,802	6,574	5,409	4,443
1994	10,368	9,111	6,509	5,097	4,059
1995	9,965	8,420	6,599	4,891	3,946
1996	9,726	8,370	6,190	4,919	4,004
transfer decline 1992-1996	$–567	$–643	$–435	$–334	$–135

Maybe if you stood on your head that bottom row of figures might look okay. But to any rational Canadian, there's something rotten here. The Chrétien government's policy was to chop transfer payments, knowing full well the terrible impact such an action would have on poor Canadians.* So, whose transfer payments were cut the most? Naturally, it was those of the very poor and the next-lowest income quintile.† A drop in income of $600 may not seem like a lot to some, but to the poor it will often mean nothing to eat.

How utterly bizarre. How grossly unfair. Anyone who has worked with the poor knows all too well the devastating impact the loss of only

---

* In constant 1997 dollars average family transfers amounted to $7,215 in 1993 and $6,474 in 1997.
† Statistics Canada, *Income after tax, distributions by size, 1996*, Cat. #13-210-XPB.

a few dollars can have. In 1996, about 934,000 Canadians had after-tax income of under $10,000, and 62.5 per cent of what they lived on came from transfer payments. Another 2,544,000 Canadian individuals and families had income of between $10,000 and $19,999, 52 per cent of their income coming from transfer payments.

In a 1997 study, Grant Schellenberg and David Ross showed that, without government transfers, Canada would have had almost 23 per cent of all its families living at an average of about $13,850 below the LICOs line. This depth of poverty would have a debilitating impact across the country, in every region and in every province. The human suffering and the deprivation would be immense.

In the summer of 1998, Statistics Canada advised that "earnings advances in the last few years have not benefited families with lower incomes to the same degree as during the recovery of the late 1980s. As a result, inequality in pre-transfer income continued to increase."[*] So for the poor, market income is down, and government transfers are down. Some Liberals might be tempted to point to Paul Martin's 1998 and 1999 budgets and the increased Child Tax Benefits. But these recent increases in help for the poor have only brought government help back to the level of over ten years ago. It was totally inadequate then, and it's totally inadequate now. That poor Canadians have figured in such a pathetic minor way in the most recent budgets speaks volumes about the federal government's priorities. As for other social spending – health care, for example – the promise of new money reverses some of the cuts made four years ago, but fails to keep pace with the growing demand of an aging population, inflation, and overall population growth.

"Ripping the heart out of democracy" is right.

Perverse is the word.

---

[*] *The Daily*, June 22, 1998.

PART SIX

Six Reasons the Poor Are Ignored

The Poor Must Sing for Their Supper

They have four kids. Neither parent is well educated. Both have worked at minimum-wage jobs or jobs paying only slightly better than minimum wage. At best the two bring in about $2,200 a month if they get full-time work. The problem is that their rent is $750 a month and child care $1,200 a month. As she says, that doesn't exactly leave a whole bunch for food. After a lot of effort trying to find better jobs, they figured it would work out best for all if he stayed home and looked after the kids, especially since his wife's job was more secure than his and one of the boys looks like he might be headed for trouble. Despite all their problems, in her words they're really into family values. It would be good for the kids, instead of their being parked in what would essentially be low-quality daycare not much better than babysitting. Social services would help.

But social services wouldn't help. The father was deemed "non-compliant." Either you get yourself a job or you're cut off. So now she's at work earning her $1,100 a month, and that's their income. The rent is still $750 a month, but they're thinking of moving to X street, in a crummy part of town, where they can get a two-bedroom apartment for the six of them for $500 a

month. The guy from social services was rude. Most aren't, but
he sure as hell was. An arrogant bastard.

The most important reason that the poor in Canada are so badly ignored is that we have now had fifteen years of very conservative government in Ottawa. Previously, over the years, both Liberal and Conservative federal governments brought in progressive, enlightened, and compassionate social programs. These policies were one of the key reasons that Canada has been such an admired country around the world. In many ways, we were on the way towards creating a model civil society of social justice and egalitarianism.

Beginning with the election of Brian Mulroney in 1984, that all changed. Then, after campaigning with a deceitful Red Book full of phony election promises, the Chrétien government, elected in 1993 by voters who desperately wanted change, not only adopted almost all of the Mulroney policies, but proceeded to move even further to the right. Jean Chrétien's Liberals are easily the most conservative Liberal government in the history of Canada.

Small-c conservative governments care little about the poor.

The second reason the poor are largely ignored in Ottawa has to do with political power. Poor people rarely donate to political parties, constituency associations, candidates, leadership conventions, fundraising dinners, and other political activities. For the most part, poor people are not active participants in constituency affairs or election campaigns; they're too busy trying to survive. Go to any national convention of the only two parties that have ever held majority power in Ottawa, and you will find that the upper-two income deciles dominate. Across the country, lawyers and other professionals, corporate executives, developers, and other well-to-do men (mostly) and women run the political machines that have governed this country since Confederation. The poor are out of sight – and out of mind.

Politics is all about power. Poverty means having no power.

Why has the percentage of *seniors* living in poverty in Canada declined, while the percentage of children living in poverty has risen so dramatically? Between 1980 and 1996, while the senior population in Canada increased by 59 per cent, the number of low-income seniors actually decreased by 3 per cent. This trend is in stark contrast to the fate both of the population in general and of children under the age of eighteen in particular.* In 1970, more than 28 per cent of Canadians aged sixty-five and over lived below the LICOs line. Figure 40 covers the last twenty years for which statistics are available.

FIGURE 40

Persons in Low Income After Tax, 65+

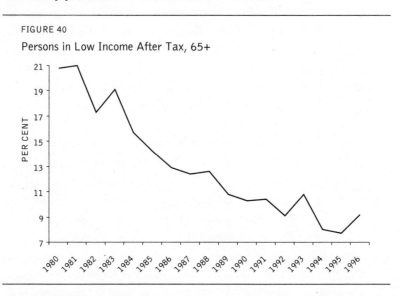

While poverty levels for children, families, and individuals increased, the political strength of seniors resulted in lower poverty rates.

During the mid and late 1960s, the federal government was seriously concerned about the fate of low-income seniors. A host of programs, including pension, disability, and survivor benefits, evolved. Seniors were an important priority – and they were voters. Most seniors vote in federal elections. Children do not. Seniors tend to know how to organize and be vocal when upset. Children are virtually invisible in political matters. Seniors know how to mobilize and to target politicians. Remember when, in 1985, "four-foot something Solange Denis stood nose to chin with Brian Mulroney on Parliament Hill and told him, 'You lied to us. I was made to vote for you and then it's good-bye Charlie Brown.'"† Mulroney, who had promised in the 1984 election campaign

---

* Statistics Canada, *The Daily*, December 22, 1997.

† *Toronto Star*, October 31, 1989.

that social programs were "a sacred trust," caught on television, replied "I'm listening to you, madame." That was the end of Mulroney's plan to de-index senior pension benefits. While partial de-indexation has seriously eroded the Child Tax Benefit and the GST low-income credit, senior benefits have maintained their value. Today, the Canada Pension Plan, Old Age Security, and the Guaranteed Income Supplement provide, on average, about half of all monthly income for seniors. Under these programs about $40 billion will go to about 4.5 million Canadians in 1999.

Many seniors have had a chance to build up their own savings for retirement. Poor children have no savings.

It's not that most seniors are now wealthy. On average they have a gross annual income before taxes of about $24,000, and in 1997 some 662,000 seniors (including almost half of all senior single women) had incomes below the LICOs line and a large number had incomes just above the line. But one thing is certain: no politician in Canada today would dream of cutting back senior benefits. In the next election they would be wiped out.

The third, fourth, and fifth reasons the poor in Canada are largely ignored relate to protracted, forceful campaigns by big business and by much of the conservative print media to convince Canadians that

- Canada's social programs are far too extravagant and too costly.
- The federal government spends far too much money, and
- Taxes in Canada are far too high.

If we're going to bring pressure to bear to help the poor in Canada, we need to address these interrelated and frequently stridently ill-informed claims. Let's start with social spending.

In Paul Martin's February 1998 budget speech, he told Canadians:

Our country is anchored in shared risks and shared benefits, in lending a hand knowing that, some day, we too may be in need. . . .

The Canadian spirit of coming together is not something that only appears now and then in response to great natural disasters or disruptions. It abides. It is there in every community, in every corner of the country, every day. And it is there in the great national programs that have come to define who we are, and what we want to become.

Time magazine has told us that "Martin harked back to his father's populist tenets. He [Junior] chose the working-class Montreal suburb of LaSalle as his constituency in an attempt to identify with Canada's neediest."*

Some identification!

In its 1998 Geneva presentation, NAPO advised: "The past five years has seen the most dramatic reversal of social and economic equalization initiatives since Canada's social security system was conceived over thirty years ago." Previously, in relation to Ottawa's funding to the provinces,

> there were specific criteria in place that protected certain economic and social rights for Canadians. . . . With the repeal of CAP [Canada Assistance Plan], these standards, conditions or administrative requirements no longer exist (except in health care).
>
> The repeal of CAP has resulted in the proliferation of requirements that must be met by people who are in need in order to receive financial assistance.
>
> The poor are being told to "sing for their supper."

When the Liberal government abandoned CAP and replaced it with the Canada Health and Social Transfer in April 1996, it also abandoned most of its ability to control standards and assign conditions to Ottawa's funding for social assistance.

When Martin announced his dramatic 1995 budget cuts, the influential right-wing Queen's University economist Thomas Courchene, in a C.D. Howe Institute study, advised that Martin's proposal would "preserve and promote" the nation's social safety net.† But the National Council on Welfare called the Canada Health and Social Transfer "the worst social-policy initiative undertaken by the federal government in more than a generation."

---

* December 29, 1997.

† *Globe and Mail*, November 15, 1995.

If you believe Courchene's assessment, I have a nice swamp I want to show you.

In a 1995 paper published shortly after Martin's budget, Ken Battle and Sherri Torjman of the Caledon Institute of Social Policy wrote:

> The 1995 federal budget is a turning point towards a new social policy for Canada . . . [which] has its roots in a succession of Conservative Budgets that date back to 1985.
>
> Conservative Finance Minister Michael Wilson will be remembered as one of the chief architects of a leaner Canadian welfare state. . . . Paul Martin is simply finishing the job for him. The continuity between these two powerful cabinet ministers from different parties was furnished by their officials at the Department of Finance. . . .
>
> In successive Budgets, Finance Minister Wilson put in place changes that radically reduced federal transfers for provincial social and health programs. . . . He also made substantial cuts to Unemployment Insurance. . . . He harnessed the power of inflation to siphon millions of dollars each year from child benefits and to wring millions more from taxpayers in federal and provincial income taxes – the working poor included. He handed the poor a leaky umbrella in the form of a partially-indexed GST credit that is falling steadily in value each year and thus imposing a growing GST burden on those least able to carry it.

A leaky umbrella indeed. With huge holes in it.

Meanwhile:

> The Conservatives also lowered the marginal tax rate for upper-income taxpayers and enriched several tax breaks that most benefit the well-off . . . [and they] substantially boosted the tax deduction limits for contributions to RRSPs and removed the limit on the tax deduction for contributions to Registered Pension Plans.
>
> Major changes to social programs . . . were made with no advance notice and little effective public debate. . . .

> The changes [the Liberals] have made to date and those announced in the 1995 Budget would indicate that the Liberals are basically following the Conservative road.

So, the bottom line? "The poor cousin of social policy, welfare and social services, will rank consistently at the bottom of the priority list. . . . Programs for people who are poor or vulnerable no longer will be deemed worthy of public support."

> It is no exaggeration to say that the Liberals brought in a budget that harks back half a century to a time when the federal government played a much smaller role vis-à-vis the provinces and when charity and the private market played a much more prominent role in social policy. The future of Canadian social policy may well resemble the past more than the present.
>
> This no doubt will please the international financiers in Tokyo, New York, and London – but raises serious questions as to why we have a federal government and its role with respect to its own citizens, particularly the most vulnerable. The future of Canada's income safety net for the poor and its health care system for everyone is being traded off in the frenzy to please Wall Street men in suits – who chalk up the numbers on a ledger but have absolutely no interest in the well-being of people, especially poor Canadians.
>
> The 1995 federal Budget represents a fundamental turning point in Canadian social policy. It was the Liberals who created the foundation of our social security system in the 1950s, 1960s and 1970s. It was the Conservatives who fundamentally weakened that foundation in the 1980s by putting federal transfer payments to the provinces on a down escalator. It is now the Liberals of the 1990s who are shaking that foundation to the core.[*]

After Martin brought in his 1995 budget, former Liberal cabinet minister Warren Allmand rose in the House of Commons and said that

---

[*] Caledon Institute of Social Policy, "How Finance Re-Formed Social Policy." Ken Battle and Sherri Torjman, April 1, 1995.

what Martin was doing was "completely contrary to what we said in the Red Book during the election campaign."

> I am opposed to these provisions, first of all because social programs in this country are not the cause of the deficit, so why are they being attacked . . .? Second, I am opposed to these provisions in the budget . . . because they will cause severe harm to those in need. They will widen the gap between rich and poor. . . . I cannot contribute to tearing down a system that for my 29 years in the House I helped build up. I just cannot do it.*

The claim that Canada spends too much on social programs is nonsense. The last year for which detailed international comparisons from the OECD are available is 1995. That year, of the twenty-seven member countries, nineteen had higher social spending to GDP than Canada, and only seven had lower spending, including, of course, the United States, along with countries such as Korea, Mexico, and Turkey. If Canada had spent only *the average* of all the OECD nations on social spending as a percentage of GDP in 1995, the extra amount would have been $40.8 billion for the one year!

The next time you hear someone say Canada's social spending is far too generous, tell them that they don't know what they're talking about.

Figure 41 (overleaf) shows the most recent OECD social-spending comparisons. Contrary to what we have so often been told, federal spending on social services and health care in Canada has not mushroomed out of control. Nor was it responsible for the huge buildup of debt. In 1975, combined federal spending on social services and health care amounted to 38.7 per cent of all federal expenditures. Twenty-three years later it was down to 37 per cent. But the Michael Wilson–Paul Martin cutbacks have hurt badly.

NAPO puts the impact of the cuts in perspective:

> Dramatic cuts to federal transfer payments mean provinces have cut equal (or in some cases greater) amounts from already meager budgets for social support programs. As a result,

---

* House of Commons *Hansard*, March 14, 1995, and June 5, 1995.

FIGURE 41

Public Social Expenditures as a Percentage of GDP, 1995

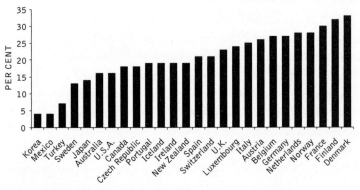

SOURCE: OECD, Social Expenditure Database, 1980 –1995.

Canada spends less on social programs than most developed countries, and far less than many.

choices are being made to fund politically popular health care and post-secondary education services over income support programs such as welfare.[*]

So, the poor remain last in line. In the words of one journalist: "Welfare recipients and the beneficiaries of other social programs – the disabled, legal aid clients, day care, parents and children – have trouble mustering the same lobbying clout as advocates for heath and education."[†]

By 1998, provincial per capita social-services spending had fallen about 12 per cent from mid-decade levels, with Alberta and Ontario making the biggest cuts. In Alberta, as but one of a thousand awful examples,

First it was the hospitals that were kicking the mentally ill out before they should have.

[*] NAPO, November 1998.
[†] The *Globe and Mail*, January 11, 1999.

Now the programs that were designed to help ease these same people back into society are turning them away because of lack of funding.

"The mentally ill are falling through the cracks," says Gerry Raymond, a well-known, experienced service provider.[*]

Not only have the spending cuts directly degraded the meagre standard of living of poor Canadians, but the quality of service to the poor also has sharply deteriorated. Overworked social workers trying to cope with funding cuts and reduced staff in the face of substantially increased demand are worn out. Columnist Michael Valpy summed it up nicely:

> When Canada stopped building its welfare state in the early 1970s, most of the Europeans were already ahead of us – advanced beyond Canada in public health and job-training programs, in pensions, in family support and shelter allowances. They have stayed ahead of us (while Canada has retreated from what it built). What is more, most European corporations and publics have put up sufficient tax dollars to pay for their welfare states.[†]

Public social spending and poverty rates are directly connected. Most European countries have adult- and child-poverty rates below Canada's. The Netherlands and Norway are but two of several excellent examples of how a high level of social spending has drastically reduced poverty rates and helped raise the overall standard of living. Both countries maintain consistently low unemployment rates (around 4 per cent at this writing) even though their tax rates compared to GDP are among the highest in the OECD. That's not the way it's supposed to be, according to the neo-cons and the old cons as well. Generous social programs are supposed to encourage idleness and raise the unemployment rate. High tax levels are supposed to discourage investment and contribute to unemployment. If only Canada had been fortunate enough to have had the Netherlands' or Norway's unemployment rates and poverty rates for the past decade!

---

[*] *Edmonton Journal*, June 24, 1998.
[†] *Globe and Mail*, April 21, 1993.

When the right wing in Canada says that we Canadians spend too much on social programs, the immediate response must always be, "Compared to whom?" If they reply that we must compare ourselves to our next-door neighbour and largest trading partner, you will likely already know how to respond, but, after reading part seven in this book, you will have some extra ammunition.

The following is the lead paragraph from a *Globe and Mail* story, April 1998:

> A $37-a-month allowance for pregnant women on welfare is being scrapped to stop them from squandering the money on beer, Ontario Premier Mike Harris said yesterday.
>
> The move to dump the pregnancy allowance, which was supposed to pay for sometimes expensive groceries like fresh vegetables and dairy products, usually in the final six months of pregnancy, came as a surprise.[*]

If this story isn't indicative of selfish, cruel, and stupid policy-making, I don't know what is. But for all their uncaring, ignorant attitudes and behaviour, provincial politicians like Mike Harris and Ralph Klein have every right to point to Ottawa as the source of at least part of their budgetary problems. As Tom Kent put it, "For 20 years . . . Canadian social policy has been marked by more retreats than advances. This is not because of forces beyond our control." Rather, "we have faltered in national purpose . . . our pursuit of the public interest has flagged . . ."[†]

The International Covenant on Economic, Social and Cultural Rights commits countries that sign on to recognize "the right of everyone to social security, including social insurance; the right of everyone to an adequate standard of living for himself and his family, including adequate food, clothing and housing . . . and the right of everyone to be free from hunger." By these standards, Canada's social policies are a dismal failure. And, rather than overspending on social programs, we spend too little.

---

[*] Margaret Philp and Richard Mackie, April 18, 1998.
[†] Caledon Institute of Social Policy, *Social Policy 2000*, January 5, 1999.

Government Spending:
In the Middle of the Pack

He said as far as he could tell (and he reads three papers a day)
there's just no way the country is going to survive much longer
if the government keeps spending our money like it grows on
bloody trees. Those tax-and-spend fools are going to drive us all
into bankruptcy. He was just leaving for La Quinta and he was
going to read up on government waste and all that incredible,
useless, mindless spending in Ottawa and Victoria. Thank God
we've got at least a few politicians who understand that we're
spending so goddamn much more than other countries there's
no way we can be competitive, no way we can be productive.
There's just no incentive left.

When we left the Pan Pacific after our lunch his chauffeur
brought his Jag around and they dropped me off at my hotel.

If we're going to do a much better job of helping poor Canadians, it's
going to take money. But how can we manage that? We're constantly
told that government in Canada *already* spends far too much money.

Do Canadian governments spend too much? Again, the question
must be asked, "Compared to what country?" And again, by international standards, the answer must be a firm no.

FIGURE 42

General Government Outlays as a Percentage of Nominal GDP

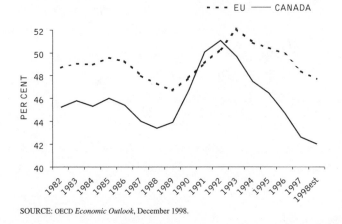

SOURCE: OECD *Economic Outlook*, December 1998.

Total government spending in Canada is now well below European levels.

FIGURE 43

General Government Total Outlays to GDP

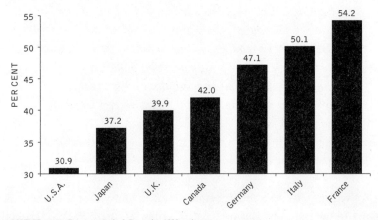

SOURCE: OECD, *Economic Outlook*, December 1998, estimates.

Canada is in the middle of G-7 government spending as a percentage of GDP.

Figure 42 shows how Canada compares to the average of the European Union countries. For much of the past two decades our total government spending has been well below E.U. levels, and the difference has been growing during most of the 1990s.

Figure 43 shows how Canada compared to the G-7 countries in 1998 in terms of total government outlays as a percentage of GDP. Once again, we're in the middle of the pack. By the year 2000, total government spending in Canada will likely have dropped closer to 41 per cent of GDP.

Figure 44 shows Ottawa's spending on goods and services (1992 prices) compared to GDP. Once again, if we believed the financial press, we would be in no doubt that the federal government has been avariciously gobbling up the Canadian economy. Not so.

FIGURE 44

Net Government Current Expenditures on Goods and Services
Ratio to Real GDP

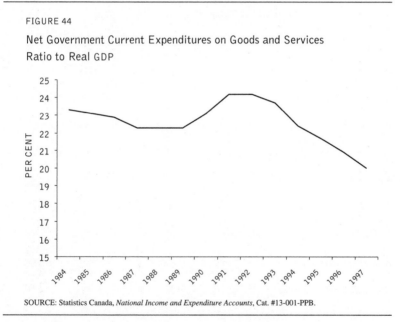

SOURCE: Statistics Canada, *National Income and Expenditure Accounts*, Cat. #13-001-PPB.

Despite much propaganda to the contrary, federal government spending as a ratio of real GDP has declined substantially since the early 1990s.

If you prefer a similar measurement without adjusting for constant dollars, the ratio of total budgetary expenditure to GDP fell from 22.9 per cent in 1991-92 to 17.3 per cent in 1997-98 and is headed lower. By either measurement, federal spending to GDP has been declining, not increasing. Ottawa's spending between 1991-92 and 1997-98 fell by some $6.7 billion.

Another way of looking at federal government spending is on a real per capita basis. In 1993 Ottawa spent more than $6,000 per capita. By 2000 that figure will be below $5,000.

To sum up, when you read or hear that government spending in Canada is far too high, you must point out that in international terms we're in the middle of the pack, have been in the middle of the pack for many years, and that total government spending to GDP has fallen considerably, down to levels not seen since the 1960s.

"We Can't Afford to Help the Poor"

They were sitting around the nineteenth hole after the game. The topic of taxes came up. X said he was in great shape since he had moved almost everything to the Cayman Islands. Y said he had him beat. He stayed out of the country for one day more than half a year, including all winter, so he didn't pay a cent in Canadian income taxes. Z said, but you came back to Canada for your triple bypass, didn't you? Z said, well how about the Bronfman deal, all that money leaving the country untaxed. People should be strung up over that one, passing up hundreds of millions of dollars in tax money in a closed-door, no-minutes meeting. X said, big deal; suitcases stuffed with cash leave the country every day for tax havens. Y said it's no wonder with taxes being what they are in this country. X said the big theft is the way the branch plants here book their profits out of the country so they don't pay big taxes here. Y said, careful! Remember who I work for.

The conversation turned to their children. Together they had eight kids going to Canadian universities.

The fifth reason our politicians have so blatantly ignored the poor is that any important measures to assist poor men, women, and children in

Canada are going to require money and we're already "Taxed to Death."* A day doesn't go by without a shrill newspaper editorial or column or Chamber of Commerce speech deploring the plight of "our overburdened taxpayers" and outlining the urgent need to reduce taxes so we can be more competitive and more productive. I don't think it's an exaggeration to call many of the media comments about our tax system bordering on the hysterical. Or simply hysterical. One thing is for sure, many of these comments are without foundation or just plain ridiculous.

Week after week, month after month, Canadians are bombarded with inflated claims about how overtaxed we are and how urgent it is that we cut taxes by huge amounts before the entire economy sinks into oblivion. Many of the most strident complaints come from right-wing organizations such as the Fraser Institute or the Reform Party, or from the wealthy. But principally they come from the print-media business sections and editorial pages and columnists who cater to and work for the wealthy.

Let's examine one typical column, "Canada can't afford not to cut taxes," by media favourite Sherry S. Cooper, chief economist at Nesbitt Burns. Cooper tells her readers that our "tax millstone" and "pernicious taxes" are damaging our economy. "Countries with low tax rates are the countries with low unemployment rates. . . . The tax burden has discouraged foreign investment in this country. We have lagged behind the major industrial countries of the OECD in attracting foreign business" having been "suffocated by an overwhelming tax burden."†

Interesting. In 1998, Canada had an all-time-record amount of direct foreign investment, amounting to $22.94 billion, far eclipsing the previous record by about $10 billion. That's some suffocation. Moreover, Canada has many more entire industries that are majority foreign-controlled than any other developed nation in the world. That's some lagging behind. As to countries with low tax rates having low unemployment rates, when you see Figure 46, you will see many countries with higher taxes than Canada that have, over the years, averaged lower rates of unemployment than Canada.

* *Financial Post Magazine*, February 1999.
† *National Post*, February 19, 1999.

Diane Francis, another of the right wing's favourite columnists, describes Canadians as being "among the world's most over-taxed citizens."*

According to the editor of the *Financial Post Magazine*, "We suffer the most oppressive tax regime in the industrialized world. Anyone up for a tax revolt?" he asks. Later on, in the same issue, we read, "Despite the 1998 tax cuts, we still have the highest income – and profit – tax rates in the industrialized world as a percentage of GDP."†

How does all this hyperbole stack up to reality? Let's consider first a longer historical period and compare total government current receipts as a percentage of GDP. Figure 45 shows an OECD thirty-five year comparison, from 1960 to 1995 inclusive.

FIGURE 45

Current Government Receipts to GDP, 1960 to 1995

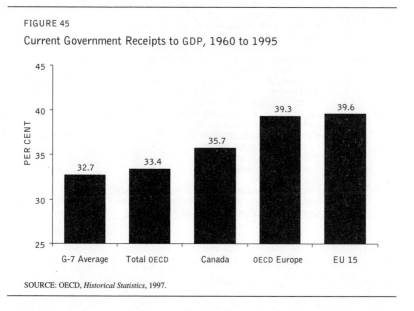

SOURCE: OECD, *Historical Statistics*, 1997.

This thirty-five-year comparison of government revenue as a proportion of GDP again shows Canada with receipts well below European levels. Claims that we're far too highly taxed are often misleading.

---

* *Edmonton Journal*, January 31, 1999.
† February 1999.

Figure 46 shows the comparisons for 1996, the most recent available at this writing.

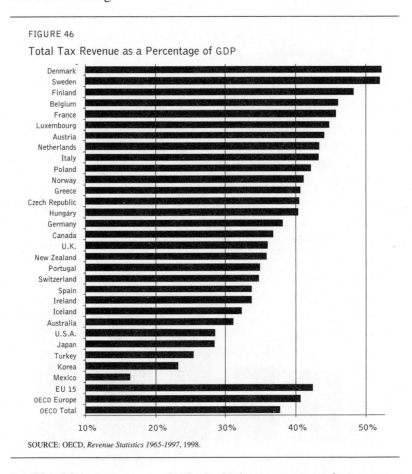

FIGURE 46

Total Tax Revenue as a Percentage of GDP

SOURCE: OECD, *Revenue Statistics 1965-1997*, 1998.

In 1996, fifteen OECD countries had a higher percentage of tax revenue compared to GDP than Canada. By 1999 Canada will have dropped further down the list.

Contrary to all the baloney, we're in the middle of the pack again. In 1996, fifteen OECD countries had higher tax revenue to GDP than Canada, and thirteen were lower. Moreover, Canada's total taxes were lower than the average for the E.U., the OECD countries in Europe, and below the average of the total OECD. Hardly what you've been told over and over and over again in your morning paper.

As I pointed out in *The Betrayal of Canada*, personal income taxes in Canada *are* higher than the OECD average; corporate taxes to GDP tend to be lower. Readers should note carefully, however, that tax *rates* and taxes effectively *paid* are often miles apart. We're constantly told about tax rates of 50 per cent or more that afflict the wealthy. But the following table presents quite a different picture.

In 1995, the 45,000 Canadians who earned more than $250,000 paid federal and provincial income taxes at the combined rate of 38.5 per cent. For all fourteen million taxpayers, the total combined income tax averaged 19.3 per cent.*

Here are the average total money incomes and average income tax paid by the five income quintiles in 1996.†

	Average Money Income	Average Tax	Taxes to Income
Lowest quintile	$17,447	$687	3.9%
Second quintile	33,855	4,328	12.8
Middle quintile	49,565	9,019	18.2
Fourth quintile	68,191	14,563	21.4
Highest quintile	114,095	29,388	25.8

New figures show that in 1997 Canadian families paid an average of 20.2 per cent of their total income in income taxes, with the top quintile averaging 26 per cent.

What about the oft-repeated contention that Canadian corporations are overtaxed? In 1996, thirteen OECD countries saw corporations contribute a higher percentage of total taxation than in Canada, while fourteen had lower corporate contribution levels. So, again, we're in the middle.** In the 1990s, corporate taxation in Canada as a percentage of GDP was well below the average levels of the previous four decades.

For corporations in Canada, in the words of the Canadian Tax Foundation, "the overall tax burden on business was less than the averages for the European OECD countries and the G-7 countries."

---

* *Finances of the Nation*, Canadian Tax Foundation, Table 3.3, 1998.
† Statistics Canada *Income after tax, distribution by size in Canada, 1996* Cat. #13-210-XPB.
** OECD, *Revenue Statistics, 1965-1997*, 1998.

I find it amazing that almost all media tax commentary treats tax revenue as confiscation of money which is to be poured down a sewer. The *Financial Post Magazine* editor asks, "Why strive for excellence at work when you know that a good percentage of what you earn will end up in public sector coffers to be used for who knows what?" Who knows what? Let's consider, for example, health care, pensions, education, medical research, highways, sewers, police, national defence, job training, the environment, national parks, and so on.

Taxes paid are only one side of the coin. Measuring combined take-home pay plus direct benefits received, Canadians do much better than the citizens of four of the G-7 nations and once again are about right in the middle of the international pack. The one-sided, far-right perspectives of the Fraser Institute and some of our editorial pages usually totally ignore the fact that most of our taxes go for things that Canadians want. Poor Sherry Cooper seems puzzled by the fact that most Canadians "are unconcerned about our stifling tax burden." She shouldn't be. The polls taken over a period of years have yielded consistent results. Canadians rarely put tax reduction at the top of their lists of priorities and concerns. One national poll put more transfer payments, more help for young people trying to find jobs, new health-care programs such as home care or pharmacare, increased benefits for children in low-income families, and new scholarship funds to improve access to education all well ahead of reducing income tax.*

In December 1998, Campaign 2000 estimated that it would require about $7.5 billion "to lift every poor child in Canada out of poverty." That's a lot of money. But let's compare that amount with the surplus in our EI fund, now well over $31 billion. Or let's suppose total tax revenue in Canada to GDP was just the same, no more, as the average of all the twenty-nine OECD countries. That would mean additional revenue of over $9 billion that we could use to help poor children. Could there possibly be a better investment for Canada's future, not to mention the suffering and deprivation that could be alleviated?

Whenever you raise the question of helping the poor, you always hear that we can't afford to do much because our taxes are already so high. *Where* are we going to get the money? Well, we already *have* the

---

* *Globe and Mail*, February 7, 1998.

money, but it's unfairly distributed. Nobody enjoys paying taxes. Certainly there's abundant evidence that government at all levels could operate much more efficiently. But, when you hear or read the distorted comments like the examples you read earlier in this chapter, when people say we Canadians are badly overtaxed, ask them once again, "Compared to where?" Then, perhaps, if you're bold enough, when they answer, ask them how come they haven't moved there already.

We'll come to the sixth reason why the poor are ignored in Canada, shortly, but first a look at the frequently brain-dead debate about "the brain drain."

Brain Drain or Brain Gain?

*They went to McGill medical school together. One went on to
take a post-graduate degree in the U.S. and became a very successful orthopedic surgeon. The other became a popular family
physician with a big practice. In their mid-forties they were
both recruited by a big Texas clinic. The salary was huge, the
taxes lower than in Canada, and there was a lot of research
money available. Both doctors liked Canada a great deal, had
family here, were doing well financially, but the offers were just
too good to turn down.*

*In Texas they lived in gated communities which had their
own security patrols. They could play golf and outdoor tennis
for most of the year. And they were making big bucks. The
surgeon was a big fan of Ronald Reagan.*

*Nine years later, the family physician returned to Canada.
The health maintenance organizations (HMOs) had taken
over. Now the doctors were told who they could see and could
not see; they received incentives to cut back on "unnecessary"
tests and procedures; they needed authorization before referring patients to specialists. The managed-care companies
believe that there are far too many doctors, too many surgeons.*

The name of the game is cost-cutting. The bottom line is not health but profit. About half the doctors now complain they've lost control of their medical decision-making and can't spend adequate time with their patients. The HMOs are even beginning to cut back salaries. Now the managers and insurance companies are in control.

What does the so-called "brain drain" have to do with poverty? Plenty.

The same people who have provided us with so many years of misinformation about taxes have recently escalated their loud laments about Canadians being driven out of their own country by high taxes. As usual, many of the conservative think-tank and media comments on the brain drain have ranged from the highly hyperbolic to the wildly hysterical.

Among others, the conservative and continentalist C.D. Howe Institute (which, like the Fraser Institute, absolutely refuses to reveal the sources of its funding) says Canada's tax burden has been a major factor in the brain drain. According to the *Financial Post*'s editor-at-large, "Those who think the brain drain problem isn't serious . . . should read the C.D. Howe Institute's latest report on the issue. . . . BCNI President Tom d'Aquino says the problem has reached 'near crisis' proportions."[*] For *Canadian Business* magazine, "This brain drain is a loss to our economy, and further threatens our innovative and economic potential. . . . Cutting taxes is something that governments can and should carry out."[†] I could give you a fat volume of similar comments, but you've likely heard or read most of them already.

In early October 1998, Scott Murray and his colleagues at Statistics Canada produced an important paper, *Brain Drain or Brain Gain? What Do the Data Say?* Given the newspaper frenzy on the subject, one would have thought that the Press Gallery and other journalists across the country would have leaped at the opportunity to report Murray's findings. Not so. Only David Crane of the *Toronto Star* gave the report any prominence. Those who had been loudly beating the brain drain drum either entirely or largely ignored it.

Let's see what Murray's study showed:

---

[*] Neville Nankivell, October 24, 1998.
[†] Jason Myers, December 11, 1998.

Is there a brain drain to the U.S.?

Yes, but this drain is offset by a brain gain from all over the world, especially in the high-tech sector, where the gain is many times greater than the drain. Given the severe shortage of workers in the high-tech sector, this gain is making an important contribution in meeting the high demand.

Emigration of Canadians to the U.S. in the 1990s [has been] small in a historical sense and small in relation to the inflow of immigrants.

Here are Murray's figures for the annual averages in the years 1990 to 1996:

Emigration to the U.S.	Immigration from the U.S.	Immigration From All Over the World
21,732	6,493	230,581

During the same years, there was an annual average of 9,770 Canadian emigrants destined to the U.S. labour force, while there was an annual average of 122,701 immigrants destined to the Canadian labour force. Moreover, Canadian emigration to the United States in the 1990s was the *lowest* since the 1950s as a percentage of immigration to Canada. As well, there has been no increasing trend of emigration to the U.S. in the 1990s. Once again, not exactly what you've been reading and hearing!

But what about all those university graduates we're losing? For every graduate who moved to the U.S. in the 1990s, we gained four immigrant university graduates.

But what about the quality of these immigrants? Compared to Canadian-born university students, almost twice as many immigrants had bachelor's degrees or higher, and about three times as many had master's, Ph.D., or medical degrees. According to Murray, "The savings for Canadian tax payers in education costs for these immigrant university graduates are very substantial . . . in 1995 alone $5.3 billion in total."

But hasn't the brain drain to the U.S. hurt us badly in certain key areas such as health care and computer sciences? Here are Murray's average annual figures of emigration to the U.S. in the years 1990 to 1996 as a fraction of the Canadian labour force total stock:

Physicians	5/1,000
Nurses	3/1,000
Computer Scientists	1/1,000
Engineers	3/1,000
Managerial workers	1/1,000

In terms of emigration as a percentage of *the new supply* of workers, it looked like this:

Physicians and other health-diagnosing professionals	5.1%
Nurses	2.1
Engineers	1.8
Computer Scientists	0.5
Managerial workers	0.6

Murray returns to the question of immigrant quality. Let's deal with computer science, which has been "at the heart of the current brain drain debate. . . . After ten years, immigrant computer scientists earn slightly more than their Canadian-born colleagues at every age. . . . Their estimated annual average earnings in a lifetime are only one per cent less than that of Canadian born computer scientists."

There is one area where Canada does have a net brain drain, and that is health. How much of that has to do with the Chrétien government's and provincial health cutbacks is unknown, but there's every reason to believe that it's been a major factor. So too has been Canada's terrible record in funding medical research although Ottawa seems to have at last woken up to this problem.

One final point from Murray's paper. Press reports about migration to the U.S. are often based on misleading information.

The U.S. Immigration and Naturalization Service produces a count of entries of border crossings and not unique individuals.

... An individual who migrates to the United States on a temporary work visa, and who then travels outside the U.S. (including back to Canada), regardless of the reason for the travel, or the duration, is re-counted on each return to the U.S., other than returns by motor vehicle. Clearly, multiple entries by the same individuals do not reflect the annual flow of workers to the U.S.

One frequent claim is that a quarter of all Canadian doctoral students leave the country. Perhaps they do. But as Murray points out, "Almost an equal proportion of these graduates are foreign students. This raises the possibility that a considerable portion of the doctoral graduates departing from Canada may, in fact, be foreign students returning to their country of origin." Similarly, many foreign graduate students in the United States return to their homes around the world.

Three important points need to be made about immigrants. First, most Canadians had immigrants as ancestors; Canada was largely built by immigrants. Second, even though in the 1990s immigrants have had increasing poverty rates in Canada, most immigrants are not poor. Third, the evidence is clear that each generation of immigrants generally fares better than the previous one.

John Kenneth Galbraith writes: "There is a strong current of thought, or what is so described, that deeply deplores immigration, is deeply resentful of the migrants and campaigns ardently against their entry and continuing presence."* Canada is no exception. Certainly we have our own racists and bigots, but fortunately they are a small minority.

Andrew Cardozo, a past president of the Pearson-Shoyama Institute, has written:

> The studies on the economic contribution of immigrants range from those that report immigration has no effect on the economy to those that conclude it is positive. No credible study suggests a drain on our economy. Immigrants also use fewer social services than they pay for, relative to other Canadians.
>
> Small business: The engine of economic growth and job creation; estimates are that 50 per cent to 80 per cent of the

---

* *The Good Society*, Boston, Houghton Mifflin, 1996.

small business owners are immigrants and an increasing number are in the high tech sector with incredible ties to export these goods to other countries.

Medicare: Not only are studies showing that immigrants use the health-care system less than Canadian-born folks, but immigrants play a major role in staffing the health-care system.

Education: Immigrants on average have more university education than those born here, and like health care, a sizeable number of immigrants teach in colleges and universities, especially in faculties like science, business and medicine.[*]

Here's Jeffrey Simpson:

Dismiss the canards that immigrants take massive numbers of jobs from Canadians. No study shows that; in fact, studies tend to show the contrary. Immigrants add vitality to the country, give us links with places far from our shores, inject purchasing power to the economy and make the country generally a more interesting place.[†]

But hasn't the percentage of immigrants in Canada been growing rapidly? The 1996 census showed that immigrants made up 17.4 per cent of the population, a small increase over the 15- to 16-per-cent level of the period 1951 to 1991. Figure 47 looks at immigrants this century.

In an excellent paper for the City of Toronto Homelessness Task Force in July 1998, Mendelson Associates comments on a relatively recent development relating to the welfare of immigrants:

Until 1989, the incidence of poverty of families headed by someone born in Canada was roughly the same as the incidence for families headed by someone born abroad. Since 1989, however, the incidence of poverty for families headed by non-Canadian-born residents has increased much more rapidly than for families headed by a person born in Canada.

---

[*] *Toronto Star*, September 8, 1997.
[†] *Globe and Mail*, October 29, 1997.

FIGURE 47

Immigrants as a Percentage of Canada's Population, 1901 to 1996

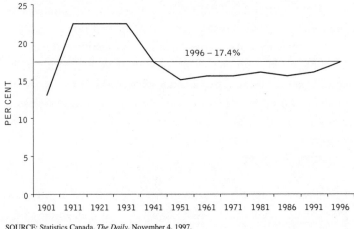

SOURCE: Statistics Canada, *The Daily*, November 4, 1997.

Immigrant-to-population levels have been increasing only modestly and remain well below the percentages in the early 1990s.

In 1986, the difference was small. By 1996, there was considerably more poverty among non-Canadian-born families and individuals. If one considers immigrants who arrived in Canada after 1989, the difference is huge. "Despite recovery from 1994 on, poverty among immigrant families has continued to increase and the gap between immigrants and non-immigrants continues to grow." Why would that be? Michael Mendelson believes "the brunt of the downturn in the early 1990s was very unevenly spread. Many immigrants and particularly refugees are the least able to protect themselves and have much increased vulnerability since most are much less entrenched in the work force." [*]

So, summing up, immigrants make an important contribution to Canada, adding to our economy in a substantial way. While the immigrant population in recent years has suffered from increasing poverty,

---

[*] Conversation with the author, February 26, 1999.

most working-age immigrants have jobs and do not live in poverty. Should the increasing number of immigrants who do live in poverty lead us to curtail new immigration? Hardly.

In another recent paper, three McMaster University economists, Frank Denton, Christine Feaver, and Byron Spencer, show that due to the aging of Canada's population and a fertility rate below the natural replacement level since the early 1970s, both the "population and labour force growth rates are on long-run downward paths. . . . Net immigration has accounted for a variable but substantial share of population growth since the early 1950s. Since the mid-1980s it has accounted for almost half the total growth, thus offsetting, in large measure, the effects of continuing low fertility rates."[*] The three economists produce a startling table:

Estimated Contribution of Net Immigration to Labour Force Growth

1976-81	9.6%
1981-86	13.4
1986-91	45.6
1991-96	71.0

Figure 48 (overleaf) is even more startling. Given a continuation of the present patterns of fertility and immigration, Canada's labour force will have virtually zero growth in the not-too-distant future. Increases in immigration above historical levels will be essential if Canada's economy is to grow. Unless Canada's productivity growth somehow far exceeds its recent performance, new immigrants will play an increasingly vital role in our country's future and in our efforts to achieve a higher standard of living.

Just as this book was being sent off to the publisher a new study by the noted U.B.C. economist John Helliwell was released.[†] Among its conclusions are

---

[*] "Immigration and Population Aging," *Canadian Business Economics*, February 1999.
[†] *Checking the Brain Drain: Evidence and Implications.*

FIGURE 48

Five-Year Percentage Labour Force Growth Rates

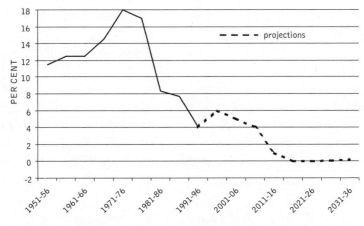

SOURCE: *Canadian Business Economics*, Immigration and Population Aging, February 1999.

Because of our declining labour-force growth rate, if Canada is to grow immigrants will have to play an even greater role in the future.

• the flow of Canadians to the United States is now smaller than it has been in almost any other period of our history.
• there are now some 260,000 fewer Canadians living in the U.S. than there were in 1980, and most Canadians living in the U.S. emigrated before 1960.
• in 1930 about twelve per cent of Canada's population had migrated to the U.S. Today the figure is under two per cent.

But surely, from all that we've heard and read, Canadians have been moving around. Helliwell is very clear. Canadians are "70 times more likely to be living in another Canadian province than in a U.S. state of similar size and distance."

It is true that Canada is losing some fine people to the U.S. In some cases this is because of taxes, in others it is because of job opportunity, in others it is because of research funding or personal and family reasons. But the vastly overblown brain-drain scare is highly misleading. It is just one more reflection of the continuing campaign to lower

Canadian taxes to U.S. rates. If that campaign is successful, it will certainly destroy much of what most Canadians value about our country. It would also finally destroy any last chance of doing anything meaningful to help millions of Canadians living in poverty.

PART SEVEN

The War Against the Poor

Hostility, Extremists, and the Denial of Need

The food bank head said that although the same threads run through the lives of many food-bank recipients, each person's story remains unique. Many clients anticipate the arrival of EI cheques, pension or insurance payments, only to find out at the last moment that the cheque has been held up for any number of reasons. Peter was working in the oil industry and had been laid off. With a wife and two children, he was desperately searching for employment and living on EI benefits. His wife held a part-time minimum-wage job and they were just managing to pay their bills and rent. Because of a computer glitch, Peter's EI cheque, as well as several hundred others, did not arrive. They were told that there would be a delay. He had to turn to the food bank for assistance. This was a very difficult step to take, as he had never had to ask for help before and felt humiliated. He was treated with respect and dignity and left the premises with his head held high.

Pretty well every food-bank story is different. But after years in this job we know that unemployment and poor wages are the main culprits. We also know that the government cutbacks

have been devastating. What kind of society takes so much
away from the poor?

Wasn't it supposed to be a war against poverty?

Instead, there's abundant evidence that in Canada there has been and is a war against the poor. This is the sixth reason the plight of the poor in Canada is largely ignored. In almost all of my interviews for this book, people have told me that our country has changed. There's now a widespread denial of need. The words social assistance have become pejorative. Instead of help for the poor, there is scapegoating of the underprivileged. Compassion and altruism are in decline.

In the words of Carol Goar, after their election, the Mike Harris Ontario government "treated . . . poor people like social parasites."* In Alberta, Ralph Klein brought terrible, widespread suffering to tens of thousands of poor men, women and children through draconian cuts to social-services spending. We've already reviewed Jean Chrétien's and Paul Martin's uncaring contributions to human misery and deprivation.

What is so amazing is that, as poverty has grown in Canada during the past decade, the poor have increasingly been blamed for being poor. Not only has indifference grown, but so has outright hostility. Not only has hostility towards the poor grown, but blatant hate-mongering now exists, even on the pages of some of our newspapers. According to this view, the poor themselves are responsible for their own desperate circumstances. If they *really* wanted to work, they could find jobs. Most of those on welfare are lazy; they drink too much and they quickly squander the overly generous assistance that they receive.

It has been more than two hundred years since Adam Smith's definition of poverty: "By necessaries I understand, not only the commodities which are indispensably necessary for the support of life, but whatever the custom of the country renders it indecent for creditable people, even of the lowest order, to be without."† Two centuries later, some people in Canada are saying that such a definition of poverty is far too generous; assistance to the poor should be based only on what they require to survive.

---

* *Toronto Star,* January 9, 1999.
† *The Wealth of Nations*, Book Five, Revenue of the Sovereign or Commonwealth, 1776.

According to the U.N.,

Human poverty is deprivation in multiple dimensions, not just income. . . . Food, shelter, water, sanitation, medical care and clothing are necessary for leading a long and healthy life. Schooling and access to information through books, radio, newspapers – and, increasingly, electronic networks – are necessary to acquire language, literacy, numeracy and up-to-date information. Transport and energy are critical inputs to all these things and virtually all other human activity. There is growing evidence that lack of mobility and access lie at the heart of economic and social disempowerment of women.

But now, the likes of the Fraser Institute, cheered on by the right-wing national editorial pages, say that the number of poor in Canada is exaggerated and the real needs of the few truly poor are deemed to be vastly overstated.

One upshot of the well-organized campaign against the poor is that public-opinion polls reflecting the concerns of Canadians rarely mention poverty. In the June 1999 Ontario provincial election, poverty ranked far down the list of topics raised by either the politicians or the public. There was much debate about education, health care, and taxation. But Ontario's poor men, women, and children were, for the most part, of little consequence in the campaign. In terms of public policy, the war against the poor has been a great success; for a great many Canadians, the poor (except when you encounter panhandlers or men pushing grocery carts down back alleys) are invisible.

A few years ago, the Vancouver-based Fraser Institute was regarded by more than a few as an extremist organization with little credibility. Today, the media, for the most part, prominently report each of the institute's press releases and studies as if they were gospel. Fortunately, there are still quite a few people who are smart enough to know better.

In a 1997 internal document leaked to Linda Goyette of the *Edmonton Journal*, the Fraser Institute explained just how successful they'd been in penetrating the media. "As everybody now knows, we have outpaced not only each and every one of our competitors but the sum total of their efforts in this area." Among the institute's goals is "to enlist the help of no less than 25 multinational companies in supporting the development of the index" of their far-right-wing economic interpretations. And one of their principal objectives will be "to convince Statistics Canada to publish our measurement of poverty as the poverty lines for Canada so as to stop the use of the LICOs lines currently misused by most commentators."

The object of the exercise is to drastically reduce the number of poor in Canada by using an ultra-right definition of poverty.

If there are headquarters for the war against the poor, they have to be in the Department of Finance in Ottawa and in the offices of the Fraser Institute. Linda McQuaig summed up the attitude of the finance ministry: "With so many generous support systems out there, it was hard to imagine why anyone bothered working any more. . . . After all, many of the unemployed were simply not in the mood to work – too lazy, listless and unwilling to give up afternoons by the pool."

The idea of a so-called "natural rate of unemployment" being an acceptable level, and then abandoning those below that level as being beyond concern, could only come from neo-classicist, tenured, blinkered Milton Friedman economists who wouldn't know a food bank or a youth shelter or a hungry child even if they somehow got lost and blundered across one.

For economist Christopher Sarlo and his associates at the Fraser Institute, the number of poor in Canada have been woefully exaggerated. This exaggeration is largely the fault of those in the "poverty business." The higher the supposed number of poor, the more jobs there are for those who claim they are there to fight poverty.

But if poverty has indeed been so exaggerated, why has there been such a dramatic increase in dependency on food banks across the county? Why are there now so many more homeless? Why do social workers complain about their vastly increased caseloads? Why do inner-city teachers and churches tell of so many more poor and hungry children?

As to the notion that the poor have themselves to blame, perhaps the Fraser Institute would like to tell us how that theory applies to a poor child. Or to a young mother and child forced to flee an abusive husband. Or to a downsized fifty-year-old who can't find another job. Or to a handicapped person whose best job in the past five years was part-time and paid less than six dollars an hour. Or to a woman suffering from mental illness who lives on the street because she was kicked out of her hospital and has nowhere else to go.

For Sarlo, the narrowly defined poverty line in 1995, for a family of four, was $16,032, less than half the CCSD's poverty line and well below the LICOs line. His conclusion is that his data "overwhelmingly support the view that poverty, as it is generally understood, has been largely eliminated in Canada." The idea "that poverty is a widespread and growing problem in Canada is a myth. . . . Poverty is not a major problem in Canada."*

Unfortunately, there are quite a few people in Canada who believe that such statements are true.

David Ross, the dedicated, articulate executive director of the CCSD, has done an excellent job of dissecting Sarlo's ideas:

Poverty is more than just starving slowly, or freezing in the cold. . . . In the rich countries of the industrialized world, the income level [for defining] poverty is many times the level required to assure bare physical survival.

The Fraser Institute's analysis is probably attractive to fiscal conservatives who would prefer not to redistribute income through government programs, but rather let the free market provide to each person according to their abilities. For such thinkers, corporate and individual philanthropy and small-scale, strictly targeted government programs for only the very worst off are sufficient to ensure that no Canadian children appear with swollen, malnourished bellies on CNN. But this line of reasoning is dangerously simplistic.

The views of right-wing thinkers such as Chris Sarlo of the Fraser Institute are dangerous because they obscure the breadth and depth of the problems Canada faces.†

Richard Shillington writes:

---

* *Poverty in Canada*, 2nd edition, The Fraser Institute, 1996.
† *Perception* 21.3.

Sarlo is consistent in assessing only bare physical needs. "I had no difficulty in excluding products such as radios, television, VCRs, newspapers, magazines etc., from the list. These cannot in any way be described as physical necessities. Similarly, such items as children's toys, books and writing materials would not qualify as physical necessities." This constricted focus on basic needs implies subsistence level incomes – warehousing costs.

Sarlo compares welfare rates to his poverty lines and concludes: "There are a great many problems with our welfare system but inadequacy is not one of them."

Sarlo calls for equal access to education while using a poverty line that excludes books and television to conclude that welfare rates are adequate. A flexible mind indeed.*

For the Fraser Institute, or as Dalton Camp calls them, "the right-wing, make believe, Vancouver think-tank,"

our social problems appear intractable largely as a consequence of excessive government involvement. . . . Our priority should be to replace with private alternatives those government operated social programs that have proved themselves inefficient and ineffective.

Private alternatives? For-profit welfare? For-profit unemployment insurance? For-profit food stamps?

Let's look more closely at the define-poverty-away standards of the Fraser Institute. First, compare average household spending with spending of low-income Canadians. In 1996, Canadian households spent 17 per cent of their household budgets on shelter, 12 per cent on food, and 4 per cent for clothing. So the average household spent about one-third, or $16,367, of household spending for the essentials of food, clothing, and shelter.

By comparison, the fifth of households with the *lowest* income spent a *total* of almost the identical figure for the three above essentials, but their total income of $16,400 somehow had to *also* provide for bus

---

* *Toronto Star*, December 30, 1997.

tickets, recreation, insurance payments, pension contributions, utility bills, telephone, household furnishing and equipment, health and personal-care products, education, reading material, school supplies, taxes, and so on.

The $16,400 figure is also close to the figure Sarlo calculated for a family of four's *total* required income for the year. Doesn't exactly leave much for the other things, does it?

More recently Sarlo seems to have modified his views somewhat. His "basic needs" market-basket indicator seems more reasonable, but "the further away we get from the basic needs, the less credible is our poverty line." And the government must "remember that setting poverty lines is not . . . an exercise in compassion." God forbid!

For Sarlo, the LICOs lines are far too high and "clearly exaggerate the problems of poverty . . ." And what about child poverty in Canada? Here Sarlo's true colours show through:

> When a basic needs measure is used to determine child poverty in Canada, we find that the clear trend has been down over the past 20 years or so. I have estimated the rate of child poverty to be about 9 per cent in 1973; about 8 per cent in 1984 and about 5.6 per cent in 1994. This solid decline over the past couple of decades comes after more impressive decreases in real poverty in Canada between 1951 and the mid-1970s.[*]

(By the way, when we inquired yet again about where the Fraser Institute gets its funding, we were told, as in the past, most emphatically that the list "is quite private.")

If the Fraser Institute and the Department of Finance have led the war against the poor in Canada, the editorial pages of our two national newspapers have not been far behind. It's important to make the distinction between most Canadian journalists and the editorial pages. I happen to think that we have some good newspapers in Canada. But some of the editorial pages often read like material from the depths of the Dark Ages. All across the country we have many first-class journalists who produce consistently fine writing in their news reports and their

---

[*] Fraser Institute, *Fraser Forum*, October 1998.

analytical material. True, there are some columnists who make Preston Manning look like a rabid socialist, but for the most part, the newsroom and commentary staff present interesting, informative reading every day. If some of the editorial pages were half as balanced as the rest of the paper, thousands of readers across the country wouldn't simply skip over them, knowing full well the unbalanced right-wing ideological tilt they can expect.

Of course, some of the tilt will often appear elsewhere in the paper. In 1996, when the CCSD released *The Progress of Canada's Children* showing one in five Canadian children – about 1.4 million – were living in poverty, and that 40 per cent of welfare recipients were children, the headline for the *Globe and Mail* story proclaimed "CANADIAN CHILDREN DOING WELL, STUDY SAYS."*

In 1995, all 99,000 net new jobs for the year were part-time, while over the entire year there was a net loss of 22,000 full-time jobs. One result was that the number of Canadians who fell below the LICOs line increased by about 264,000 as the population grew and as family income dropped. In October 1996, the Washington, D.C.–based Economic Policy Institute reported that Canada's child-poverty rate was second only to that of the United States. On November 26, the Vanier Institute of the Family called for an urgent, radical redistribution of money and effort to prevent rising child poverty from creating a lost generation.

A few days later, the editor of the *Globe and Mail* outraged many readers with a remarkable column "about the behavioural roots of poverty" and "behavioural dysfunction among the poor"; it could have been written during the time of Charles Dickens. "Cutting welfare payments appears to shift many of the poor back to work." The remedy? "A supply-side approach to poverty" that would improve "parenting skills of poor parents." And then, the ultimate wisdom: "Arguably the biggest obstacle to breakthroughs in social policy is manners. It is almost always bad manners to go to the root of things."† It boggles the mind.

At the same time, *Edmonton Journal* columnist Linda Goyette put matters in perspective:

---

* *Globe and Mail*, November 13, 1996.
† William Thorsell, November 1996.

Back in 1989, after a unanimous resolution in Parliament, Canada promised the United Nations that it would work tirelessly to eradicate child poverty by the year 2000.

In their curious wisdom, Ottawa and the provinces decided to reach this goal by cutting billions of dollars out of health, education and social programs; reducing unemployment insurance and welfare payments to families; replacing the Canada Assistance Plan with a watery substitute; and abandoning the promise of a national day-care program.

Federal and provincial governments have been working overtime to make life harder for the poorest families in the country.[*]

Soon after, the national editorial pages were at it again. "The good news about child poverty is that it has been this bad before. The bad news is that it is not getting any better."[†] "The good news"? Some good news!

Nadine Gordimer describes the tendency to blame the poor as "the hardening of the heart and narrowing of the mind." Outraged reaction greeted the *Globe and Mail* column. "If his language sounds offensive it is, because I am sure that it is offensive to the hundreds of thousands of poor parents whose problem is not that of appropriate parenting skills, but that of an economy that does not create enough decent paying jobs. . . ."[**] Other letters to the paper spoke of the long history of blaming the poor for their own condition and "the smug, comfortable classes" with no knowledge of poverty.

Strangely enough, Canadian editorial writers are often sympathetic to poverty *outside* of Canada. In a lead editorial in June 1997, the *Globe and Mail* commented on the 1997 U.N. *Human Development Report* relating to world poverty: "The existence of such want amid the world's overflowing riches is a scandal."[††] A scandal elsewhere, but O.K. here.

Five months later, in another lead editorial, the *Globe* returned to the question of poverty in our own country. "What Ottawa decides to do about child poverty will determine, for better or worse, the broad course

---

* Fall 1996.
† *Globe and Mail*, Editorial, January 16, 1997.
** Letter from Lynne Toupin, *Globe and Mail*, December 4, 1996.
†† June 14, 1997.

that government will take in this country for many years to come. . . . Will we surrender to the age old logic that a cheque writing machine will solve every social ill . . .? Unfortunately, attempts to improve the lot of the working-age poor who are able to work by sending them cheques consistently . . . create dependency. . . . And the more generous the program, the worse the effects. Dressing it up as a 'child poverty' program changes little. . . ."*

For the *Globe*, lower taxes are needed to encourage job creation and productive investment. Minimum wages should be kept low and labour markets deregulated. Unemployment and welfare cuts "ensure that the balance of self-interest lies in working in preference to collecting state cash." The *Globe* goes on to praise the United States for its low unemployment rates. The paper failed to mention that year after year the U.S. has the highest poverty rates among all the developed nations in the world.

The *Globe and Mail*'s editorial writers echoed the Fraser Institute's line in July of 1997.†

Try to have a reasoned discussion about welfare and income inequality in Canada and you are bedevilled by an appalling lack of hard information. Discussions based on evidence are rare because that evidence is either narrow or simply non-existent. People therefore stake out their positions on the basis of either prejudice or emotion or individual self-interest or both.

The editorial goes on to discuss "those who abuse the low-income statistics to exaggerate the extent of real poverty in Canada."

In response to yet another Ronald Reaganesque *Globe and Mail* editorial on poverty later in the year, Michael Farrell, the acting executive director of NAPO, wrote to the paper:

I have become increasingly concerned with the *Globe*'s prescriptions for addressing the problems of poverty in Canada.

---

* November 13, 1997.
† July 10, 1997.

Your most recent editorial seems to be suggesting that by lowering social assistance rates further, it will "encourage" people to find work. By lowering minimum wage rates, it will encourage businesses to hire more workers.

The idea that social assistance rates are so high that recipients are discouraged from finding paid employment would have some validity if rates were high enough to provide an adequate standard of living. Currently, the average social assistance rate for individuals in Canada provides about $600 a month; hardly a life of leisure. In fact, the historical demand by the unemployed and social assistance recipients for government training or work placement programs has always overwhelmed the supply. There has never been any indication in Canada that the majority of people who are unemployed or on social assistance are in any way unwilling to re-enter the work force.

The suggestion of lowering minimum wages to reduce poverty in Canada would be amusing if not for the fact that there are actually some people who give it serious consideration. The average provincial minimum wage rate provides about $800 a month after taxes, which barely provides a subsistence existence for families. Is it not reasonable to expect that if you have a full-time job you should be able to receive a wage that provides you with a life of dignity?[*]

For the then-editor at the *Globe and Mail*, "inflation, not unemployment must be the core reference point in driving monetary policy. . . . Indeed, many observers fear that inflation is bound to rise next year."[†] Well, many observers were dead wrong. Canada's inflation rate in 1998 was a mere 1 per cent, one of the lowest in our history.

The editor's column went on to advise, once again, that among other things we could increase the supply of low-paying jobs by reducing the minimum wage and eliminating payroll taxes on those jobs. He's got it half right – the last half. But the impact on the poor of reducing the minimum wage would be disastrous, causing an immense increase

[*] November 15, 1997.
[†] November 22, 1997.

in human suffering. The idea that reducing already near-starvation wages would be a cure for poverty is egregiously cruel.

Two days after Paul Martin's February 1999 budget, which ignored the homeless crisis in Canada and did little or nothing for most poor single mothers, a *Globe and Mail* headline reported, "World's poor overlooked." The article went on to advise that the Canadian foreign aid budget was too low.[*]

Not to be outdone by the *Globe*, the *National Post*, responding to *The Growing Gap*, told us in an editorial that those "who profess concern about 'inequality' . . . are less concerned with the poor being poor than with the rich being rich." Moreover, "it is because of government programmes that the poorest have been lured into permanent dependency." For the "'we-the-socially-concerned' cabal . . . executive incomes may be the object of envy masquerading as social justice. . . . The main argument against entitlement programmes remains not their enormous costs to those who must pay for them, it is their disastrous effects on those they are allegedly designed to help."[†]

Right on! And food makes people hungry, medicine makes people sick, education makes people dumb, and good jobs make people poor.

For the *National Post*, the "shocking revelation" is that "the poor have stopped working almost completely. . . . The average number of weeks worked by the poorest 10% of families plummeted [while] the richest decile has doubled their hours of work relative to those of the poorest. . . . It is because of government programmes that the poorest have been lured into permanent dependency. . . . The whole obsession with 'inequality' is frequently bogus."

Somehow, the *Post* hasn't been able to figure out that the number of weeks worked is directly related to the labour-market factors already covered in this book. As for the poor being "lured into permanent dependency," the *Post* writer should try living for a month on a welfare subsistence allowance to determine exactly how alluring it is.

For the *National Post*, the move to redefine poverty with the proposed Market Basket Measure will be great:

---

[*] *Globe and Mail*, February 18, 1999.
[†] October 30, 1998.

Finally, a step forward in the war against poverty, and this time, miraculously with no funds attached. The federal, provincial and territorial governments have quietly drawn up plans to change the standard of poverty measurement in Canada so as to drop 1.5 million from the rolls of the poor, reducing the poverty rate from 17% to 12%. . . .

Confusing the harsh and serious condition of true poverty with what's been labeled as "humble circumstances" only makes it more difficult for charities and government to find and assist those in real need.

Predictably, anti-poverty groups are up in arms over the new formula. An exaggerated measure of human misery suits their interests, though it does nothing to help the poor.[*]

A friend in Toronto faxed me after reading this editorial: "It's a big relief to know there's no big problem and that those pitiful souls you're tripping over on your way to the bank are but trifling figments of your overly-active imagination."[†]

National Post owner Conrad Black has been consistent in his views. In May 1992 he advised that "caring and compassion really means socialism, wealth confiscation and redistribution."[**] Speaking in Edmonton in fall 1997, Black warned his audience about "extravagant welfare programs which cause money to be skimmed to people who haven't earned it." And, more recently, declaring victory, "the great effort to promote a socialist fable of a more compassionate society has deservedly failed."[††]

Let's hear now from one of Conrad Black's columnists writing about "the modern welfare industry":

A friend who has interviewed thousands of politicians, academics and experts in his career, says that anytime one of them claims he is acting on behalf of the children you can bet his motivation is self-interest.

---

[*] *National Post*, mid-December, 1998.
[†] Fax from David Shaw, December 16, 1998.
[**] *The Financial Post 500*, May 1992.
[††] Institute for Research on Public Policy, *Policy Options*, January/February 1999.

After making that comment, the Southam writer goes on to quote a book by a Chicago professor (*What Money Can't Buy: Family Income and Children's Life Chance* by Susan E. Mayer, published by Harvard University Press, 1997) who writes that "most people are poor because of themselves. Dishonesty, apathy, laziness, lack of self discipline, inability to hold a job, marital breakdown and father absence are the factors most likely to lead to poverty. None is alleviated by welfare. . . . The welfare industry provides . . . cushy academic, civil service or tax-supported lobby jobs. . . . They aren't interested in programs that work, only in programs that reflect well on them."*

Tom Flanagan, professor of political science at the University of Calgary, who has been director of research for the Reform Party, makes a similar case:

> Canada, I hope, is nearing the end of a long and disastrous experiment with no-strings-attached charity. First came the efforts of government to abolish poverty by taxation and redistribution, based on the false but seductive belief that poverty is caused only by a shortage of money. The result was the equalization of after-tax income statistics, but also family disintegration, welfare dependency, more poverty, homelessness and squalor. Then came well-meaning private citizens with food banks, street clinics, drop-in centres and overnight shelters – facilities that may be needed in the circumstances, but ultimately encourage further dependence unless they challenge the recipients of assistance to amend their lives.†

So, let's close the food banks and let people starve and close the shelters and let people freeze. It will be good for them.

Most readers will already be very familiar with the extent of Mike Harris's social cuts in Ontario. For Harris, children are hungry in part "because working mothers don't cook hot breakfasts for their families like they once did."** Moreover, "There's been no particular link

---

* Lorne Gunter, *Edmonton Journal*, August 19, 1997.
† *Globe and Mail*, December 31, 1998.
** *Globe and Mail*, June 3, 1998.

between children hungry at school and the unemployment rates and welfare rates."[*]

Now let's turn our attention to Ralph Klein's Alberta.

As a gauge of the Alberta government's attitude towards the poor, Child Services Minister Pearl Calahasen advised, "I don't know of any children that are in need at this stage of the game." When a furor broke across the province after her statement was reported, Calahasen claimed she was misquoted. Not true, said the *Edmonton Journal* reporter: "Those were her exact words."[†]

And those words are an accurate reflection of the ultra-conservative attitude of the Ralph Klein government towards the poor. Bernd Walter, who was Alberta's children's advocate, says Alberta's child-welfare system is crippled by an "anti-child atmosphere. . . . The attitude says we really don't care about our children."[**] According to the C.D. Howe Institute, the rest of Canada should look to Alberta as an example when it comes to reforming social assistance. "This success has important lessons for other provinces. . . . The 1993 Alberta welfare reform is one experiment from which all Canadians and their governments can benefit."[††] Saying that other provinces could benefit by copying Alberta is like saying that Slobodan Milosevic should be awarded the Nobel Peace Prize.

Since the Alberta "reforms" (meaning the draconian cutbacks of the already-modest social-assistance funds that had gone to the poorest Albertans) were instituted, demand at food banks across the province has risen dramatically, far more than doubling in Edmonton. Brian Bechtel, director of the Edmonton Social Planning Council, calls the C.D. Howe report "a superficial analysis" and says most of the people who were cut off social assistance are living in extreme poverty.

Alberta is one of the three wealthiest provinces in Canada and in recent years has had the highest or one of the highest growth rates. There is no sales tax and no government net debt. Here are just a handful of items reported in the province since the Klein cutbacks:

---

[*] Tom Walkom, *Toronto Star*, November 7, 1996.
[†] The *Edmonton Journal*, November 29, 1998.
[**] The *Edmonton Journal*, Fall 1997.
[††] Kenneth Boessenkool, *Back to Work: Learning from the Alberta Experiment*, 1997.

- A jail in Calgary is being used as a youth shelter. A Calgary lawyer reports that a social worker called her to say, "Better that your client gets convicted because [then] we can access a specialized treatment bed."*
- A recent study showed very long waits for medical care. One person had scheduled surgery cancelled four times. A mother waiting for the removal of an aggressive ovarian malignancy died before a hospital bed was available.†
- The Edmonton Food Bank and the Salvation Army both say they have been overwhelmed by demand for assistance. The Salvation Army director says, "The economy is supposed to be better. . . . I don't really have an explanation other than we have more working poor."**
- Five years after Alberta's 1993 cutbacks, over 2,200 more children from poor families have been turned over to government care. Brian Bechtel says, "It's a factor of the extreme stress that comes with trying to raise a child with $200 or $300 of income after you pay the rent."
- Of those denied welfare after the 1993 cutbacks who were able to find employment, over 83 per cent reported difficulty paying for food and shelter, and more than half were forced to rely on a food bank.
- Of those who remained on welfare, two-thirds reported that they were unable to find decent shelter given the low shelter allowances, increasing rents, and decreasing vacancy rates.
- Since the cutbacks, the number of Alberta families living with incomes less than half of the LICOs has doubled, and the number of children more than tripled.
- The Edmonton Inner City Housing Society has been turning away seven families for every family it could help.
- One Edmonton church food bank had an increase of more than 1,000 per cent in people served over a four-year period.

---

* The *Edmonton Journal*, January 29, 1999.
† The *Edmonton Journal*, February 1999.
** The *Edmonton Journal*, December 20, 1998.

- Alberta's welfare rates for single parents with one child are the lowest in Canada.*
- By mid-October 1997, "Alberta's child welfare system [was] so overwhelmed with abused and neglected children that some [were] being placed on waiting lists for protection, allowing only those in immediate danger to receive help."† Alberta's children's advocate described "an anxiety-plagued child welfare work force, whose members are leaving and being replaced by less experienced workers."
- The children's advocate also reported that he "is seeing an increasing number of youths who are homeless. In addition to being without food, clothing and shelter, they have no direction in their life." The *Edmonton Journal* asks, "What kind of province are we that we let this happen, despite the economic recovery all around us? What kind of government drives families into poverty, cuts a program to teach job skills to handicapped people, cuts funding to the Head Start Program?"**

Good questions. "A wealthy province that cares little about the poor" is the only possible answer. But the C.D. Howe Institute says Alberta provides "important lessons for other provinces . . . from which all Canadians and their governments can benefit."

I asked the C.D. Howe study's author if he had interviewed *any* people from the food banks, shelters, churches, inner-city schools, social agencies or, indeed, any front-line people. He answered, "No, it was a macroeconomic study."

What could possibly motivate the institute to say that the rest of Canada should follow Alberta's cruel example? It's no secret. Right-wing organizations like the C.D. Howe, funded secretly by big business and probably from the U.S. as well, approve of big government cutbacks, regardless of the painful human consequences. They also have their own reliable authority to turn to: "I think we've done a good job in terms of alleviating poverty in this province," says Premier Ralph Klein.†† In

April 1999, a new study showed that more than 45,000 children in Klein's home city of Calgary were without enough food every day, experienced intermittent hunger, or lived in such low-income families that proper nutrition was a serious problem.

How can we possibly explain all of this? We are not dealing with stupid people. In fact, most of them are clever. But most of them are in favour of curtailing government spending and dropping taxes to U.S. levels. Let the poor pull themselves up by their own bootstraps. Or sink with the rafts.

There is another explanation. In the 1997 U.N. *Human Development Report* there was an interesting boxed item entitled "Vested interests in perpetuating poverty":

Poor people are often seen as an economic burden on society. Yet poverty often serves the vested interests of the economically powerful, who may depend on the poverty-stricken to ensure that their societies run smoothly. A mobile pool of low-paid and unorganized workers is useful for doing the "dirty, dangerous and difficult" work that others refuse to do. In industrial countries many jobs considered menial are taken by immigrants, legal and illegal. With no legal protection or opportunity for collective action, workers are often exploited, receiving wages far below the minimum.

The poor can also be politically convenient. In some countries they serve as scapegoats for the ills of society, as immigrant workers do in Europe and North America. But they can also serve as a useful pool of voters for politicians who claim to serve their interests – even if they never consult them.

In the end, poverty reduction must involve some redistribution of resources – economic, social or political – and that will sometimes be vigorously opposed. Any strategy to eradicate poverty must therefore take into account the fact that many people have a vested interest in the perpetuation of poverty.[*]

---

[*] All quotes from the United Nations *Human Development Report* are courtesy the United Nations and Oxford University Press, Inc., New York.

To properly understand the war against the poor in Canada, we must understand that most of our right-wing establishment and some of their leading journalists want us to be more like the United States: less government, lower taxes, let the market decide. Certainly since the FTA was implemented in 1989, we've moved much closer to the U.S. in many ways, including privatization, deregulation, and harmonization of standards, while American control of business in this country has continued to expand. If Canada continues to move even closer to the U.S. model, the prospects for ever doing anything important about the poor in Canada will soon diminish to nil.

"Building Bigger Prisons to House the Poor"

"In the United States, the war against the poor has been won."

– John Kenneth Galbraith
speech in Toronto honouring
Senator Keith Davey, January 1997

Do Canadians want to adopt even more American standards and values? If we did, what would be the impact on the poor in Canada? How should Canadians react to the growing pressure from the far-right economic elite in Canada to abandon our own social-program standards and move to the American models?

No one would deny that since the FTA was implemented Canada has grown much closer to the United States in economic, social, and cultural terms. The investment provisions of the agreement have allowed growing American control of our corporations and resources. A vast array of policies and standards have been modified to avoid conflicts with those in the U.S. There is continuing pressure from the right to accelerate that process.

For many Canadians there is much to like about the U.S: their entre-preneurial energy, some of their great sports heroes, their excellent novelists and musicians, their scientists and scholars. Yet every public-opinion poll shows that the vast majority of Canadians have no desire to become Americans. They want Canada to remain a separate country and wouldn't move to the U.S. if they had the opportunity to do so. Most Canadians still think there are important differences between the two countries that are worth preserving. But a large number of our conservative economic elite disagree. Moreover, some of our most prominent formulators of public opinion receive large amounts of their funding from right-wing American corporations, organizations, and foundations that are determined to convince Canadians that the American way is the path to heaven.

At the same time, most Canadian newspapers and television stations are owned by conservative continentalists who have voiced their desire to see Canada move even closer to the U.S. For some editorial writers, columnists, and politicians, any criticism of the United States smacks of anti-Americanism. If what follows echoes the words of such distinguished Americans as Robert Reich, Paul Krugman, Lewis H. Lapham, Ralph Nader, John Kenneth Galbraith, Senator Daniel Patrick Moynihan, John R. MacArthur, Mario Cuomo, Lester Thurow, and the U.S. National Council of Churches, then I plead guilty.

The United States has been blessed with its lowest unemployment rate since 1973, eight straight years of strong economic expansion, and, in the words of *Fortune* magazine, is "Paradise Found: The Best of All Possible Economies."

At the same time, the U.S. has consistently tolerated poverty rates that can only be described as outrageous. The 1997 U.N. *Human Development Report* produced the following comparisons based on a conservative OECD measure.

Distribution of Income Poverty
Share of population in income poverty 1989-94

United States	19%
United Kingdom	15
Australia	13
Japan	12
Canada	12
Spain	10
Netherlands	7
OECD Average	9

Despite the booming American economy, child-poverty rates in the U.S. have doubled since 1974. Meanwhile, in 1996 President

Clinton agreed to major welfare changes that allowed U.S. states to reduce help for poor children. Since the early days of Ronald Reagan's presidency, while some ten million more Americans were added to the poverty rolls, billions of dollars have been cut from federal food aid. State welfare benefits are at ridiculously low levels, the number of homeless across the country has risen every year, and, in the words of *The New Yorker*, "when it comes to protecting our children (the U.S.) is now an underdeveloped nation."* *New York Times* columnist Anthony Lewis wrote,

> President Bill Clinton's decision to sign the bill ending the national commitment to help poor children . . . signals a change in basic American attitudes.
>
> Optimism and generosity have been the hallmarks of the American character. . . . The welfare bill is the opposite. . . . For generosity it substitutes callousness. . . . What the legislation will do is victimize poor children.

Democratic senator Daniel Moynihan of New York says that what the U.S. government has done will make "the lives of children as wretched as possible. . . . Hundreds of thousands of children will be forced to live on the streets . . . children on grates because there is no money in the states or cities to care for them." For Democratic representative John Lewis, the victimization of children will return to haunt U.S. society: "Where is the sense of decency? What does it profit a great nation to conquer the world, only to lose its soul?"†

In the words of *The Economist*,

> America tolerates greater inequality than exists elsewhere, and the percentage of its citizens who live in poverty is around twice the average for rich countries. Given all this, you might expect that Americans would be willing to give up some dynamism in order to diminish poverty and inequality. Far from it. . . . Neither President Clinton nor his aides refuted a

---

* *Edmonton Journal*, January 27, 1996.
† *New York Times*, early August 1996.

recent study suggesting that [the new legislation] would push 2.6 [million] people into poverty.*

While President Clinton and the U.S. Congress were slashing assistance for the poor, the Bread for the World Institute was reporting growing hunger among children in the U.S. According to *Time* magazine, "in spite of prosperity and job growth, a new study warns of a festering crisis among the working poor. Hunger in America in times of plenty?" Food banks are reporting sharply increased demand. "Who are swelling the ranks of the hungry? . . . It's the working poor. . . . The job market is there. The income isn't."†

By early 1999, *The New York Times* was reporting that more stringent rules have sharply cut the number of people who have sought food-stamp assistance. Those who have lost access to public food aid now are forced to rely on soup kitchens.**

In 1998, the U.S. Census Bureau reported that 13.3 per cent of Americans (35.6 million) lived below the official American poverty line. But the official method of defining poverty is hardly a reflection of reality compared to even conservative international standards. One study suggests that while the U.S. government classified 38 million Americans as poor in 1994, the more accurate figure was more than 65 million. The U.S. definition of poverty has been a threshold as much as 50 per cent lower than the LICOs base. (For more on this subject, see Appendix Three).

Cities like New York and the nation's capital, Washington, D.C., have appalling levels of poverty. Some 27 per cent of people who live in New York live in poverty, with an average poor family of four having to get by on $14,763 a year. Some 100,000 poor inhabitants find themselves homeless over the course of a year. In the borough of Queens, says Mario Cuomo, children growing up "will hear the sound of gunfire before that of an orchestra" while the "people on Park Avenue do not see that they have any relation to poor children."

Washington, D.C., has a higher infant mortality rate than Havana, Cuba. Christopher Hitchens, writing in *Vanity Fair*, said,

---

* *The Economist*, August 3, 1996.
† July 21, 1997.
** February 25, 1999.

Here [is] a city that has *contempt* for its citizens . . . a place that has banana republic levels of infant mortality . . . schools that [have] levels of illiteracy and innumeracy that would disgrace many cities in the Southern Hemisphere.

For *The Economist*,

The heart of Washington, D.C. is the American nightmare. Unemployed blacks sit on grimy front-steps of crumbling houses that were once grand; old sedans skirt the potholes. . . . By the standards of Europe and Japan, [American cities] still suffer appalling crime, yawning social disparities and remarkable underachievement in education. . . . There were 767 murders in New York in 1997; in London (which is about the same size) there were 129 in the year. . . . In Europe, no one talks of cities "dying." In America, however, respected academics and planners have sometimes suggested that inner cities should simply be abandoned.

Meanwhile, the well-to-do are moving out. In the 1960s, the District of Columbia's population was about 825,000. Today, it's down to about 545,000. Poor blacks are left in an inner city of squalor and decay. In New York, a lawyer for the Legal Aid Society's Homeless Family Rights Project advises, "The city seems bent on making assistance so miserable to seek that people simply won't seek it."*

Allan Fotheringham and I have both written about the big sign we have encountered at Washington's National Airport: "WELCOME TO THE MOST IMPORTANT CITY IN THE WORLD." The most important city in the world has been the murder capital of the United States for years and has among the lowest school-test results in the country.

In California there are thousands of gated developments with high fences and security floodlights and their own security patrols. They are, says Christopher Parkes of the *Financial Times*, "fortress communities" whose numbers are expected to double within five years: "White-only segregation, buried by federal legislation more

---

* *The Economist*, July 6, 1996.

than 30 years ago, is being restored by consumer demand. . . . 'You will see the walls go up wherever you see large numbers of immigrants' says the dean of the University of Southern California urban planning school."

President Clinton's 1996 legislation had a direct impact on about 13 million Americans receiving welfare and twice that number who were dependent on food stamps. The fifty states were now in control. Benefits could be limited to five years in a lifetime, and monthly cash payments from Washington to poor Americans ended. Benefits to immigrants were denied or cut back sharply. *Edmonton Journal* columnist Linda Goyette wrote, "The United States spends $260 billion on its military budget while it pretends it can't afford the most basic social support for ghetto children."* Over 430,000 U.S. families with no other income faced deep cuts in public assistance.

John R. MacArthur, publisher of *Harper's Magazine*, described the impact of turning welfare over to the states:

> This is bad news. [The result will be] the unsmiling commercial exploitation of human misery, particularly among disturbed, bereft and defenseless children. . . . In states like Texas, the ultimate goal will be the further enrichment of the already rich, and [to] drive the poor off the welfare rolls, or at least reduce their payments. Less money for welfare can then translate into more politically popular programs such as building bigger prisons to house the poor, imposing more death sentences on the poor and purchasing additional guns and ammunition with which to suppress the poor if they riot.†

For John Kenneth Galbraith, the debate about welfare assistance to the poor "always boils down to the slightly improbable case that the rich are not working because they have too little income, the poor because they have too much."**

In late February 1999 the *New York Times* reported that

---

* August 22, 1996.
† *Globe and Mail*, May 16, 1997.
** *The Good Society*, Boston, Houghton Mifflin, 1996.

Wisconsin drives its welfare rolls to record lows. . . . Unwilling or unable to work for public aid, many of the state's most troubled mothers have lost their benefits. . . . No anti-poverty idea has animated the last decade as much as "ending welfare." . . . Both President Clinton and his Republican adversaries have celebrated the dwindling rolls [while] homeless shelters are running out of beds.

We've already looked at the distribution of income in the United States, but let's return to the topic briefly. According to the *Globe and Mail*'s columnist Marcus Gee:

- The incomes of the poorest 5 per cent of Americans dropped by 34 per cent from 1969 to 1993. The incomes of the richest 5 per cent rose by 43 per cent.
- Company presidents now earn 225 times the salary of the average employee.
- In recent years the gap between rich and poor has become a canyon.
- Poverty breeds crime, drug abuse, poor health, and more poverty. It costs middle-class Americans a fortune in income transfers, health care expenditures, and policing costs. Poverty is not only wrong, it is expensive.

Why then is no one talking about it?[*]
Galbraith puts it this way:

A reliably growing economy begins, but it by no means ends, the agenda of the socially concerned. There is a very specific flaw in the market system against which we must rally political strength and action. The market system distributes income in a highly unequal fashion. The United States, it is now clear, exercises an adverse leadership in this regard.

There is the inescapable fact that the modern market economy (in the now-approved terminology) accords wealth

---

[*] *Globe and Mail*, October 23, 1996.

and distributes income in a highly unequal, socially adverse and also functionally damaging fashion. In the United States, now the extreme case among the major industrial countries, the Federal Reserve, an impeccable source said, as reported in the *New York Times*, that the top 1 percent of American households owned nearly 40 percent of the nation's wealth in 1989, the top 20 percent more than 80 percent.

This, the good society cannot accept. Nor can it accept intellectually the justification, more precisely the contrivance, that defends this inequality.*

In his book *The Work of Nations*,† Robert Reich says that the top 20 per cent of Americans are "quietly seceding from the rest of the nation." In the *New York Times*, the former U.S. Secretary of Labor suggests that "when the going gets rough again, we will notice that the gap between rich and poor had widened into a chasm, nobody has job security, and there is no safety net. Even in these frothy times, more of our children are impoverished than before the expansion started, and fewer Americans ever see a doctor."**

Now let's look at what has been happening to worker's wages in the U.S. According to Massachusetts Institute of Technology economist Lester Thurow, 60 per cent of Americans now receive 20 per cent less in real wages than they did twenty years ago, while during the past decade the number of U.S. billionaires jumped from thirteen to more than 250. Meanwhile, many families who formerly relied on a single breadwinner now must have two full-time workers to maintain a decent standard of living and both work longer hours.

Moreover, Thurow says that while many well-to-do Americans send their children to private schools, across the U.S. school budgets are being defeated by a growing population of seniors and the growing cost of higher education is causing many students to abandon university.

Despite the numerous reports of the surging U.S. economy,

---

* *The Good Society*, Boston, Houghton Mifflin, 1996.
† Alfred A. Knopf, New York, 1991.
** *New York Times*, January 3, 1999.

after adjustment for inflation the median household annual income, $37,005 in 1997, is roughly where it was in 1989, the final year of the last expansion the Census Bureau reported last month.

What's more, the 1997 level was only $1,260 above 1973's income. . . . Many households in the 1960s added more to their incomes in a single year than their counterparts today have added in 25 years. And they did it with one wage earner, not two or three, working fewer hours than the average jobholder does today.[*]

According to the *New York Times,* "While wealthier families enjoyed big gains, particularly from the booming stock market, most households find that their incomes, adjusted for inflation, are no higher today than they were in 1989. . . . Americans, for the most part, have been running in place for 25 years."[†]

The *New York Review of Books* echoes the same theme: "The average full-time worker in U.S. business now makes $440 per week. Twenty-five years ago the average worker made $517 a week in today's dollars. . . . Little wonder that so many Americans have lost their sense of getting ahead, and that so many parents now fear for their children's financial future. . . . Corporate employees who consider themselves lucky to have jobs that give increases of a percent or two beyond the cost of living know that their firms' top executives are making millions in salary and further tens of millions on stock options."[**]

As Lewis Lapham, editor of *Harper's,* points out:

Most of the country's best-known social theorists hold fast to the belief that government should remain as unobtrusive as possible, and that all decisions of importance should be referred to the custodians of private wealth or the officers of corporate management. . . . Why tinker with a system that pays $18 billion for the broadcast rights to the next eight years of

---

[*] *New York Times,* October, 18, 1998.
[†] October 17, 1998.
[**] October 8, 1998.

professional football games and awards the senior vice-presidents of *Fortune 500* companies salaries of $2 million, $4 million, $10 million per annum?*

Let's look more closely now at the U.S. standard of living. According to *The Economist*,

> Despite rapid job growth and falling unemployment . . . the typical worker's financial situation has continued a long decline that began in the late 1970s, mainly because of erosion in wages. During the 1980s, three out of five American workers saw their real hourly wages fall. . . . Since 1989, the fall in men's wages has grown more acute. . . . The bottom 80% of men have seen a decline.†

When asked in a 1996 *Business Week* poll if "the American dream of equal opportunity, personal freedom, and social mobility has become easier or harder to achieve in the past ten years," by a more than two-to-one margin those polled answered that it was harder. *Time* magazine revealed that "Americans are working 160 hours more each year than they did 20 years ago."** One hundred and sixty hours would add about four weeks of work in the year.

Economists Michael Wolfson and Brian Murphy looked at standards of living in both Canada and the United States. The heading for their article reads, "Analysis reveals that, from 1974 to 1995, a large portion of Canadian families had absolutely higher purchasing power than their U.S. counterparts. . . ."

> A number of intriguing results emerge from the analysis. One is that, even though the U.S. economy appears better off in terms of total output per capita, families (including unattached individuals) living in the United States are not necessarily better off, in terms of disposable income, than their Canadian counterparts. Indeed, roughly half of Canadian families had

---

* The Canadian Centre for Policy Alternatives (CCPA) *Monitor*, July/August 1998.
† September 7, 1996, based on *The State of Working America*, Economic Policy Institute, Washington, D.C.
** December 29, 1997.

disposable incomes in 1995 that gave them higher purchasing power than otherwise comparable U.S. families. The reason is that the very rich in the United States pull up the average income much more than in Canada, while those at the bottom of the U.S. income spectrum have less purchasing power than those at the bottom in Canada.

What matters more directly to families than individual labour income, inequality or polarization, is their disposable income – labour income, plus investment returns, plus government transfers, less income taxes and payroll taxes. . . . From this perspective, Canada is clearly "kinder and gentler": both inequality and polarization are considerably lower, and incomes at the bottom of the spectrum are higher than in the United States.

The U.S. incidence of low income was about 50 per cent higher than Canada's. . . . This general result, that up to roughly the halfway mark in the income spectrum Canadian families are better off, is particularly striking, given the prevailing view that Canada has a considerably higher level of taxation than does the United States.

Canada's universal public health care system was larger and distributionally more progressive. Thus, had the value of publicly provided health care benefits been included in the analysis, Canadian family income levels would have moved higher relative to those of U.S. families, and inequality would have fallen more in Canada.

With respect to family incomes, the most striking result is that a substantial fraction of Canadian families was *absolutely* better off in 1995 than their U.S. counterparts at similar points in the income spectrum.

On the basis of the most widely used (purchasing power parity) measures . . . about 60 per cent of Canadians (ranked in terms of their disposable incomes, adjusted for family structure) have *higher* incomes than their similarly defined U.S. counterparts.[*]

---

[*] *Monthly Labour Review*, Washington, D.C., April 1998.

Two other respected economists, Canadian Andrew Sharpe and Larry Mishel of the Economic Policy Institute in Washington, D.C., presented another paper in October 1998. According to them, the well-being of Canadians in 1997 was almost 9-per-cent higher than that of Americans.

> A key finding of the paper is that while the United States enjoyed greater increases in economic well-being than Canada over the 1971-97 period and particularly in the 1990s, the level of economic well-being in 1997 [still] appears higher in Canada when importance is given inequality and economic security aspects of economic well-being.*

The economists' measurements included family income, taxes, wages and benefits, type of jobs, wealth and poverty, risk of illness, personal consumption, life expectancy, medical costs, cost of crime, and other social and economic indicators: "In 1994, inequality . . . for all persons was 23 per cent less in Canada than in the United States. The poverty rate in Canada was 41 per cent less . . . the level of the overall equality index was 37 per cent higher in Canada than in the U.S. in 1994."

Now, how does all of this match up to the constant bellyaching of our journalistic Americaphiles about the need to move to U.S. tax rates and a more *laissez-faire* Ayn Rand economy? Despite all the baloney to the contrary, the median Canadian family makes about $700 more a year, after taxes, then a comparable U.S. family. If family health-care costs are considered, the Canadian advantage is even greater.

What about the income extremes? If middle-class Canadians are better off than middle-class Americans, how do the rich and the poor in each country compare? As might be expected, the rich in the U.S. are better off, the poor in Canada are better off. While the distribution of income in Canada is pretty bad, in the U.S. it's awful. While poverty in Canada is terrible, in the U.S. its appalling.

Aside from the additional financial advantage that Canadians have in their health-care costs, Andrew Sharpe pinpoints another major

---

* *A Comparison of Trends in the Economic Well-Being of Canadians and Americans*, Centre for the Study of Living Standards, October 1998.

advantage: "Public education is another cost worth noting too. . . . Often in the U.S., people end up sending their kids to private schools because their public schools aren't good enough. Tuitions are higher in the U.S. too."* Let's turn now from standard of living to quality of life.

---

* *Globe and Mail*, December 21, 1998.

The Quality of Life and the Quality of Death

To what extent are poverty and crime related? Ask any experienced police officer. Poverty can and frequently does produce a sense of hopelessness and despair. The United States has the highest poverty rates, violent-crime rates, and murder rates among the developed nations. Poor people aren't born criminals; most poor people are good citizens, but locked-in poverty often produces hungry, desperate people and a social environment infested with crime and violence.

According to the U.S. magazine *Atlantic Monthly*, "Nearly a half million Americans have been murdered in the past two decades alone – and we are now accustomed, perhaps almost inured, to such grim statistics."*

Elliott Currie in *Crime and Punishment in America* says that "by the mid-1990s a young American male was 37 times as likely to die by deliberate violence as his English counterpart" and 26 times as likely as a young Frenchman and 60 times as likely as a young Japanese. Every year more than two thousand American teenagers use a gun to kill someone.†

Figure 49 speaks for itself:

---

* September 1997.
† Metropolitan Books/Henry Holt & Company, 1998.

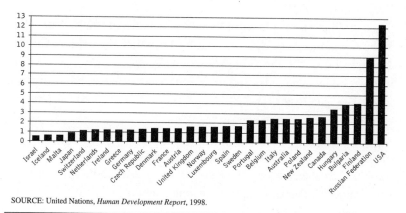

FIGURE 49

International Homicides by Men Per 100,000 People,
1985 to 1990

SOURCE: United Nations, *Human Development Report*, 1998.

The United States is in a class by itself when homicide rates among developed nations are considered.

The next table also speaks for itself.

Comparative Homicide Rates Per 100,000 population*

	U.S.	Canada		U.S.	Canada
1981	9.8	2.7	1989	8.7	2.4
1982	9.1	2.7	1990	9.4	2.4
1983	8.3	2.7	1991	9.8	2.7
1984	7.9	2.6	1992	9.3	2.6
1985	7.9	2.7	1993	9.5	2.2
1986	8.6	2.2	1994	9.0	2.0
1987	8.3	2.4	1995	8.2	2.0
1988	8.4	2.1	1996	7.4	2.1

In 1990, there were 2,245 murders in New York City, and 23,440 in the United States. The same year there was a total of 660 murders in Canada.

* Canadian Centre for Justice Statistics, Ottawa.

In 1996, the murder rate in Louisiana led the country at 17.5 murders per 100,000 population. The same year, the U.S. rate was 7.4 per 100,000. The next closest country was Finland at 3.2 per 100,000. Britain's rate was 0.5.*

In 1996, two people were killed by handguns in New Zealand. In Japan the number was 15, followed by 31 in the U.K., 106 in Canada, 211 in Germany. In the United States, in the same year, 9,390 people were killed by handguns. Around 35,000 deaths are caused by firearms in the U.S. each year. The FBI says that there are about half a million gun-related incidents each year.†

About 40 per cent of Americans have a gun in their home; about 25 per cent have handguns. Around one in ten Americans carries a gun away from home and "on any given day, one adult in 50 will be carrying a handgun. . . . Gunshots are the second commonest cause of death for Americans aged between 10 and 24."**

Here are some more international comparisons.

Firearm Deaths Rate per 100,000
1994-95††

Japan	0.07
Vietnam	0.18
U.K.	0.57
Spain	1.01
Germany	1.47
Sweden	2.31
Australia	3.05
U.S.	13.70

And here are some recent headlines:

Arkansas:	5 DIE AS GUN-TOTING BOYS AMBUSH SCHOOLMATES
Louisiana:	A BURST OF VIOLENCE LEAVES 3 DEAD IN A CHURCH

---

* *New York Times*, July 25, 1998.
† *The Economist*, April 4, 1998.
** *The Economist*, September 26, 1998.
†† *Globe and Mail*, Coalition to Stop Gun Violence, February 12, 1999.

Virginia: SECURITY MEASURES IN SCHOOLS ON RISE TO EASE
               FEARS OF VIOLENCE
New York: WHY DO KIDS KILL?
Mississippi: 16-YEAR-OLD IS ACCUSED OF KILLING MOTHER
               THEN SHOOTING NINE CLASSMATES
California: TWO U.S. YOUNGSTERS GUNNED DOWN
Colorado: DOZENS DEAD OR WOUNDED IN SCHOOL RAMPAGE

True we have our own Pierre Lebruns and Marc Lepines and the school shooting in Taber, Alberta, but compared to the U.S. they're few and far between. According to Sarah Brady, whose husband, James, was shot in the Ronald Reagan assassination attempt, "Every day in the U.S. fourteen children are killed in gun homicides, suicides, and unintentional shootings – that's an entire classroom of children every two days."* In Washington, D.C., in 1998 there were 260 homicides. In Ottawa–Carleton there were two.

According to the U.S. Center for Disease Control and Prevention in Atlanta, children in the U.S. are five times as likely to be murdered and twelve times as likely to die because of a firearm than those in other industrialized countries. "The United States has the highest rates of childhood homicides, suicides and firearm related deaths of 26 countries studied."† And from the *New York Times*, "Over the last decade, gun makers have found that what would sell best are higher caliber, more rapidfire pistols that can be easily concealed. . . . The gun industry has deliberately enhanced its profits by increasing the lethality – the killing power – of its products."**

As a direct result of an intensive National Rifle Association lobby, more than thirty U.S. states now allow people to carry handguns. Today, most U.S. gun producers have developed

> powerful new pistols that fit in the palm of the hand. . . . These ultracompacts are less than 18 centimeters long and can hold as many as 10 large-calibre cartridges. . . . "They have more killing power per ounce, per bullet, per buck than any other

---

* *The Economist*, April 24, 1999.
† *Edmonton Journal*, February 7, 1997.
** Tom Diaz, "Making a Killer," February 14, 1999.

gun," said David Kairys, a Temple University law professor. . . .
"Easy to conceal. Easy to fire. Easy to acquire," says a Beretta
ad for its new Cougar pistol. . . . "Lighter. Completely conceal-
able. Plenty of firepower."*

What great news!

In the United States the powerful gun lobby intimidated U.S. sena-
tors and representatives for decades. If ever a country desperately
needed tough gun control, it's the U.S. Yet any attempt to significantly
tighten the current hopelessly weak legislation collapses in the face of
the National Rifle Association and their well-financed lobby.

In Canada, there's an entirely different story. Dalton Camp writes
about Canada and

> the failure of the gun lobby in its campaign to hunt down des-
> ignated MPs who had supported C-158, most of them Ontario
> Liberals. In Ontario, all but two Liberal candidates were
> elected. This should serve as an example of the need for public
> men and women to stand up and speak up for what they believe
> . . . rather than weasel, waffle, and grovel for the support of a
> dubious special interest.†

But, in the United States,

> After the tragic shooting in the Oregon high school last week, I
> saw a Georgia state legislator on television proposing that
> teachers carry guns in school, thus – the man said – sending the
> message to "criminals" that if they brought their weapons to
> school, they could be outgunned by the faculty.**

The violence, high crime rate, and widespread use of illegal drugs
in the United States have had a major impact. In 1970, the U.S. prison
population was about 250,000. Ten years later it had doubled. By 1992,

---

* Louise Palmer, *The Boston Globe*, in *The Globe and Mail*, March 10, 1999.
† *Toronto Star*, June 12, 1997.
** *Toronto Star*, May 24, 1998.

it was about 1.25 million. Six years later the number had jumped to 1.8 million, having doubled again since 1985.

By 1998, the U.S. prison population was about fifty-five times Canada's prison population. In addition, about 575,000 people were held in local American jails awaiting trial or serving sentences of less than a year. The U.S. incarceration rate is six to ten times higher than in most developed nations; only Russia now has a higher percentage of its citizens behind bars, and the U.S. is expected to pass Russia next year. Moreover, "contrary to popular belief, the greatest source of growth in state prisons is in violent offenders, not drug violators," according to Allen Beck of the U.S. Sentencing Project.[*] Today, most U.S. prisons are operating at far over capacity.

The U.S. Bureau of Justice statistics looked at some comparative incarceration rates as shown in Figure 50.

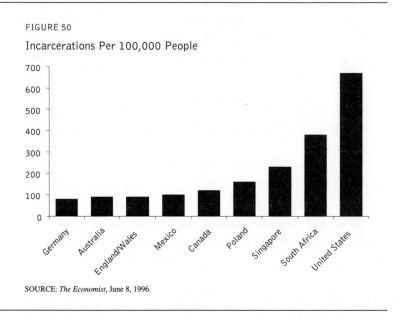

FIGURE 50

Incarcerations Per 100,000 People

SOURCE: *The Economist*, June 8, 1996.

On average, every week a new jail or prison is built in the United States.

---

[*] *Edmonton Journal*, August 3, 1998.

In *With Liberty for Some: 500 Years of Imprisonment in America*,* Scott Christianson writes that one in every 163 Americans is in jail or prison, a rate six times the average in Europe.

> In his final chapter, Mr. Christianson describes the burgeoning prison-industrial complex, based on prison labour, which has brought wealth to many smaller towns and cities where prisons are based. America seems to have come full circle – imprisonment is once again as much about profit as punishment. As this book makes clear, popular support for mass incarceration and ever longer prison sentences is not merely a by-product of the past two decades' war on crime, but a consistent and ugly side of American society which has remained unquestioned for far too long.†

In February 1999, the *New York Times* reported that in Pennsylvania a first-year teacher makes about $18,500 a year while a prison-guard trainee is paid $22,300. Every year for the past fourteen years the state has added at least one new prison, while the corrections budget has jumped to over $1 billion a year and rising: "Every 20 seconds someone in America is arrested for a drug violation. Every week, on average, a new jail or prison is built to lock up more people in the world's largest penal system."

As a record number of people are locked up, money is shifted from schools to prisons. In California alone, the prison system costs about $4 billion a year (compared to just over $2 billion for all of Canada). Since 1984, the state has added twenty-one prisons and only one university campus. At universities, salaries have stagnated; meanwhile, pay for prison guards has doubled. According to the *New York Times*,

> A prison guard now makes about $51,000 a year, while a first-year professor in California's once-vaunted university system is paid $41,000. Over the past 10 years, as the state's population grew by five million people, state university enrollment fell

---

* Northeastern University, 1998/99.
† *The Economist*, February 13, 1999.

20,000. "Most of our buildings are literally falling apart and we've lost 1,500 full time faculty members" said Jeri Bledsoe, general manager of the California Faculty Association. "You bet there's been a price to pay for the prison boom."*

Meanwhile, the American Library Association called California's school libraries "the worst of the worst" full of outdated books depicting savage Indians and happy slaves, sexist material and books suggesting that man will some day land on the moon and John F. Kennedy is alive and well living in the White House.†

Today, there are some 3,500 inmates on death row in the United States. "Since 1976, 75 American men and women have been convicted of murder, sentenced to death and later found innocent – roughly one in every seven prisoners who have been executed. . . . Most of the 75 were accused of heinous crimes for which prosecutors, who are elected officials, were under pressure to find someone to blame. . . . Minorities fare particularly poorly in capital cases. . . . Public defenders are underpaid and overloaded with cases; at worst they are incompetent."**

In the fall of 1998, Amnesty International reported that U.S. prisons were overcrowded, inhumane places where beatings, rape, and torture by guards are frequent. Government officials in the U.S. are well aware of these human-rights violations, but have failed to do much about them. According to Amnesty International, the "U.S. police forces and criminal and legal systems have a persistent and widespread pattern of human rights violations. . . . Across the country, thousands of people are subjected to sustained and deliberate brutality at the hands of police officials. Cruel, degrading and sometimes life-threatening methods of constraint continue to be a feature of the U.S. criminal justice system. . . . The death penalty . . . is often enacted in vengeance, applied in an arbitrary manner, subject to bias because of the defendant's race or economic status."††

Today, increasingly, U.S. prisons are being run for profit – if you can imagine. Among those investing in prisons are General Electric and

---

* *New York Times*, February 28, 1999.
† *National Post*, June 2, 1999.
** *The Economist*, November 28, 1998.
†† *Edmonton Journal*, October 5, 1998.

American Express. Some of the predictable results are even more over-crowding, much poorer food, far less security, and inadequate rehabilitation programs. Then, of course, some of the predictable results when prisoners are released are greater hostility to society and more crime.

Sometimes They Come Back Dead

The severely burned child was brought to the L.A. County Hospital by his mother and grandfather. The little two-and-a-half-year-old boy came from a poor family; he had second- and third-degree burns to his leg and needed skin grafts. The mother explained that the boy had climbed up onto the kitchen counter and climbed into the sink and turned the hot water on.

But the doctors and nurses were skeptical. If the child was strong enough to climb up to the sink he would be strong enough to pull himself away from the hot water. It looked like an obvious case of child abuse, especially since the burned areas looked as if someone had held the boy's leg under the hot water.

The Child Protective Services were called and looked into the case briefly. But, as happens often, they were over budget and didn't have the money for a proper investigation. The little boy was treated and released back into the mother's custody.

One of the doctors told me that this sort of thing happens often. "The kids are sent right back to an environment where they get injured again. Sometimes they come back to the hospital dead."

How would you like to be poor and sick in the United States?

The right wing in Canada continues its perennial, persistent lobby for private health care in Canada. The very well-to-do like the idea. But even they generally rush home from Florida or Hawaii when they need medical treatment. Fortunately, the majority of Canadians understand why they would suffer if more private health care were allowed to erode Canada's public system further. For most Canadians, the results would be higher costs, poorer quality care, longer waiting periods, less competent medical staff, and a two-tier system where the rich have priority and better quality treatment, and the rest have longer lineups. And the poor? According to Henry Sporn, editor-in-chief of the U.S. *Healthcare Business News*: "In California, mothers on Medicaid giving birth were denied epidurals as they writhed on the birthing table because Medicaid reimbursement wasn't sufficient. Similar denials of treatment, drugs or therapies occur constantly, and people die, deteriorate or stay in pain because they can't afford treatment."* Sporn points out that Medicaid is the program "which provides coverage for Americans who earn less than the incredibly low U.S. poverty line of $16,050 for a family of four."

Dalton Camp has reported on a Harvard Medical School–Cambridge Hospital study "not likely to be found in the reception room at the Fraser Institute, or on a coffee table at Stornaway."

> Titled "For Our Patients, Not for Profits: A Call to Action," the American study is a stinging indictment of health care for profit, summed up in the preface with the indictment: "Declining Coverage, Rising Costs, Increasing Inequality."
>
> The report lists some typical advice from U.S. health consulting firms: "Don't have cataracts removed in more than one eye unless the patient is young and needs both eyes to work; don't stay overnight for a mastectomy; allow one day's stay for vaginal delivery, two days for a Caesarian; don't allow more than three days for a stroke, even if the patient is unable to walk."†

---

* *Montreal Gazette*, late July, 1998.
† *Toronto Star*, January 20, 1999.

According to the *New York Times*, "State health insurance regulators are reporting surging numbers of formal complaints from patients and doctors against health insurers, primarily health maintenance organizations. . . . What troubles the commissioners more than the volume of complaints is . . . that 'Now it's about whether you get the service at all.' "*

In Jeffrey Simpson's words, "Four years into the world of HMOs, the hatred of them is palpable everywhere in the medical profession and beyond." Clerks routinely say no to medical tests that doctors require. Competing companies require a multitude of forms to be completed, adding mountains of paperwork. Moreover, "HMOs are not keen on covering patients with pre-existing medical conditions. . . . HMOs demand much higher premiums claiming they cannot make adequate profits and businesses small and large are screaming. . . . leaving employees to fend for themselves." And the poor? "The working poor don't qualify for state aid. . . ."†

According to the CCSD:

Public health insurance enables Canadian children at all income levels to make the same average number of visits to doctors. By comparison, one-third of American children did not have health insurance at some point in 1995 and 1996, and *they were eight times less likely than insured children to visit a doctor.***

The emphasis is mine. Pathetic is the word.

In September 1998, the U.S. Census Bureau reported that about 43.4 million Americans, or 16.1 per cent of the population, had no health-care coverage and that the number was growing by an astonishing 125,000 people a month. "In Ohio, 500,000 seniors recently saw their state health-care coverage cut off. . . . Jonathan Ross, an internist from Toledo, Ohio, and a spokesman for Physicians for a National Health Program . . . said it's a myth that care is better in the United States than in Canada for those who can afford it. . . . Doctors are being

---

* October 11, 1998.
† *Globe and Mail*, January 22, 1999.
** *The Progress of Canada's Children*, 1997.

subverted . . . to be the executioners rather than the helpers of their patients."* Another member of the program, president Dr. Robert LeBow, told of

> a 28 year old woman who was pregnant but didn't have the money to pay for pre-natal examinations. When she felt her baby stop moving, she went to the hospital and found she was two weeks past term and that the baby had died. The woman had to have a Caesarian section to remove the dead fetus, and she didn't survive the operation. "She died and her baby died because she felt she couldn't afford the care."†

About 11 million American children have no health-care coverage and another 33 million men and women have no coverage. Add every man, woman, and child in Canada together, then add another 50 per cent, and you will have about the number of Americans who have no health coverage in the richest country on earth.

Health-care costs in the U.S. are consuming an increasing percentage of the GDP, now about 14 per cent and rising, while in Canada they're at about 9 per cent. Canadian costs per capita are about half those in the U.S., about $2,095 to about $4,090 (U.S.) in 1997.

In terms of total per capita health spending among developed nations, in 1997 Canada was sixth, behind the U.S. (by far the most costly), Switzerland, Luxembourg, Germany, and France. But in terms of *public* spending on health to GDP, Canada was below the average of the OECD, and well behind Britain, Sweden, France, Germany, and Japan, and also below the Netherlands, Italy, and Australia. Far back in the pack, at the bottom of the twenty-nine-country OECD list, was the United States, at about half the public spending rate for Britain. At the same time, *total* U.S. health spending as a percentage of GDP is some 100 per cent higher in the United States than it is in Britain.

While we all know U.S. income-tax rates are lower than Canada's, social-insurance taxes and health-insurance costs are considerably higher. According to the OECD, in 1996 employee social-security

---

* *Globe and Mail*, November 17, 1998.
† *National Post*, November 18, 1998.

contributions in the U.S. were twice as high as those in Canada as a percentage of total taxation – 10.6 per cent to 5.3 per cent. The highest average cost over the years for small U.S. companies, ahead of taxes, wages, and other costs, are health-insurance costs.

Tens of millions of Americans live in fear of illness. Some are totally uninsured. Millions more have inadequate insurance. The cost of one major operation will frequently bankrupt an entire family. Insurance companies often refuse to pay all costs for operations, even if the patient, as is frequently the case, thought he or she had full coverage. Many poor families are obliged to pay four-figure upfront costs, even for childbirth. Some insurance companies refuse to cover a variety of illnesses, for example, AIDS. A neuroblastomic child seeking a last-chance bone-marrow transplant must have parents who will put up $50,000 prior to hospital admission. For one American nurse, the impact of illness on poor families was all too often devastating: "It wasn't unusual to see a mother reduced to tears in response to the hospital bill collector calling into the sick child's room and forcefully demand immediate payment." According to the *New York Times Magazine,* "Most Americans doubt that they will be able to afford health care in the next 10 years."*

Earlier I wrote about a Canadian doctor who left Canada for the U.S., only to return in disgust after the HMOs had gained control. Many if not most Americans now feel that managed care has been a failure. Previously, most of those insured could select their own doctors. Now the big insurance companies are in control of the selection of physicians, procedures, referrals, and other aspects of health care, much to the dissatisfaction of millions of doctors and patients.

Moreover, in the U.S., being poor and not being white is bad for your health. In a recent article on the state of health care in the U.S., *The Economist* writes:

> On average black children are more than twice as likely to die in infancy. . . . 40% more black men die from coronary heart disease.
>
> Poverty – which brings with it a poorer diet and less access to medical care – is largely to blame for poor health. And, there

---

* November 1, 1998.

are three times as many blacks and Latinos living in poverty as whites. Although some receive state-financed health insurance or Medicaid, many have no coverage at all, even if they are employed . . . Without insurance, patients tend to put off seeing a doctor until the last moment and end up in hospital with far more serious conditions.*

In 1997, life expectancy at birth in the United States was 76.1 years. In Canada it was 78.7 years. In 1996, infant mortality in Canada as a percentage of live births was 0.6 per cent; in the U.S. it was 0.8 per cent.† Low-income Canadians also have a much higher cancer-survival rate than low-income Americans.

Certainly Canada has had its own health-care problems. But, despite these problems, the vast majority of Canadians are unquestionably better served by Canada's public health system. Even if you're politically on the right, well-to-do, and wish to dispute this, there can be no denying that the poor in Canada are infinitely better off than the poor in the U.S. when it comes to health care. Anyone who argues differently must either live in a cave, or work for the Fraser Institute.

Many respected American health-care experts have warned Canadians about moving to more private health care. Dr. Claudia Fegan of Chicago asks Canadians, "How can you be so foolish as to not learn from our mistakes?"** U.S. groups advocating Canadian-style health care say, "The Canadian system is so far away and yet here it is right across the border. . . . Canadians should be proud of what they have, understand why it's good and work to defend it."††

Readers who want to take a good look at what's wrong with the U.S. system should go to their public or university library and read back issues of the *New England Journal of Medicine*.

Briefly, to education. Just as the United States has some of the finest hospitals and best doctors in the world, it also has some of the finest universities and the best educators. But as in the case of health care, where most poor Americans suffer greatly, the U.S. education system leaves

---

* February 27, 1999.
† *OECD in Figures*, 1998.
** *Edmonton Journal*, February 19, 1999.
†† *Globe and Mail*, November 17, 1998

much to be desired when it comes to low-income children, poor youths, and underprivileged young men and women.

The public education system in the United States ranks low in international esteem. A January 1998 study by a non-profit Washington-based organization, Education Week, reported dismal results:

A public education study considered one of the most thorough ever conducted in the United States, confirms parents' worse fears: Not only are schools falling apart, so are students.

In major cities, more than half the public school kids in grade 4 and 8 standard tests can't read or do math and science at the most basic level. . . .

In urban schools where a majority of students live below the poverty line, two-thirds or more fail to reach even the "basic" level on national tests.

America's 11 million urban students – about one in four public school kids – have fewer funds, poorer resources, more class room violence and chaos, fewer qualified teachers and less parental involvement than students in suburban and rural schools, the survey concludes.[*]

A Canadian who left for the U.S. and returned wrote the *Globe and Mail*:

I too departed Canada at 24, and climbed the ladder of success in urban America as an advertising executive – three kids, a happy marriage, a rosy future in a glamorous profession. What more could one ask for? Well, a neighbourhood school would have been nice. Or, barring that, a school without metal detectors or regular weapons searches. Or a commute through part of town that was less terrifying.[†]

Of course if you are wealthy or have a high salary, you send your kids to expensive private schools. Readers should not be misled by some

[*] *Toronto Star*, January 9, 1998
[†] Letter from Chris Copp, Waterloo, Ontario, December 13, 1996.

comparative education-spending statistics of Canada and the U.S. At all levels, the U.S. spends more. But many more expensive private schools and very expensive universities skew some international comparative statistics.

We've already looked at how poor Canadian kids get shortchanged in the Canadian educational system. Don't for a moment imagine that poor American children are better off. As a percentage of the total population, there are more of them and that's an important factor in how they are treated and mistreated.

John Kenneth Galbraith writes,

> There must also be firm recognition of yet another major flaw of the market system. That is its allocation of income as between public and private services and functions. In the United States, private television is richly financed; urban public schools are badly starved. Private dwellings are clean, tolerable, and pleasant; public housing and public streets are filthy. Libraries, public recreational facilities, basic social services – all needed more by the poor than the rich – are seen as a burden.[*]

Much has been written about how low the U.S. unemployment rate is. But the U.S. has always had a relatively low unemployment rate, never reaching 10 per cent during the past half-century and averaging only 5.7 per cent since the Second World War. Yet, as we have seen, poverty rates in the U.S. are the worst in the developed world, and *far* worse than those in most developed nations. You don't have to be a rocket scientist to figure out that very low wages are a continuing built-in factor in the American economy. And for those who are unemployed, U.S. benefits are far lower than those in Canada, as is the ratio of successful unemployment claims to the number unemployed.

While U.S. unemployment rates look excellent, the October 1998 issue of *Atlantic Monthly* had quite a different perspective on low U.S. unemployment, calling the official rate a "dubious measure" and a "gravely misleading statistic" that failed to recognize millions of the unemployed and the prison population.

---

[*] *The Socially Concerned Today*, University of Toronto Press, 1998.

One last point about the American attitude towards the poor. Figure 51 is a chart published early in 1999 based on 1997 OECD statistics. The wealthiest country in the world is at the bottom of the barrel in aid to developing countries.

FIGURE 51

Net Official Aid: Disbursements as a Percentage of GDP

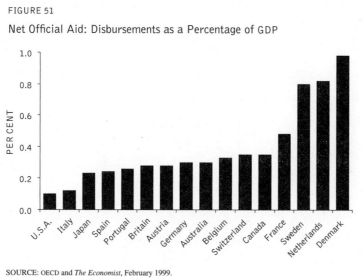

SOURCE: OECD and *The Economist*, February 1999.

Just as the United States has the highest poverty rates among developed nations, it also has the worst record in assistance to developing nations.

Summing up, those who want us to be more like the Americans are asking for even more and deeper poverty, and a society in which there are even greater disparities in income and a poorer quality of life for most citizens. A Southam–Global poll late in 1997 showed that "88 per cent of Canadians doubt they or a family member would ever move to the U.S. . . . Three quarters of Canadians surveyed thought they enjoy a better quality of life than Americans, a number that rises to 84 per cent among young people."[*] I don't know about you, but I'm with the 88 per cent.

---

[*] Southam Newspapers, late December, 1997.

PART EIGHT

Under Poor Management

The Country Is Humming,
Money Is on the Move, We're on a Roll

We've seen that poverty in Canada is much worse than it is in many other developed countries, and that despite abundant rhetoric from our politicians, poverty has increased and the income gap has been widening. We've also looked at the main causes of poverty, and reasons poverty has been so ignored in Canada. What we need to do now is look at policy changes that are necessary to bring the poor out of poverty and allow them the opportunity to attain a decent standard of living. First let's take a brief look at how Canada and Canadians have been doing as a whole so that we can put suggested solutions in the context of what has been happening in this country in recent years.

In the summer of 1997, economist Sherry Cooper described Canada's economy as "red hot."* At the time there were 1.4 million Canadians unemployed.

At the end of 1997, Prime Minister Chrétien told Canadians, "We are more relaxed at this moment because it's less tough. . . . Economically the country is going quite well. . . . People feel good."†

---

* *Toronto Star*, August 5, 1997.
† *Edmonton Journal*, December 27, 1997.

About the same time, three of the *Globe*'s best journalists told readers:

> Need proof that the national economy is sizzling this Christmas? Go no farther than Bloor Street West, Toronto's chi-chi shopping district, where the good times are rolling and conspicuous consumption is most definitely back in vogue.
>
> In Secrett, the custom jeweller catering to high-end indulgences, the rich are on a spending spree. The store's $10,000 sapphire-and-diamond bracelets, sets of $15,000 diamond earrings and $8,000 onyx panther sculptures – and things worth much, much more – are leaving the glass display cases faster than they have since, well, the greedy eighties. . . .
>
> When the gemstones start moving this quickly on Bloor Street, it's a sign that the country's larger economy turbine is humming. . . . It boils down to one fact: Money is on the move at a terrific clip mainly because consumer and business spending has been on a tear for the past year.*

The following spring, John McCallum, the Royal Bank's chief economist, joined the chorus: "If anyone doubts that the Canadian economy is on a roll, I guess this evidence [the unemployment rate dropped to 8.4 per cent] is likely to end that."†

April Lindgren of the *Ottawa Citizen* wrote from quite a different perspective:

> There's just one problem with the good economic news trumpeted by Bay Street bankers, forecasters and the Liberal government in Ottawa.
>
> Many Canadians don't buy it.
>
> Respondents to a year-end . . . poll on Canadian attitudes to a wide range of issues painted a much darker picture of their personal economic reality than the one that emerges from national economic statistics.

---

* Brian Laghi, Miro Cernetig, and Bruce Little, December 20, 1997.
† *Globe and Mail*, May 9, 1998.

>Respondents . . . said they were working harder than five years ago but were not being rewarded with either increased pay or job security. . . . Many Canadians . . . believed their children will have a lower standard of living than they do.*

Now let's hear from the Department of Finance in Ottawa in October 1998:

>The central objective of economic policy is to enhance the well-being of people through higher living standards.
>The best measure of the living standards is real gross domestic product (GDP) per capita.

Among the government's "accomplishments" and "policies to promote higher living standards" that Finance listed were NAFTA, privatization of de Havilland and Canadian National, being a leading player in the World Trade Organization, and other great success stories.†

For a moment let's take Finance's word for it and use real GDP to see just how the country has been "humming." Figure 52 is clear. Some "humming." Some "on a roll."

The Department of Finance's suggestion that the best measure of living standards is real GDP per capita is plain nonsense. Suppose, for example, the GDP increases by $10 billion and ten billionaires each get $1 billion of the increase and transfer most of it to tax havens, while the other thirty million Canadians get zip. How is that supposed to be a good overall measure of our standard of living? Granted, I've used an extreme example, but measuring standard of living by taking the country's GDP and dividing it by the population is about as valid a way of looking at national well-being as saying that bank CEOs' retirement packages are indicative of the generosity of average seniors' pensions in Canada.

Taking an increasing national GDP and dividing it by the population will not translate into lower poverty rates or improved average incomes

---

* *Edmonton Journal*, December 20, 1997.
† *Strengthening Productivity and Improving the Living Standards of Canadians.*

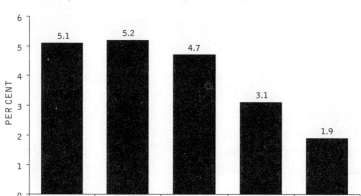

FIGURE 52

GDP Growth, Annual Per Cent Change

SOURCE: Statistics Canada, *National Income and Expenditure Accounts*, Cat. #13-001-PPB; and Statistics Canada, Canadian Economic Observer, *Historical Statistical Supplement*, Cat. #11-210-XPB (1999 forecast).

Under the governments of Brian Mulroney and Jean Chrétien, Canada's economic performance as measured by growth in GDP has been dismal compared to previous decades.

if income distribution is unfair. If most of the dividends of economic growth accumulate only in the hands of the already well-to-do, even higher poverty rates are possible. As GDP rises, profits may increase, and CEOs will inevitably receive larger salaries, big bonuses, and even bigger option packages, but the market economy provides no guarantee that average Canadians will be better off. The reality is that rising GDP has effectively been delinked from poverty and greater wealth hasn't trickled down to the poor.

Let's see how Canada's GDP growth has been, compared to other nations in the decade before the Free Trade Agreement, and in the first decade of free trade. Following are the GDP growth totals for the two decades.*

---

* OECD, *Economic Outlook*, 1998 and 1993 editions; Statistics Canada, *National Income and Expenditure Accounts*, fourth quarter, 1998.

	Canada	G-7	Total OECD	E.U.
1979-1988	+31.7	+28.1	+27.3	+22.7
1989-1998	+19.4	+22.3	+24.3	+21.4

You can see that in the decade before the FTA, Canada outper-formed the G-7, OECD, and the E.U. by a good margin. However, in the first decade of the FTA, Canada fell behind all the same countries. Quite a change! Tell us again, Brian Mulroney and Tom d'Aquino, just how great free trade has been for Canada.

In October 1998, economists Lars Osberg of Dalhousie and Andrew Sharpe produced an important paper, *An Index of Economic Well-Being for Canada*. From the paper, here's a look at GDP per capita in Canada, measured in 1992 dollars.

1979	$21,765	1989	25,755
1980	21,794	1990	25,438
1981	22,172	1991	24,648
1982	21,262	1992	24,526
1983	21,626	1993	24,815
1984	22,634	1994	25,470
1985	23,634	1995	25,709
1986	24,018	1996	25,728
1987	24,691	1997	26,394
1988	25,550		

At first glance, it would appear that the overall economic welfare of the average Canadian has been rising (although just barely in the 1990s). This is deceiving. Sharpe and Osberg go on to chart GDP per capita and then economic well-being (a multi-faceted measure includ-ing consumption flows, wealth, economic security, and income inequal-ity) to present quite a different picture (see Figure 53). In the conclusion to their paper, the economists write, "A key finding is the economic well-being of Canadians . . . has increased at a much slower rate over the last 25 years than real GDP per capita, a widely-used indicator of eco-nomic well-being." In fact, "the index shows a large 10 per cent absolute deterioration of economic well-being in Canada in the 1990s."

FIGURE 53

Trends in Economic Well-Being and GDP Per Capita Indexes

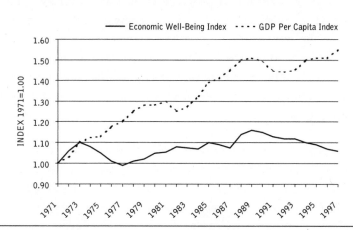

Over the past century, the well-being of average Canadians has failed to match per capita GDP increases.

Which helps explain, along with the factors mentioned in Part Four of this book, the increasing poverty in Canada.

In the U.S., a San Francisco group, Redefining Progress, has developed a "genuine progress indicator" (GPI), that includes measurements relating to health, the environment, welfare of children and seniors, quality of life, crime, and other factors as a better measurement of how a country is doing. While the GDP in the U.S. has been increasing, the GPI has fallen for over twenty years.

And, what about the future? The OECD's 1998 report on Canada* presents a gloomy forecast. If the OECD's projections are accurate, and if we're doing very little for the poor now (when we're supposed to be in such great shape), what, then, will be the prospects for the poor in the future? And for the many millions of other Canadians with high personal and household debt, declining savings and decreased disposable income?

For many years after the Second World War, Canada's standard of living, as measured by taking GDP and dividing it by population, was

---

* OECD Economic Surveys, 1997-1998, *Canada*.

consistently number two in the world, ahead of all other nations but the United States. Today we're twenty-first or twenty-second. According to the OECD, unless Canada makes significant changes in economic policy, within less than a generation our national income will be as much 15 per cent below the average of the 29 OECD countries.

A better measure of GDP in defining standard of living is real GDP purchasing-power parity (PPP), which measures what money can really buy. In 1995, in real PPP, Canada stood sixth among the OECD nations, behind Norway, the U.S., Japan, Switzerland, and Luxembourg. By 1997 we were down to eighth place.

Does that make us a poor country? Hardly. Even though our ranking has fallen in recent years, we are still one of the wealthiest countries in the world, ahead of twenty other OECD countries and well ahead of scores of other countries around the world.* But declining GDP, no matter how interpreted, is a clear sign that our "red hot" country has been under poor management for many years. The 1990s has been the worst decade for economic growth in Canada since the 1930s – the decade of the Great Depression.

---

* OECD, *National Accounts*, 1998.

Debt, Savings, and Disposable Income

Economists Anthony Myatt and David Murrell of the Department of Economics at the University of New Brunswick put economic well-being in this perspective:

> One way of feeling the pulse of an economy is to look at the financial state of health of households. Analysts who have done this recently have reported three potentially worrying symptoms: increasing household debt, increasing personal bankruptcies, and a declining household savings rate. Real household liabilities (consumer credit, bank loans and other loans) as a proportion of personal disposable income have risen substantially in the last 10 years. . . . At the same time the cost of servicing this debt has ballooned. Some analysts argue that these costs are unmanageable and point to the number of overdue mortgage payments, credit card delinquencies and consumer bankruptcies.
>
> Along with an increase in debt and bankruptcy is a decline in the personal savings rate (total personal savings as a percentage of personal disposable income). From the 1981-82 recession, when savings hit a historic high of almost 18 per cent

of disposable income, by 1997 they had fallen to less than 2 per cent. The bottom line is that some analysts are afraid households are becoming more and more vulnerable to adverse shocks, whether in the form of future increases in interest rates, or downturns in employment.*

By the end of 1996, household debt in Canada, which had been about 50 per cent of disposable income in 1985, had risen to a record-breaking 94 per cent. By 1998, Canadians were in debt to the extent of about 115 per cent of after-tax income, an increase from 76 per cent in 1985.

The Vanier Institute on the Family produced an analysis of personal debt (Figure 54) early in 1999. A similarly ominous trend is reflected in the numbers pertaining to household debt (Figure 55):

In early 1999, Eric Beauchesne of Southam Newspapers in Ottawa was reporting:

FIGURE 54

Personal Debt as a Percentage of Disposable Income

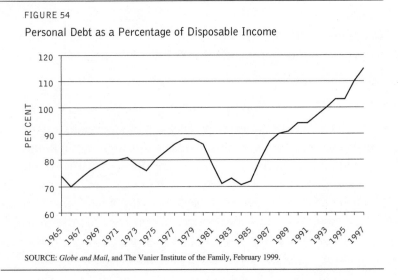

SOURCE: *Globe and Mail*, and The Vanier Institute of the Family, February 1999.

You're not likely to hear Jean Chrétien or Paul Martin saying much about this chart: the indebtedness of Canadians is rising drastically. Too many individuals can no longer make ends meet.

---

* *Canadian Business Economics*, November 1998.

FIGURE 55

Household Debt as a Percentage of Personal Disposable Income

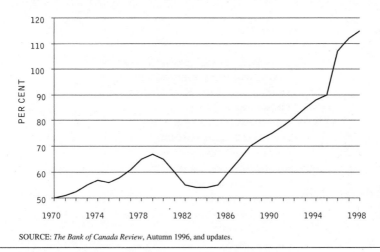

SOURCE: *The Bank of Canada Review*, Autumn 1996, and updates.

As with individuals, Canadian families have fallen increasingly behind under the Mulroney and Chrétien governments. A recession or rising interest rates could produce disastrous results for millions of Canadians.

FIGURE 56

Household Savings Ratio as a Percentage of Disposable Income

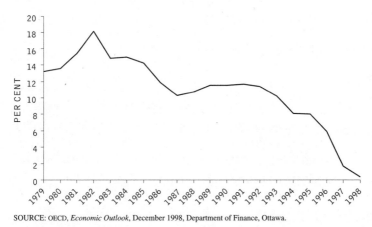

SOURCE: OECD, *Economic Outlook*, December 1998, Department of Finance, Ottawa.

As personal and household debt soared through the roof, savings plunged into the basement.

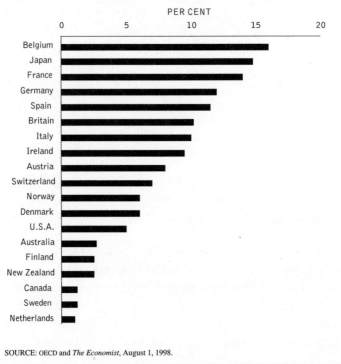

FIGURE 57

Savings Ratios, International Comparisons
Household Savings as a Percentage of Disposable Household Income

SOURCE: OECD and *The Economist*, August 1, 1998.

Not so long ago, Canadians were among the top savers in the world.
Today we're near the bottom of the list among developed nations.

> Families are spending more than they earn, sinking deeper into debt, and going bankrupt in increasing numbers. . . . Personal debt and bankruptcies have soared this decade, while the savings rate has plunged. . . . Personal bankruptcies climbed to nearly four per 1,000 adults by 1997, from less than one per 1,000 in 1976.[*]

Between 1960 and 1994, Canada's household savings as a percentage of disposable income averaged 9.4 per cent per year. But by 1996, they were

---

[*] *Edmonton Journal*, January 13, 1999.

FIGURE 58

Annual Percentage Changes in Personal Disposable Income

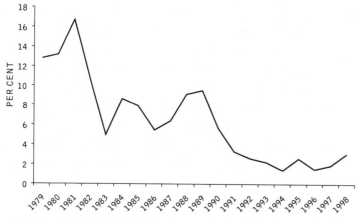

SOURCE: Statistics Canada, *National Income and Expenditure Accounts*, Cat. #13-001-PPB.

Personal disposable income is a key indicator of the welfare of Canadians. This figure shows the drastic decline in what Canadians have to spend over the past decade.

down to a fifty-year low and in 1997 and 1998 plunged to almost zero.

Let's look at our household savings ratios (Figure 56): How does Canada compare to other countries, in savings as a percentage of GDP? Figure 57 shows that of the twenty-nine OECD member nations, Canada is now in twentieth place.

It is true that as the household savings rate has plunged off a cliff, real household net worth for many has increased. But the precipitous decline in savings leaves Canadian households in the most precarious position since the Great Depression. Low savings rates leave Canadians highly vulnerable to market corrections, rising interest and mortgage rates, tighter bank credit, and a host of other potential economic problems. Increased RRSPs represent an important factor in increasing net worth, but most Canadians can't afford to buy RRSPs. Between 1991 and 1997 fewer than one-third of eligible Canadians purchased RRSPs (82 per cent of those with incomes over $100,000, 5 per cent with incomes under $10,000). In 1997 only 11 per cent of Canadians made the maximum eligible contributions.

Another useful way of measuring how Canadians are doing is to look at their disposable income, the money they have to spend after taxes and after payroll deductions. In April 1998, Statistics Canada reported that disposable income per person in 1997 had dropped again, the sixth decline in seven years, for a total decrease of 6.7 per cent since 1990. Figure 58 is a dramatic indication of the declining well-being of Canadians. In the ten years before the FTA, real disposable income increased at an annual average rate of 9.6 per cent. In the first ten years of the FTA, it increased at an annual average rate of only 3.5 per cent.

Another indicator of the health of the economy is the number of personal bankruptcies. In the ten years before the FTA, they averaged 23,300 per year. During the last ten years they averaged over 61,000 per year.

Treading Water or Sinking

For decades after the Second World War, Canadians, with good cause, believed that things were getting better and that they had every reason to believe that this trend would continue. Because we had relatively abundant natural resources, because we had mobilized well, and because we were so much better off than we had been before the war, optimism reigned. As shown earlier, we were clearly outperforming most of the world. But, as we have seen, recently the Canadian standard of living has fallen. The employment figures you read earlier in Part Four of this book are a major factor.

Before we go on to look at policy considerations, let's do one last standard-of-living overview, beginning with a look at what has happened to personal income in Canada during the past twenty years.

In the decade before the FTA, increases in total personal income averaged 10 per cent a year. During the past decade, they averaged only 3.9 per cent a year.* After tax and after inflation, average income in the 1990s dropped by about 7 per cent, the largest decline since the Great Depression. While it is true that increased taxes were a factor in declining real income, most of the decrease came not from taxes but from falling

---

* Statistics Canada, *National Income and Expenditure Accounts*, Cat. #13-001 PPB.

273

market income. By 1995, individual average income was below the level of 1980. So fifteen years of work resulted in a declining income.*

What impact did these events have on poor families? During the first half of the 1990s, the total number of families in Canada increased by about 6 per cent; the number of low-income families increased by more than 30 per cent! Figure 59 is a look at their combined income shortfalls below the LICOs line.

FIGURE 59

Aggregate Income Deficiency

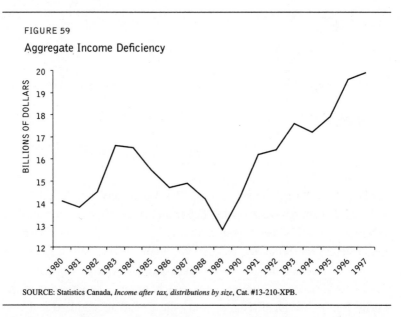

SOURCE: Statistics Canada, *Income after tax, distributions by size*, Cat. #13-210-XPB.

This figure shows the total amount necessary (in constant 1995 dollars) to bring all low-income Canadians up to the LICOs line.

The average income of all families and unattached individuals, after tax and after transfers, was $39,367 in 1980. By 1996, this had fallen to $36,946. Once again, many years of work produced a drop in income.† Note that the decline was $2,421, a great deal of money to the average Canadian.

In June 1998, Statistics Canada reviewed the results: "The outcome of these developments in earnings was a trend towards greater inequality

---

* Statistics Canada, *The Daily*, May 12, 1998.
† Statistics Canada, *Income after tax, distribution by size, 1996*, Cat. #13-210.

before transfers and taxes between 1980 and 1996. . . . Future trends in income inequality depend on developments in distributions of pre-transfer income, especially earnings."* According to Armine Yalnizyan, author of *The Growing Gap*,

> Between 1981 and 1996, 60% of Canadian families with dependent children experienced a real (inflation-adjusted) decline in their average earnings from the market. The real earnings of the bottom 20% of families were cut in half over the period. In 1980 the poorest 20% of the population made the equivalent of about $12,000 a year from work on the average (expressed in 1996 dollars). By 1996 the average income from earnings (and returns on investments) for this group had fallen to just under $6,000.†

While average incomes declined, in 1996 some 2.8 million Canadian households were forced to spend 30 per cent or more of their income on housing, up from 23 per cent five years earlier.

Statistics Canada now measures income comparisons in constant 1996 dollars. By 1996, average family income before transfers and taxes dropped from $53,080 in 1989 to $49,988 in 1996. Taxes were a factor in the final net decline for family income, but they accounted for a decrease of only $229 compared to the drop of $3,092 in market income.** According to Statistics Canada, "When the losses and gains of economic swings during the 1980s and 1990s are taken into consideration, real average income after tax for families in 1996 was nearly 5% lower than in 1980." So again we can see that over almost twenty years, Canadian families not only failed to gain ground in their standard of living, they lost it.

Now, one gets the clear impression from the financial press that increased taxes are responsible for this decline. Taxes have increased, but, according to Statistics Canada, "Average after-tax family income in 1996 was $45,032, about 5% less than in 1989, the peak year for income. Average transfer payments were $6,641, down 6.5 per cent

---

* *The Daily*, June 27, 1998.
† Centre for Social Justice, *The Growing Gap*, Toronto, 1998.
** *Income after tax, distribution by size in Canada*, 1996 Cat. #13-210 XPB.

from the peak in 1993, while average income tax was $11,597, 1% above the previous peak in 1990."* We can see that declining market income and reduced transfer payments are the main contributors to declining family income.

For some families, the results have been even worse. Gordon Cleveland and Michael Krashinsky report, "The pressures on young families have been even greater. . . . The average family incomes with the head aged 20 to 24 were 17.6 per cent worse off in 1991 than similar families in 1980."† Bear in mind that all of this has been happening despite a huge increase in the number of dual-earner families, from about 32 per cent of two-partner families in 1967 to over 60 per cent in 1996.**

In September 1998, a COMPAS poll for the CIBC showed that "most Canadians – 64 per cent . . . believed they were either treading water or sinking when it came to their personal finances. Only 36 per cent felt they were getting ahead."††

Reporting on the studies of Osberg and Sharpe, Bruce Little wrote:

> Canada's economic well-being has fallen in every year of the 1990s, even though the economy as a whole has recovered from the latest recession. . . .
>
> The biggest reason for the slow growth since 1971 of well-being is "the failure of economic equality to increase and the large fall in economic security."

Osberg and Sharpe "figured that there was a huge decline in economic security for Canadians – about 52 per cent between 1971 and 1997, and almost all of the decline occurred in the 1990s."***

Setting aside purely economic measurements, how are Canadian families doing in general? In an October 1998 survey, Canadian families reported huge increases in stress levels over previous eras, largely due to lack of money and to unstable jobs, as well as parents having to

---

* *Income after tax, distribution by size in Canada*, 1996, Cat. #13-210 XPB.
† *The Benefit and Costs of Good Child Care*, March 1998.
** Statistics Canada, *The Daily*, October 23, 1998.
†† *Maclean's*, October 26, 1998.
*** *Globe and Mail*, October 28, 1998.

work both too hard and for too many hours. One of the results was a sub-stantial increase in chronic emotional ill-health.*

Somehow, it all isn't working. As indicated earlier, we have had huge increases in exports (and imports), low inflation, comparatively low nominal interest rates, a drop in the official unemployment rate, and yet, as Dalton Camp has written, "when will the drip – as in drip down economics – put food on the family tables of the poor?"†

Good question. And what will happen to the poor and to all Canadians in a future recession?

---

* Southam News, COMPAS poll, *National Post*, November 24, 1998.
† *Toronto Star*, May 17, 1998.

PART NINE

*What Can We Do About
Poverty in Canada?*

"At a Crossroad"
– The Best Possible Investment

What can we do about poverty in Canada? Let's start with children.

When I began the research for this book, I knew there were large numbers of children living in poverty across our country. But I had no idea just how terrible and widespread the suffering is, how very deep the poverty is in so many homes and communities, how hundreds of thousands of Canadian children are being damaged for life. Let me quote from a letter to me from Doug McNally, the knowledgeable executive director of the Edmonton Community Foundation:

> When many poor children arrive at the schoolhouse door in kindergarten or grade one, they are often not ready to learn. It isn't unusual that they don't know letters or colours. Lacking the early development opportunities found in most Canadian homes, the brains of these children may simply not have developed. Recent research has revealed that infants' brains are immature at birth and that seventy per cent of development will occur in the first three years of life. Different areas of the brain will mature in sequence. The sequence is genetically set, but use-dependent. The windows of opportunity for development of attachment, self-regulation and vocabulary close at eighteen

months, twenty-four months and three to four years respectively. After the windows close, change can occur, but it is difficult to achieve.

In addition to being behind their classmates and continually struggling to learn, many of these children will misbehave and provoke disciplinary reactions in the school. The discipline is usually mild at first, but escalates over time as the child ages and progresses through the elementary and junior high grades. Combined with poor school performance, this often results in the child dropping out of or being expelled from the school system.

Some of the results: far higher rates of major mental disorders; of those afflicted, only about half report symptoms to a physician or mental health professional. Many also suffer from a substance abuse problem. In the case of some high-risk children, there is a background of neglect, conflict, child rejection, alcoholism, violence, parental absence and poor parental emotional or physical health. Half of prison inmates' files showed that the offenders had been victims of abuse or had frequently witnessed family violence. One result is a victimization-offender cycle.

Poverty is a common denominator.

McNally, a former police chief, is quick to point out that most poor children have loving parents who do their best to provide a caring, supportive family environment. But for the poor this is often extremely difficult, if not impossible.

McNally ends his letter with advice about the future, based on his many years of working closely with the poor:

I believe, in terms of criminal justice, that we are at a crossroad. We can either march down the road taken by our American neighbours and lock up increasing numbers of individuals at ever-increasing cost, or we can invest in children and families. At some point I hope we recognize that imprisonment is the most expensive and least effective strategy. Doing nothing will likely mean increased numbers of repeat and violent offenders, making all of us feel less secure in our homes and neighbourhoods. It will lead to ever increasing costs for policing, courts, prisons, parole, probation and insurance, as well as increased needs for private security firms, alarm systems, etc.

We must recognize that this problem is intergenerational. The parents I've described are frequently parenting in similar ways to their parents. The cycle will continue until we find the time, will, energy and resources necessary to give every child an equal opportunity to succeed in school and succeed for life. We must ensure that every child is ready, intellectually, physically and emotionally, to succeed the day they enter the grade one door.

From a hundred different sources we know that investment in early childhood development is the best possible investment we can make. We know it will lead to a better, happier, healthier, more productive society and country. We know that child poverty often produces a wide range of anti-social behaviour and results in adults who can't compete in society or in the job market. There are dozens of studies that show the enormous overall benefits reduced child poverty can bring: lower welfare costs, health-care costs and justice-system costs, not to mention the substantial betterment of the quality of life that can be achieved.

What should we aim for? What should our goals be? There is no reason why Canada should not become *the* number-one country in the world in its care for and respect for children. The resources can be mobilized; all that is lacking is the political will and leadership.

Where do we begin? Let's start by reminding Prime Minister Jean Chrétien of two resolutions passed at the 1998 national Liberal Party convention. The first resolution was sponsored by the national Liberal caucus. It began, "Whereas it is estimated that three million children in Canada arrive at school hungry," and ended with, "Be it resolved that the Liberal Party of Canada urges the federal government to take action to establish a national child nutrition program." The National Women's Liberal Commission urged the government "to ensure initiatives" which would lead to "the establishment of adequate child care facilities across Canada."

It's no secret that the value of resolutions passed at political conventions in Canada evaporates about as quickly as the early-morning dew on a hot July day. But let's also go back to Finance Minister Paul Martin's 1999 budget address: "This budget demonstrates that the finances of the nation are now in better shape than they have been in a generation – and that further progress lies ahead." The finance minister has also told us that "few countries are as well positioned as we are" and that "the economy is entering a period of strong growth."

What better time, then, to do something really important about poor children in Canada? And poor adults too. Here are some things that should be a priority.

First, the prime minister and the cabinet should agree to a two-day, televised meeting with representatives of the National Council of Welfare, NAPO, CCSD, Campaign 2000, the Canadian Association of Food Banks, the Caledon Institute, the Assembly of First Nations, the Centre for Social Justice, the newly formed Campaign Against Child Poverty, and other organizations concerned with poverty in Canada. Then the prime minister and cabinet should meet with finance and poverty experts from European countries that have low poverty rates to review the taxation, income distribution, and social policies that have successfully produced low poverty rates in these other countries.

I have my own list.

As our first priority we should establish Canadian Child Care Community Centres across the country. The centres should be located not only in low-income communities but in most communities. This is necessary since studies now show that poverty exists not only in the inner city and on aboriginal reservations, but also in the suburbs and in rural areas. The new centres should be open to all children between seven in the morning and seven in the evening. In announcing the centres, the government should proclaim that it will no longer tolerate a situation where so many Canadian children are forced to go hungry. Breakfast, lunch, dinner, and snacks will be provided without charge to children in need. No child will be turned away. The centres, where possible, will seek the co-operation of hospitals in preparing nutritious food (in much the same way that Edmonton's School Lunch Program works closely with a local hospital).

Each centre will have a full-time nurse and receive regular visits from a pediatrician. When required, children will be referred to medical specialists or to an optometrist, speech pathologist, or dentist. Transportation will be provided, without charge, as will all other services. When the doctor prescribes drugs for the children, the centres will obtain these drugs and provide them to the parents without charge.

Each centre will have a playroom, infant and toddler facilities, a library, computers, and recreational facilities.

Each centre will have well-trained, properly paid early-childhood educators, child-care staff, and quality child-care facilities, which will be provided at no charge. The federal government should plan a conference of child-care specialists, educators, and early-childhood-intervention specialists to help draft detailed plans for the centres.

The centres will not only provide substantial benefit for children from low-income families, they will also provide valuable assistance to single parents, allowing them a much better opportunity to enter the workforce and/or to improve their education. The large number of working-poor families will also gain great benefit from the centres.

It is important to stress that the centres should not only have staff devoted to early-childhood development, they will also serve as a community centre for mothers who require advice and support. Telephones will be available for families that do not have one. Message boards will help with communications. Staff will know when outreach workers need to be called. Rooms will be available for private case conferences.

While the vast majority of parents are loving and caring towards their children, there are times when intervention is required due to physical and sexual abuse, alcoholic parents and other reasons. The centres' staff will be well-trained to recognize such situations and will be knowledgeable about the nature of the response required for children at risk.

The centres and their staffs will

- provide children with a safe place to go after school;
- help with anger-management skills;
- help children with their self-confidence;
- help avoid family violence;
- help youth problem-solving skills;
- help with delinquency problems;
- help with drug- and alcohol-use problems;
- intervene in abusive situations;

- help direct children to community services and recreational opportunities;
- help improve school attendance;
- help identify and correct developmental delays;
- help reduce family stress;
- help identify child neglect, abuse, violence;
- help arrange medication;
- help with attention deficit disorders;
- help arrange social-services involvement when required.

Each centre will welcome the active participation of community volunteers and parents. There will be clothing-exchange programs, parenting literature, parenting groups, and head-start programs for four-year-olds. Each centre will have a small bus to pick up children from their homes if necessary and deliver them, and to pick up volunteers and donated supplies.

Studies show that for every dollar invested in quality child care, there is at the very least a double benefit to society, and some studies show the benefit to be as high as seven-fold. Economists Gordon Cleveland and Michael Krashinsky have shown that through enhanced childhood development, subsequent productivity, and lower social costs, as well as greater workforce participation by single mothers, society comes out a big winner. Children do much better in school and are more likely to proceed to post-secondary education. It goes without saying that such children are much less likely to be involved in crime or to become a burden to society.

Note the economists' comments published by the Childcare Resource and Research Unit at the Centre for Urban and Community Studies at the University of Toronto:

> Studies . . . found that if child care costs were fully subsidized, the rate of full-time employment for mothers would increase from 29 per cent to 52 per cent. This finding is even more dramatic in a lifetime context because mothers who are employed part-time for a substantial part of their lives generally have lower lifetime incomes. Many mothers work part-time because of child care considerations.

> Fully subsidized child care expenses would provide an
> incentive for single mothers on welfare . . . to join the paid
> labour force, reducing the need for welfare.*

So substantial societal benefits will flow from the centres, including the alleviation of hunger, stress, and other problems associated with child poverty. Among potential benefits cited in the University of Toronto study, school-age children will be "more considerate of others, less hostile, more cooperative, more socially skilled, more able to stay focused on a task, better able to follow multi-step directions and to work independently, and are better performers on tests that measure understanding and language use."

As previously indicated, the Childcare Resource and Research unit has calculated that the future annual monetary benefits to society from a national, high-quality, public child-care program would exceed $4.3 billion, while parental employment benefits would be over $6.2 billion. These benefits of more than $10.5 billion would be *far* greater than the total child-care costs involved, likely over $5 billion greater.

The Canadian Community Child Care Centres will be more costly than child care in itself because of their more all-inclusive nature. Shortly we will explore the funding of the centres and other programs to help the poor and to help reduce poverty in Canada. However, it is important not to lose sight of the frequent suggestion that every government dollar spent on children's welfare will likely save about seven dollars down the road in future correctional, health, and social-services costs. The one-to-seven ratio originates from a Michigan study and may be overstated for Canada. Nevertheless, the evidence is that costs to society related to improving child development are small compared to the overall rewards.

Many, if not most, Canadians know that investing in children is *the best of all possible investments*. It is less well known that in Canada we lag far behind European countries in paying proper attention to child development, and the needs of single and working mothers. A January 1999 report from the Canadian Policy Research Networks in Ottawa showed that France, Germany, Sweden, Norway, and the Netherlands have much

---

* *The Benefits and Costs of Good Childcare.*

stronger family support policies than Canada. In such areas as maternity leave at full wage, family allowance payments, child-care programs, parental leave, and other family social policy areas, Canada falls behind. What was needed "was commitment to allocate resources to children and families and consensus on the need for government to actively support families. . . . But for the most part, with the exception of Quebec, Canadian governments have left families to fend for themselves. . . ."*

The federal government should make a strong commitment that we not only not lag behind in the future, but that we will lead the way in creating a truly exemplary society in our own country. (As this book was going to press, newspapers reported a leaked Health Canada document that suggested the federal government was finally considering a new national child-care program. While the media made much of the proposal, Health Minister Allan Rock and his deputy minister had not even seen it.)

After its meetings with the anti-poverty groups, the government will be aware of the estimates that place the direct cost to society of child poverty in the tens of billions of dollars per year,† and will have been yet again reminded that all recent studies show the increasing importance of post-secondary education in gaining employment. Those without high school diplomas are steadily losing substantial ground in all measurements of employment changes, and those who have university degrees or college diplomas now account for almost 80 per cent of new jobs. The blunt truth is that today poor children are being terribly shortchanged in their opportunities for a good future life. The Canadian Child Care Community Centres will help change that, as will other education initiatives that are required to solve the problem of our rapidly increasing post-secondary tuition fees.

Our government must also study a program unveiled in the United Kingdom early in 1998 by Chancellor of the Exchequer Gordon Brown, an ambitious plan aimed at the high number of unemployed youths in Britain. The program includes six months of subsidized employment including one day a week of job training, or full-time job training, or a

---

* The Canadian Press, January 30, 1999.

† A 1997 OECD study calculated that Canada would lose some $4 billion in taxes and social costs because of the 137,000 Canadian young people who dropped out of school in 1994 alone. A high percentage of the dropouts came from poor families.

six-month paid job in the voluntary sector, with time off for job training.
Each participant gets access to his or her own personal adviser. In an editorial, the *Toronto Star* comments:

> Compare this to our confusing patchwork of programs. Ottawa scatters its $400 million in youth employment initiatives over so many departments and programs that bureaucrats can't keep them all straight. (To confuse matters further, Ottawa says it spends $2 billion a year assisting youths. But this includes $643 million for student loans and $1.1 billion for native schooling).
> Britain offers unemployed young people a clear road map. Canada confronts them with an impenetrable maze.[*]

The Canadian government should quickly set out to chop down the maze and to provide our youth with much more meaningful assistance. The high levels of youth unemployment in Canada during the past decade represent a terrible waste of our young people's lives. In 1989 fewer than 10 per cent of young Canadians had no job experience. Today it's up to 25 per cent – one in four.

Alas, as columnist David Crane has written, "Unfortunately, the Jean Chrétien government has largely abandoned any serious federal training role shifting responsibility to the provinces. But few provinces have effective training programs. . . ."[†] We urgently need new policies – perhaps a combination of payroll, education, and other incentives – that can put hundreds of thousands of unemployed Canadian youths into the workforce in rewarding employment. While the federal government will continue to welcome the private sector's Career Edge and Corporate Council on Youth in the Economy programs, it will understand that they have been woefully inadequate in meeting the needs of the large numbers of young Canadians who want and need jobs. Finding a solution to the problem of youth unemployment should be an urgent priority, and another of the first places the government should turn is European apprenticeship programs, which are closely linked to high-school education.

---

[*] February 16, 1998.
[†] *Toronto Star*, January 27, 1999.

The federal government should change the name of its labour-force insurance program back to its original title, Unemployment Insurance. More importantly, the government should return the program to its original purpose of providing workers who require assistance with adequate benefits when they lose their jobs or for good reason are required to leave their jobs. The government's current policy of taking worker and business premiums to provide funds for purposes other than those intended is gross fiscal irresponsibility. Large cutbacks in benefits and excessively restrictive eligibility requirements have been major factors in increasing and deepening poverty in Canada.

The working poor are a major and increasing problem in Canada. Some European countries are seeking to cut social-assistance costs by increasing minimum wages. The federal government should meet with the provinces and territories to examine the costs and consequences of a minimum-wage subsidy.

Ottawa should have been impressed with the excellent Anne Golden task force report on the homeless and the lack of public housing in Toronto. Obviously, callously, it wasn't. How dismaying and how arrogant that the subsequent federal budget ignored the problem as if it didn't exist. Nothing important will happen to assist the growing number of homeless in Canada until the federal government makes the issue a national priority and leads the way to providing a publicly financed solution. Today, a very large percentage of those on social assistance across the country are unable to find habitable, affordable accommodation. Only about 7 per cent of those on welfare have managed to find subsidized housing. The Chrétien government rejected the recommendations of its own party's task force on housing, which should have been acted upon long ago. In June 1999 the Federation of Canadian Municipalities sharply criticized Ottawa for its failure to develop an urgently needed public housing policy. In the words of Toronto mayor Mel Lastman, "The federal government has walked away and said housing for the homeless, or any housing, is not their responsibility."[*] The construction of non-profit public rental housing should be offered to the provinces and to the municipalities with an attractive cost-sharing formula, a GST rebate, low-cost land and with

* The Canadian Press, reported in the *Edmonton Journal*, June 5, 1999.

Ottawa providing long-overdue leadership. And by the way, the construction of public housing will create many jobs.

In 1980 there were 1.3 million welfare recipients in Canada. By 1990, the number had increased to 1.9 million. Today it is closer to 2.7 million. If there were ever a clear indication of the failure of government economic policy, these numbers provide it. While it is true that handicaps or disabilities are a factor in about a quarter of welfare cases, the growing number of Canadians, almost 10 per cent, who must now rely on social assistance shows that new economic policies are urgently needed. Over a million Canadian children are currently welfare recipients. That leaves many employable handicapped persons and at least 1.1 million other Canadians, many of whom need assistance to get into the workforce. But those who find decent-paying full-time jobs will often be able to provide properly for children or other family members now dependent on welfare.

For those who believe that welfare assistance provides a bountiful life of ease, it should be noted that welfare rates in eight provinces are at least 40 per cent below the Statistics Canada LICOs line and some provinces' rates are 70 to almost 80 per cent lower than the LICOs line. In 1996, the average welfare income of a couple with two children was only about $1,390 a month. Social-assistance programs to help our disadvantaged must include adequate financial assistance to provide funds for proper food, shelter, clothing, basic transportation, personal-care and health-care expenses, and children's needs.

The 1997 report of the National Council of Welfare indicated that

> welfare incomes in all parts of Canada fall well below the poverty line. They also represent only a small fraction of average incomes. . . . As the benefit freezes and the decreases continue, people already living in poverty on welfare grow poorer.
>
> Social Assistance or welfare is the income program of last resort in Canada. It provides financial assistance to individuals and families whose resources are inadequate to meet their needs and who have exhausted other avenues of support.

The report goes on to discuss the increasingly restrictive provincial rules and regulations relating to welfare eligibility: the stringent conditions and limitations, the "needs tests," the examinations of assets, and other factors intended to make eligibility more difficult. The council's concluding analysis of benefits is clear:

> The incomes are abysmally low. . . . The only "discretion" many welfare recipients have is how to cut back on food when the money starts running short towards the end of the month. . . . Welfare incomes which reach only one-fifth or one-third of the poverty line are unacceptably low and should be raised at the earliest possible date.

In some provinces, a single employable person on welfare received as little as 11 per cent of average single employable income; a disabled person as little as 26 per cent of average.

In several provinces, reductions in welfare benefits have been disastrous. In constant 1996 dollars, an Ontario couple with two children saw their welfare assistance drop from $20,540 in 1992 to $15,428 in 1996. In Alberta, a couple with two children saw their assistance drop from $16,622 in 1992 to $14,622 in 1996. According to the council, "Welfare incomes in all provinces are grossly inadequate. Yet, instead of improving the living standards of people on welfare, the provinces have imposed freezes and cuts to welfare rates, gravitating to the lowest standards. Incomes which provide adequate standards of living covering the costs of the necessities of life must be a goal of welfare programs. . . . Paying decent welfare rates and improving incentives to work by increasing earnings exemptions is sound social policy; cutting benefits is not."

In Ontario, one of the wealthiest provinces in Canada, the 116 per cent increase in the rate of child poverty since the 1989 House of Commons resolution has been the highest in the country. According to the Ontario Campaign 2000 Report Card 1998, approximately one in ten children in Ontario were poor in 1989. By 1996 it was one in five. According to the Interfaith Social Assistance Reform Coalition, the number of youths and families using hostels and shelters in the province doubled between 1986 and 1996. Yet, while there are more homeless people and poor children in Ontario than ever before, the Harris government dumped over 370,000 people from its welfare rolls.

For those in the province who still receive welfare, the situation remains grim.

> The average Toronto single mother receives $1,071.70 a month. Out of that $680.53 goes to pay the rent in private rental housing where more than three-quarters live. . . . That leaves just $391.17 or $13.03 a day to pay for food, clothing, transportation, a telephone and other expenses.
>
> In dollars and cents, the Harris welfare cuts meant that a single mother with one child saw her annual income drop by $3,169 to 59 per cent of the poverty line.
>
> Before the cuts, two-thirds of welfare parents with children under 12 could pay the rent with the shelter allowance portion of their welfare cheques. After the cuts, only a third could pay the rent on the amount allotted for shelter.
>
> As a result, landlords fed up with tenants who can't pay the rent, applied for 15,157 eviction orders in the city of Toronto from mid-June 1998 to the end of February, 1999.*

Does social assistance dissuade people from going to work? Statistics Canada's Garnett Picot writes:

> Some have suggested that increases in social transfers actually encourage low employment earnings (resulting in more children living in low-income situations). By providing an alternative to the labour market it is argued, the welfare state creates disincentives for individuals and families to work and encourages dependency. . . . It is highly unlikely any work disincentive effect would be large enough to explain the declines in employment income among young families outlined in this article.
>
> After almost a decade of work in this area, researchers have moved away from the view that the transfer system explains declining earnings among younger and low-wage workers. Instead, attention is turning to the demand side of the

---

* *Toronto Star*, May 15, 1999.

labour market, the effects of changing trade patterns and the introduction of new technologies.*

Rather than cutting back social assistance, every effort should be made to provide extra help to those who can benefit from upgraded education, including teens and parents who wish to join the workforce, but do not have the necessary skills. The CCSD says it well:

> The end goal of every welfare program should be to reduce poverty, not simply to reduce the length of time that people are in receipt of social assistance. Welfare-to-work programs should ensure that no welfare recipient ends up poorer than before as a result of the program.
>
> [Nor should] programs be designed to encourage employers to replace their current employees with welfare recipients whose wages are lower or are subsidized by the government.

The evidence repeatedly shows that reports of welfare fraud are almost always exaggerated. One 1997 survey in Alberta estimates fraud to be a factor in fewer than 0.5 per cent of all welfare cases. According to NAPO,

> The rate of welfare fraud is approximately between 3% and 6%. On the other hand, the value of corporate crimes is approximately 88 times that of welfare fraud and tax fraud is approximately 40 times that of welfare fraud. When people are convicted of welfare frauds, 80% of them are given a prison sentence, while only 4% of individuals convicted of tax fraud are incarcerated.

Nevertheless, NAPO continues,

> Provincial governments across Canada have rolled back funding for social assistance and support programs and in many cases eliminated discretionary supplementary benefits such as furniture, transportation subsidies, and even pregnancy-related

---

* Statistics Canada, *Canadian Social Trends*, Autumn 1996, Cat. #11-008-XPE.

dietary benefits. Furthermore, provincial governments have engaged in actions that promote the growing intolerance for social assistance recipients. They have provided the press with an endless stream of rhetoric about the need for increasing policing measures to stem the "flood" of welfare frauds and cheats. Welfare recipients are barraged with images and slogans blaming them for being poor; targeting them as the cause of high debts and deficits; reinforcing notions that they are "lazy" and "worthless."*

In the words of the National Council of Welfare,

Welfare is a degrading experience for the vast majority of recipients. Applicants have to exhaust almost all their liquid assets to qualify for help. Welfare entitlements are determined by a labyrinth of rules and regulations that may or may not make sense. . . .

The National Council of Welfare recommends that the federal, provincial and territorial governments agree to a totally new package of financial agreements for social programs.†

We badly need sensible welfare reforms in Canada, and we need levels of social assistance that provide reasonable benefits to people in poverty to allow them to live without severe deprivation while they make the effort to improve their lives. (In May 1999 the *Toronto Star* reported that single welfare mothers in Toronto rental housing were paying an average of 63.5 per cent of their monthly welfare cheque, plus tax credits and any money earned, for rent. This left an average of $13.03 a day for food, clothing, and all other expenses.) How sad it is to see the actions of some provinces that force single mothers to enroll in work-fare programs without providing adequate job training or child-care assistance. In Ontario and Alberta, single mothers wishing to upgrade their education at a post-secondary institution are often forced out of welfare into loan programs where "the prospect of a $20,000 debt is

---

* Ruth Morris, Harry Glasbeek, and Dianne Martin, *We're Being Cheated: Corporate and Welfare Fraud*, Osgoode Hall Law School, 1997.
† *Welfare Incomes 1996*, Winter 97/98.

terrifying to most lone mothers who never saw $20,000 in their life," says a senior Ottawa official. "What then?" I asked him. "They're shit out of luck," he replied. And how can we justify the actions of provincial governments that try to force older citizens to re-enter the work force when jobs for older workers are very difficult if not impossible to find?

Welfare-to-work programs should be intended to produce meaning-ful, rewarding employment designed to encourage self-sufficiency and to reduce poverty. The CCSD is right when it says,

> The work or training component of welfare-to-work programs should be voluntary. The right of Canadians to choose their own work should be an underlying principle of any welfare-to-work program. Welfare programs should support people and encour-age them to participate in the economy; they should not be designed to punish people for being jobless.
>
> Recent welfare reforms appear to be contributing to wors-ening poverty in Canada by lowering benefits and forcing some people off assistance and into uncertain employment. Another concern is that most welfare-to-work programs do not pay enough attention to the needs of recipients and their children.[*]

No one should support welfare-to-work programs that result in Canadian men, women, and children becoming poorer. Moreover, there is evidence that the work-training and employment services being offered by the provinces are far less than adequate and below the stan-dards of the recent past at a time when all evidence points to greater requirements for entering the labour force, not fewer.

We should also reject the provincial trend to classify more and more people as employable. For example, the CCSD advises that in Alberta, a single parent with a six-month-old child is considered employable. Surely some basic questions must be asked. What kind of society forces single mothers with young children to go to work in poor-paying jobs without providing adequate assistance for child care, transportation, and other needs? Most governments and citizens in Western Europe would be appalled by such policies.

---

[*] Press release, March 3, 1999.

And what kind of society makes a transition from allowing single parents to stay home until children have at least finished elementary school to forcing a mother of a six-month-old to leave home for compulsory low-wage work? And what kind of society cuts training funds when everyone knows how essential they are to help lift people out of poverty? And what kind of society punishes the poor who can't find work? If there were ever clearer indications of how Canada has moved towards American standards, practices, and values, it's difficult to imagine where they might be found.

When workfare programs are not accompanied by proper training and new job creation, the inevitable result is downward pressure on wages for the working poor. Surely, this is perverse. Cheaper labour will exacerbate poverty in Canada, not address its root problems.

NAPO comments, "Workfare is based on two myths: that people receiving welfare are so lazy that they have to be forced to work; and that there are plenty of decent jobs available. Neither of these is true. Many people on welfare perform valuable work at home, nurturing children and other family members and volunteering in the community." The evidence has long been clear; the vast majority of people on welfare want work, but have been unable to find it because of an economy that has badly underperformed.

To date, there is very little evidence that workfare results in full-time, permanent jobs. There is, however, abundant evidence that forced workfare employees often replace low and medium-skill public workers who have held jobs for many years. Where once there were real, secure, long-term, full-time jobs, now poorly paid compulsory workers are the order of the day.

No Canadian should favour welfare policy that goes back to the days of the Great Depression, or of the kind found today in so many repressive U.S. states. The federal government should meet with the provinces to show its displeasure relating to workfare and to help lead the way to positive employment policies that are fairer and more productive for all concerned. We do not need coercive policies that punish the poor to save money.

Federal policies of reducing transfer payments to the provinces have placed significant pressure on provincial and territorial financial resources, which in turn has led to reduced social spending and considerable hardship for low-income individuals and families. With this in mind, a federal government that wishes to play an activist role in the reform of social policy with the objective of reducing poverty in Canada must enter into negotiations with the provinces for a new long-term co-operative social-programs cost-sharing agreement.

For new programs such as the Canadian Child Care Community Centres, the federal government should offer to contribute 75 per cent of all costs, and commit to a guaranteed minimum twenty-year term to provide funding employing the new fixed shared-cost formula. Too often in the past the federal government has lured the provinces into shared-cost programs and then withdrawn much of its share of funding, leaving the provinces in difficult circumstances. The federal government must be prepared to offer ironclad guarantees of the new 75-25 formula, and to guarantee its minimum duration. Once in place, the new centres will become as permanent and valued a fixture in Canadian society as medicare.

Social-program standards are vitally important. In all cases where the federal government agrees to pay 75 per cent of costs, it will want to have an important say in negotiating standards with the provinces and territories. At present, there are no national standards for child care, public housing, and income assistance for the disabled, among other programs. Basic standards and definitions such as those contained in the Canada Health Act are badly needed. Canada should set firm targets that will not allow its underprivileged to fall below nationally acceptable standards.

With this in mind, we should end the Canada Health and Social Transfer (CHST) as soon as possible and put in its place new, dedicated block-funding transfer programs for each separate social program such as health care, the new Child Care Community Centre program, post-secondary education, and social assistance in general.

There needs to be major changes to the Child Tax Benefit program, beginning with full indexation. The federal government should also outlaw provincial clawbacks that sharply reduce the effectiveness of the program.

In January 1997, Ottawa agreed with the provinces and territories to work together to develop a National Children's Agenda to improve the well-being of Canada's children. Such an agenda is badly needed, and long, long overdue. The federal government should put the new Child Care Community Centres and their Child Tax Benefit at the top of the list for discussions and be open to improving the Child Tax Benefit program substantially, or to replacing it with a more effective program to assist all poor children and poor families. The objective should be clear – to alleviate suffering and to ensure a level of income which would allow the development of healthy children who will have the opportunity to compete with children from better-off families. With these goals in mind, larger benefits for low-income families must be a priority. The present absurd situation where single mothers on social assistance – generally the poorest of the poor – are so unfairly treated under the Child Tax Benefit must be changed in the near future.

In all of these discussions, the federal government will have to work with the provinces and territories to the best of its ability in the spirit of co-operative federalism, while always keeping in mind Ottawa's constitutional privilege to make payments directly to individuals. If necessary, the federal government may have to examine the possibility of threatening to withhold future transfer payments to provinces or territories that insist on clawing back federal social-assistance payments. Some provinces will rant and rage about federal intrusion into provincial jurisdiction, but Canada already is the most decentralized federal nation in the world (with the possible exception of tiny Switzerland), and it's time Ottawa showed more leadership and vision. Moreover, show me a premier who turns down the guaranteed cost-sharing formula I have suggested, and I'll show you a politician who will be in big trouble in the next provincial election.

In consultation with interested Canadians, our governments should examine legislating extended, optional unpaid parental leave, with guarantees that, after a reasonable time, the worker can return to his or her job. Some additional government assistance with paid maternity leave should be considered. We should carefully study the successful programs in Western Europe which have long been so popular and so far advanced beyond those in North America and recognize the importance of a mother's ability to stay at home and nurture her young children if she desires. An excellent discussion of this and related topics is found in *Preschool Children: Promises to Keep*, a spring 1999 publication of the National Council of Welfare.

We should all be concerned that there are still a large number of seniors, mostly single elderly women, living well below the LICOs lines, despite the overall general improvement in the welfare of seniors in Canada. The federal government should appoint a cabinet minister responsible for seniors policy, a minister who will be eager to solicit input from seniors' organizations. Where necessary, Ottawa should promptly provide for additional Guaranteed Income Supplements or Spousal Allowances for low-income seniors.

According to Statistics Canada, in 1996 4.2 million Canadians (about 16 per cent of the population) had disabilities. About 20 per cent of persons with disabilities were either housebound or required assistance travelling even short distances.* According to NAPO, over 40 per cent of people with disabilities had an income of less than $10,000. About 48 per cent of the disabled had some work and about half of these worked full-time. About 60 per cent of persons aged fifteen to sixty-four with disabilities who were not in the labour force were completely prevented from working by their condition and another 20 per cent were limited in the type of work they could do.

Many of the disabled in Canada live in deep poverty, with incomes far below the LICOs line. In the words of Traci Walters, national director of the Canadian Association of Independent Living Centres, despite frequent meetings with the federal government, Ottawa "has done absolutely nothing. . . . They use a great deal of our time on meetings that go nowhere. It's an incredible insult." When Ottawa cut transfer payments to the provinces, provincial programs for the disabled were among the first to suffer, with big cuts to transportation and home care in particular. Another result was that disabled persons with few resources found themselves having to battle provincial bureaucracies with little outside help. In the words of Lucie Lemieux-Brassard, treasurer of the Council of Canadians with Disabilities, "We're wasting so much energy just to fight for what little we have now. Without national standards, we're losing ground."† Clearly we need more generous programs to help the disabled and the handicapped in Canada.**

* *A Portrait of Persons With Disabilities*, Cat. #89-542-XPE.
† *Globe and Mail*, March 1, 1999.
** An excellent report on the disabled in Canada is *In Unison: A Canadian Approach to Disability Issues*, Human Resources Development Canada, Cat. #SP-113-10-98E.

In a great many of my interviews, the subject of mental health and its correlation to poverty came up. Two aspects of mental-health problems dominated. First, the cruelty of a system that has closed down mental-health facilities, turning sick men and women onto the streets with no place to go. How could we possibly have allowed such an uncivilized thing to happen in our country? Visit any shelter, talk to any minister or priest, and hear for yourself how shameful our record is. We need more beds and more staff to look after mentally ill or mentally handicapped Canadians.

The other aspect of mental health and poverty that came up over and over again was the pervasive impact of poverty on the mental health of young children. Cherry Murray, executive director of the Crossroads Children's Centre in Ottawa, writes:

> We know that mental health problems create staggering costs to our economy, to our well-being, and to our safety and security. We also know that for children, poverty is one of the strongest risk factors for future severe mental health problems. It is time that we stop asking what it will cost to impact on poverty. The real question is what is it costing us not to?[*]

Murray quotes numerous studies showing the higher levels of depression among poor children, the increased psychiatric disorders and overall social impairment.

It's impossible to discuss poverty in Canada without examining Canada's disgraceful record in relation to our aboriginal population. In 1996, aboriginal people made up 2 to 3 per cent of our population, but over 17 per cent of inmates in federal and provincial prisons. Average native income is about half the Canadian average, infant mortality about twice the Canadian average, the death rate of pre-school aboriginal children almost four times the national average, the suicide rate over two-and-a-half times the rate for all Canadians, the adolescent suicide rate five times, and the number forced to live on social assistance six times the Canadian average. In Toronto, roughly 25 per cent of all the homeless are aboriginal people, although they make up only 2 per cent of the city's population.

---

[*] Letter to the author, March 22, 1999.

In 1992, while Canada was sixth in the world GDP rankings based on real (PPP) GDP per capita, Canada's registered Indians were thirty-first. Using the U.N. Human Development Index calculations that have placed Canada at number one, our registered Indians were forty-eighth, and in terms of life expectancy placed forty-seventh. In education Canada placed second, our registered Indians placed forty-eighth.[*]

On average, aboriginal Canadians have seven years less life expectancy than other Canadians. About 85 per cent of families on reserves have incomes below the LICOs line. Despite this, in recent years there has been some movement back from the urban centres to the reserves. The reason? Aboriginal people have great difficulty finding jobs. Meanwhile, on many reserves there isn't enough money for food, housing is appalling, and there are no jobs. According to Tony Hall of the University of Lethbridge, "Reserves, especially in Western Canada, are somewhere between Mexico and Somalia in terms of standard of living. . . . The disparity between the reserves and the rest of Canada is immense. It should be a major embarrassment."[†] Some reserves have average annual per capita incomes as low as $4,000 to $5,000, and quite a few are in the $7,000 to $8,000 range.

Most Canadians are sympathetic to the plight of Canada's indigenous peoples. But, alas, ignorance, bigotry, and racism are facts of life. Incredibly, one recent poll showed that 48 per cent of those surveyed in Manitoba and Saskatchewan thought that aboriginals have too much power. Another survey showed that about half thought that conditions on reserves were equal to or better than in most of Canada.

It's true that some good things *are* happening. More federal money is going to urban aboriginal youth centres that provide counselling, training, advice, and recreation for native youths. At the same time, there have been educational gains at both the secondary and post-secondary levels. But the gains are very modest in comparison to the overall numbers. In 1986 only about 1 per cent of Canada's aboriginals completed university; ten years later it was only 3 per cent.

Education isn't the only key to improving the lives of Canada's native people, but it's certainly at or near the top of any list. The

---

[*] Daniel Beavon and Martin Cooke, *Measuring the Well-Being of First Nations Peoples*, Department of Indian Affairs and Northern Development, 1998.
[†] *Globe and Mail*, March 1, 1999.

problem of school dropouts must be addressed. The proposed Child Care Community Centres will go a long way towards helping native children.

Most people that I've talked to who are knowledgeable about aboriginal affairs believe there must be greater recognition of native resource rights, not as a charitable giveaway but as a fundamental right. Few if any native people in Canada felt they were giving away their rights to the resources on their lands when they entered into treaty agreements with the government of Canada.

The Report of the Royal Commission on Aboriginal Peoples spells out many excellent recommendations. Ovide Mercredi, former national chief of the Assembly of First Nations, sums things up as well as anyone:

> The last thing we want to read is someone telling us that the United Nations has deemed Canada the best county in the world in which to live. It's not the best country for my people to live in. . . . Our young people should not be condemned to live in conditions of poverty indefinitely. . . . We should not have been on welfare for the last 30 years of our lives. That is totally unforgivable in the wealthiest country in the world with the highest standard of life. . . . And people keep coming in here in great influx from all over the world to make a living, a good living, a good standard of life which they do. In the meantime we live in third world conditions. We are out of mind, out of sight. It's not just the issues of land and treaties that people are ignoring. It's practical issues like a job, a house, good health, a good education. These are things that are absent in our communities.

"Where the Hell Are We Going to Get the Money?"

The title of this chapter is the reaction you're going to get from BCNI, the Department of Finance, and the editorial pages in the business press to proposals of the kind found in the preceding chapter.

The better question would be, "What can we do to make Canada a more just country and to take important steps to sharply reduce the number of Canadians living in poverty?" Two of the most important answers lie in a re-examination of our tax system and in measures to improve the Canadian economy. We'll look at the overall economy in the next chapter. Now, we'll turn to the tax system.

We have already determined, first of all, that if Canada's total tax ratio to GDP were the same as the average of the other twenty-eight OECD countries, we'd have about $9 billion a year to help pay for the Canadian Community Child Care Centres and other measures to help poor Canadians. Coincidentally, the latest Statistics Canada aggregate-income-deficiency figures show that about $8.5 billion would be enough to bring all poor families with children and all unattached elderly Canadians up to the LICOs line.*

---

* *Income distributions by size*, Cat. #13-207, XPB.

We also learned earlier that if Canada spent the average of the other twenty-eight OECD countries on social programs, we'd have over $40 billion more to spend on health, education, and social services. Of course we can't do that because the governments of Pierre Trudeau ($150 billion), Brian Mulroney ($297 billion), and Jean Chrétien ($113 billion) racked up massive deficits for a total federal debt which next year will cost us over $43 billion in annual interest payments.

Where can we find $9 billion a year to pay for the policies suggested in the last chapter?

To begin with, we need a federal government that's committed to *finally* doing something about poverty, to spelling out clear, determined national objectives and timetables to alleviate, reduce, and finally eliminate most poverty, a government that values charity, but understands that charity only brushes the surface of the deep wound in our society. And we need a government that understands that the very concept of food banks should be anathema in a civilized country.

Here's what needs to be done. The federal government should appoint a five-person commission and give them six months to recommend tax and other policy changes that will, as fairly as possible, produce $9 billion in additional annual revenue that can be used to fight poverty. (The corporate elite and the business press will of course scream blue murder. Let them go back and read "We Can't Afford to Help the Poor" in Part Six of this book.)

Perhaps the commission could be headed by the highly regarded David Perry of the Canadian Tax Foundation. Perhaps it could have both business and labour-union economists and two other knowledgeable tax experts.

Anticipated economic growth can probably provide much of the answer without even changing the tax system. Recent forecasts suggest federal government surpluses in the $5-billion to $10-billion range. Ottawa economist Mike McCracken of Infometrica is forecasting a huge federal surplus of at least $15 billion next year and even greater surpluses in the following years. Even if he proves to be too optimistic, much of the money needed to help the poor should come without tax increases. But some important tax changes are in order and some of them are long overdue.

For John Kenneth Galbraith,

the most effective instrument for achieving a greater measure of income equality remains the progressive income tax. This has the central role in accomplishing a reasonable, even civilized, distribution of income. Nothing else, it may be added, is subject to such highly motivated and wholly predictable attacks. The good society, on the other hand, affirms its purpose; it also assumes that there will be strong, articulate, even eloquent resistance from those so taxed. They will especially allege the deleterious effect of the tax on incentives. . . . It could be claimed with equal improbability that a strongly progressive income tax causes the rich and the affluent to work harder, more imaginatively, in order to sustain their after-tax income. Referring to past experience, it can, indeed, be pointed out that the American economy had one of its highest rates of growth, its highest levels of employment and in some years a substantial budget surplus in the period immediately following World War II, when the marginal rates on the personal income tax were at a record level.*

Moreover, government should "remove the present tax and expenditure concessions to the affluent. In recent times these have achieved a measure of recognition under the cognomen of corporate welfare. Included here are diverse business subsidies and tax breaks."

Should we go back and have another good look at the Kenneth Carter 1966, six-volume "a buck is a buck" Royal Commission on Taxation as a basis for taxation? That is, all sources of income, be they wages, inheritances, gifts, lottery winnings, capital gains – you name it – should be taxed at the end of the year? If your total income from all sources is $100,000, shouldn't we tax on the basis of a $100,000 income? The Carter concept was crushed by opposition from the wealthy. Big loopholes would have been closed. In the words of one well-known tax expert who asked not to be quoted by name, "Politically it became impossible [because] the big bucks fund the politicians and the big bucks hated Carter." Should we not be angry that this continues to be true today, probably even more so than in the past?

---

* *The Socially Concerned Today*, University of Toronto Press, 1998.

By using the Carter approach to broaden the tax base, might we even be able to reduce taxes for the middle class?

Let's turn to corporations. Are they paying their fair share of taxes? In the 1990s, corporate taxation in Canada as a percentage of GDP has been well below the average levels of the previous four decades. But, from everything I have learned about the subject over the years, the answer is that many (but not all) Canadian corporations pay a reasonable corporate tax, while foreign corporations operating in Canada are escaping billions of dollars in taxes that should be paid in Canada every year.

Let's look at the practice of foreign corporations piling on debt in Canada to escape paying taxes here. First, consider the oil-and-gas sector of the Canadian economy. It's well known that foreign petroleum corporations work hard to locate their profits in other countries to minimize the taxes they have to pay in Canada. They do this by loading up their Canadian subsidiaries with high debt-to-equity ratios; debt interest charges are deductible. Rather than raising equity or using retained earnings, interest on debt capital either from the parent company at non-arm's-length interest rates or interest on money borrowed from Canadian sources reduces profits in Canada. The profits and tax revenue show up elsewhere, sometimes in tax havens. While the Americans long ago instituted a stringent tax code to ensure that the same sort of thing doesn't happen in the U.S., Canada loses billions of dollars in tax revenue by failing to act on what has for many years been a well-known procedure for reducing taxes in this country. (See Appendix Four.)

The petroleum industry is not an exception. Most multinationals operating in Canada do the same thing. Incredibly, the Chrétien government, for completely unfathomable reasons, made it no longer mandatory for wholly-owned foreign corporations to publicly report their financial results in Canada. Why wouldn't General Motors, Ford, and Chrysler adopt the same tax strategy as the big foreign oil companies? About 35 to 40 per cent of the biggest corporations in Canada are foreign-controlled; why wouldn't they all? The U.S. has moved aggressively to see that profits are declared in their country. Why should Canada not act in a similar fashion relating to profits earned here? After all, Canada has a much higher degree of foreign ownership and control than the U.S. For every dollar lost through the piling on of debt, average Canadians lose a dollar from their own pockets.

The new tax commission should look at two other common practices of multinational corporations. In *The Betrayal of Canada*, I estimated that non-arm's-length transfer pricing – artificial charges the parent company levies on its Canadian subsidiary – were probably costing Canada around $15 billion a year in lost tax revenues. Even though Revenue Canada has tightened up its scrutiny of transfer pricing in recent years, since trade volumes have increased substantially and foreign ownership has also steadily increased in recent years, my guess is that we're still looking at many billions of dollars in lost tax revenue every year.

Another common practice of both Canadian and foreign corporations is to finance overseas activities where the profits will never be taxed in Canada, but the interest charges show up here, reducing Canadian profits and taxes. Again, we're probably looking at lost tax revenue in the billions of dollars.

The new tax commission should take a good close look at a subject that is almost never discussed and hasn't been publicly debated for years: capital consumption allowances. In 1998 these depreciation allowances amounted to an enormous $115 billion. By comparison, the federal government's *total* budgetary revenues for 1998-99 were $156.5 billion. Figure 60 (overleaf) shows what has happened to capital consumption allowances in Canada during the past half-century.

Do you recall any public debate about these allowances rising from under 9 per cent to almost 13 per cent of GDP? Don't feel bad if you can't. It's been a virtually silent, virtually unknown process. The tax commission should examine the impact of reducing these write-offs by 1 to 1.5 per cent of GDP. Even 1 per cent would mean a great deal of money. Would a 1-per-cent reduction drive business out of Canada? That's what you'd be told; don't believe it for a fraction of a second. What these overly generous allowances constitute is plain and simple: they're essentially a government subsidy to big business. (By the way, Figure 60 doesn't include provincial capital consumption allowances, which in 1998 amounted to $3.3 billion.)

The tax commission will no doubt want to look into the whole question of deferred taxes. Most deferred taxes never get paid, but they

FIGURE 60

Capital Consumption Allowances as a Percentage of GDP

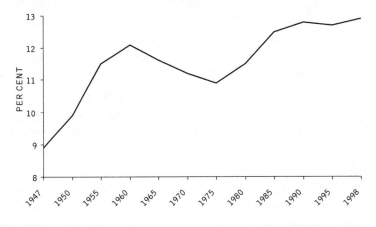

SOURCE: Statistics Canada, *National Income and Expenditure Accounts*, Cat. #13-001-PPB.

There has been virtually no debate in Canada about these enormous and escalating tax write-offs which are to a large extent fast depreciation allowances for big business.

amount to billions of dollars. Should we charge interest on deferred taxes? If not, why not? Why should wealthy corporations such as the Thomson Corp., Shell Canada, Alcan, BCE, and Canadian Pacific have hundreds of millions or even billions of dollars in deferred taxes outstanding without incurring interest charges on their debt? It would be wrong to bring in retroactive legislation that punishes investment made on the basis of previous tax policy. But why not change the system in the future?

The tax commission will also want to look at a big change made by the Trudeau government. Before 1972, interest on money borrowed by corporations to take over other corporations was deemed non-deductible. Since 1972, it has been a deductible expense. Canada already has far too much corporate concentration. Excessive corporate concentration has little to do with any theories of free enterprise or market economics. Why encourage more by giving big corporations big tax write-offs?

Tax havens should also be a focus of attention. Columnist Diane Francis tells us that wealthy Canadians' money leaves Canada regularly for tax havens. Why don't we require all financial institutions in Canada to report large withdrawals and offshore transfers promptly to Revenue Canada so that we can collect taxes on money transferred surreptitiously out of the country? And, while we're on the subject, why not substantially increase fines and penalties for tax evasion?

The auditor-general has indicated that a corporation that transfers cash to a tax haven and then buys Canadian bonds pays no tax on the resulting income. But if you buy Canadian bonds in Canada, the income is taxable. Years ago, the auditor-general identified $4.3 billion invested out of the country by only six companies, for this purpose alone. Think of what the total likely is today. The OECD *Observer* tells us:

> The number of tax havens has more than doubled. From 1985 to 1994, the value of investments into low tax jurisdictions in the Caribbean and South Pacific islands grew fivefold, to over $200 billion (U.S.).
>
> The concept of "tax havens" refers to tax jurisdictions which offer themselves as a place which non-residents can use to escape tax obligations in their countries of residence. A number of factors identify these havens, in particular the virtual absence of taxes, combined with minimum business presence requirements, and a lack of legislative and administrative transparency. Bank secrecy and other features preventing effective exchange of information are also discernable. Using these definitions, a list of jurisdictions identified as tax havens is expected to be published in October 1999. The list should help form the basis for unilateral or collective counter-measures.*

From what I can understand, Canada should be first among countries planning these collective counter-measures, and taking strong measures all on its own. To its credit, Revenue Canada has recently stepped up its efforts to address the tax haven problem, but much more needs to be done.

While we're on the subject of escaping taxes, shouldn't we all be outraged at the Mulroney government's disgusting, secret, under-the-table

---

* No. 215, January 1999.

giveaway of hundreds of millions of dollars in lost tax revenue on the transfer out of the country by the Bronfman family of what most believe should have been taxable assets? The tax commission should look into this deal and heads should roll. There should be a public inquiry into this extraordinary (or was it?) example of elite tax avoidance.

There has been much written on the subject, but Linda McQuaig's *National Post* column summed it up best.

> In a scathing ruling, Federal Court Judge Francis Muldoon attacked Ottawa's decision in 1991 to allow two private trusts, reportedly controlled by the Bronfman family, to move $2 billion in assets out of the country without paying taxes. Muldoon's ruling . . . suggests that Ottawa's action amounted to favouritism and subverted the purpose of a "free and democratic society."
>
> "Such a society is not one in which the government should be permitted to make whacking big tax concessions to the benefit of a few and to the detriment of many, who like good little serfs must just shut up and raise no complaint against their betters," the judge wrote.
>
> A basic principle of tax law is that, while assets are not taxed every year like income, they are subject to capital gains taxes when they're sold, or when the owner dies or moves them out of the country.
>
> The reason the Bronfmans didn't pay up to $700-million in capital gains taxes was because they convinced Ottawa that the assets they were moving out of the country qualified as "taxable Canadian property."
>
> Now some naïve people might think "taxable Canadian property" was something that would be subject to tax in Canada. And, in fact, this was the intention of those who designed this section of our tax laws. They wanted to make sure that foreigners would be made to pay capital gains taxes in Canada.
>
> But the Bronfman lawyers managed to twist this section around to ensure the opposite – that their Canadian client would be able to *avoid* paying capital gains taxes in Canada.
>
> Revenue Canada initially resisted. But a flurry of last-

minute meetings involving senior Finance Department officials two days before Christmas that year resulted in the Mulroney government giving its sanction to what most laypeople would consider an obvious distortion of the country's tax laws, to the benefit of one of the nation's richest families.

In [a similar case back in] 1985, the Reichmann family approached Ottawa for permission to use a complex tax deal to save $500-million in taxes in connection with its purchase of Gulf Canada. Government officials were initially reluctant, but some high-level meetings led to a favourable result for the Reichmanns – and the loss of $500-million for the Canadian treasury, in the midst of an apparent deficit crisis.*

On another question relating to corporate taxation, John Kenneth Galbraith says that "income that is widely distributed is economically serviceable, for it helps to ensure a steady flow of aggregate demand. There is a strong chance that the more unequal the distribution of income, the more dysfunctional it becomes."†

Should we then impose a higher tax on undistributed profits, at least higher than personal tax rates? We already have levels of corporate concentration in Canada that many other developed countries wouldn't accept. Our present tax system encourages the growth of corporate empires. Corporate concentration inhibits competition and keeps prices unnecessarily high. Shouldn't a really competitive free-enterprise economy put more of the corporate after-tax profits into the hands of shareholders?

What about government subsidies to corporations? Some of them are valuable to the economy. But do we really need to help build hotels in the prime minister's riding? The tax commission should have a good hard look at all transfer payments to corporations and see if some – or many – could be eliminated in the future. Transfer payments from all levels of government in the form of "business subsidies and business capital assistance" have been between $10.7 billion and $16.3 billion from 1981 to 1996.** Could we spare a billion to help the poor?

---

* *National Post*, January 11, 1999.
† *The Socially Concerned Today*, University of Toronto Press, 1998.
** Statistics Canada, *Canadian Economic Observer*, Cat. #11-210-XPB 1995/96.

Have we gone too far in giving tax breaks to the resource sector of the economy? Some knowledgeable interested parties suggest that Ottawa and the Alberta government, under heavy pressure from the petroleum industry, gave billions of dollars in unnecessary tax breaks to encourage new development in the oil sands, when such incentives weren't needed. Could we have an informed opinion from the tax commission? For that matter, why have we not seen comparative international rents for the petroleum industry from either the federal or Alberta governments? Columnist Marc Lisac of the *Edmonton Journal* writes:

> How did 90 per cent of synthetic crude royalties disappear in two years? . . . Explanations are hard to come by. . . . Businesses can get revenue breaks in the hundreds of millions of dollars with no one commenting. . . . I also think no one wants to say what royalty cuts are costing Albertans; taxpayers never had a say in the matter.[*]

In fall 1999, the Edmonton-based Parkland Institute released a new study showing that Alaska collected roughly 1.8 times more than Alberta in royalties and taxes for every unit of oil, natural gas, and byproducts produced, and Norway more than three times the amount Alberta collected.

> Had Albertans received the average Alaska rate of energy rent collection, an additional $2.4 billion per annum would have accrued to Alberta's coffers between 1992 and 1997. At the Norwegian rate, Albertans would have received $6.5 billion per annum more in revenues over the same period.
>
> What is critical is that both Norway and Alaska have realized greater returns (royalties and taxes) for every barrel of oil and gas produced while still retaining and sustaining a healthy and prosperous energy industry. . . .
>
> The sheer magnitude of the differences in energy rent collection rates warrants greater scrutiny and accountability.[†]

---

[*] March 9, 1998.

[†] *Are Albertans Receiving Maximum Revenues from Their Oil and Gas?* Prepared by Bruce Macnab for the Parkland Institute.

Of course, Ottawa can't control provincial royalty rates. But why did Justice Minister Anne McLellan talk the federal government into chipping in huge tax concessions worth additional hundreds of millions – if not billions – of dollars? Why did the Chrétien government agree?

There is a long list of other tax questions the commission might wish to examine. Why don't lottery winners pay federal income tax? Should wealthy Canadians receive the basic tax exemption? Should gambling winnings be taxed? Should RRSP money invested outside Canada be exempt? And, on the subject of RRSP tax benefits, should there be a graduated scale of tax relief so that the well-to-do still benefit, but not as much as those with low incomes? Would it not be much fairer to apply tax credits rather than tax deductions for RRSP contributions? Should the GST on expensive luxury items be higher than 7 per cent?

Next, shouldn't we make the income-tax system much more progressive? Is it really fair that someone earning $62,000 a year pays the same basic tax rate as someone earning $6,200,000? Shouldn't we re-examine the tax brackets to make them far more progressive and fairer?

What about inheritance taxes? Among major developed nations, only Canada, Australia, and New Zealand don't have them. Should we examine inheritance taxes on large estates? Why not allow reasonable basic exemptions so that average families are not penalized, but then apply a reasonable tax on the balance?

The tax commission would look not only at how to raise additional revenue, but also how it might cut taxes for Canadians, especially for low-income families and individuals. Why not index the Child Tax Benefit to inflation so its value doesn't erode? Why not raise the basic exemption for those with low incomes even further and index it as well? Ottawa brags about removing hundreds of thousands of low-income Canadians from the tax rolls through 1998 and 1999 increased exemptions, but without indexation some 1.4 million Canadians were pushed back onto those rolls in the past ten years.

On the other hand, do we really need to give high-income families big tax credits or tax deductions associated with child-care costs? In the words of Bruce Little, commenting on CCSD research,

> As a rule, most transfers from Ottawa and the provinces do go
> to the poor, but a surprising proportion of the money winds up

in the pockets of the rich. . . . Almost one-tenth of the money
paid out under the Federal Child Tax Benefit, for example, goes
to families in the top one-fifth of income earners. . . . Canadians
might wonder why upper-income families get anything – let
alone such a substantial share of transfers – if the programs are
really geared to those in need [while] only 17.6 per cent of the
CTB goes to the poorest one-fifth of homes. . . . Why are so
many households that earn over $64,000 a year getting a benefit
aimed at parents with low incomes?*

Good question. In 1996, families in the highest quintile with average
incomes over $110,000 received on average more than $4,000 in transfers. Should that money have gone to help the poor instead?

Let's not get carried away with the idea that tax cuts are the best
solution for poor Canadians. Remember, a great many poor Canadians
have little or no taxable income. In 1997 the average market income for
families in the lowest quintile was only $5,367.

Are there other important things the tax commission should look
at? Lots. Let me mention two. Why not add even more taxes to the sale
of cigarettes? If someone says that will only result in more smuggling,
my answer is let's throw more cigarette smugglers in jail with good long
sentences. We could raise a great deal of money with increased cigarette
taxes and save a great deal in health costs as well.

Everyone in the federal government will tell you that it would be very
difficult to do anything about the Tobin Tax, and even if we could we certainly couldn't do it on a unilateral basis. The proposal, by Nobel
Prize–winner James Tobin, for a tax on currency transactions, has been
the subject of much debate, and great hostility although it has received a
form of token support in the House of Commons. I think the tax commission should have another look. But suppose the commission decides that
it's not feasible? Why not apply a small tax on some domestic financial
transactions? We apply the 7-per-cent GST on almost everything else.

Can we raise some of the $9 billion to help the poor through a mix
of some of the policies listed above? Easily. Would it harm the Canadian

---

* *Globe and Mail*, May 4, 1998.

economy? No way. That $9 billion is money that the poor are going to spend, and they're going to spend it right here in Canada, not in Palm Beach living it up with billionaire Paul Desmarais, or in Rancho Mirage enjoying Frank Sinatra's old estate with billionaire Jimmy Pattison.

Will some extra taxes harm big business who will be the chief but the most reluctant donors? Hardly. It's much better that the money stay in Canada and be recirculated in this economy instead of the profits ending up in the United States or in tax havens like Bermuda, Barbados, the Cayman Islands, and the Isle of Man, to name a few of the most popular destinations for money from Canadian sources.

Besides, haven't the major accounting firm KPMG and the president of Motorola recently told us what a great country Canada is to do business in? According to Micheline Bouchard, chair and president of Motorola,

> Canada is an excellent place to do business. This is a country that provides strong support for the expansion of dynamic, high technology business. . . . To begin with, Canada has an excellent education system and a well-educated population. . . . Another advantage for Canada is our generous set of tax credits and incentives. I think we have the best research and development tax credit programs in the world. . . . Canada is a good choice for further investment because of its commitment to building its infrastructure and exploring the cutting edge of electronic commerce.*

Does anyone think that a 1-per-cent tax increase in relation to GDP would reverse such praise?

Then there's the March 1999 KPMG report, *The Competitive Alternative*, which tells us, among other things, that of all the G-7 countries, Canada has the lowest costs of doing business, almost 8 per cent lower than the U.S., as well as an effective corporate tax rate that is about average for the G-7 and (are you ready for this?) even below the U.S. rate. The report tells us that "Canada is the lowest-cost country," lower than Japan, Germany, Italy, France, Austria, the U.S., and the U.K.

---

* *Toronto Star*, March 13, 1999.

In the eastern region of North America (including Ontario), "costs in the Canadian cities examined are consistently lower than in the U.S. cities." In the western region, "costs in the Canadian cities are well below their counterparts in the U.S." Moreover, "Canada's competitive cost advantages include low land, construction, labour, electricity, and telecommunication costs." In a ten-year overall operating-cost comparison "Canada is the lowest-cost country." As well, "Canada and the United Kingdom both enjoy a significant labour cost advantage over the third-place United States," and "labour costs (including benefits) for the two software operations in Canada are less than sixty-five per cent of those in the U.S., while for manufacturing labour, Canada's costs are about seventy per cent of U.S. costs." And "electricity costs for industrial users are lowest in Canada" while telecommunication costs are the second-lowest.

Auditor-General Denis Desautel's last report showed that Ottawa and the provincial governments are losing about $12 billion *a year* to tax cheats.* Shouldn't Revenue Canada hire additional qualified tax auditors? Wouldn't it be excellent if tax cheaters' fines and interest charges made a major contribution to our Canadian Child Care Community Centres? Desautel is blunt and to the point: "Tax evasion is not a victimless crime. . . . It puts honest business at a competitive disadvantage and it causes honest taxpayers to bear the tax load of those who cheat."

Not all the money we need to help the poor in Canada must come from tax revenues. The auditor-general recently pointed out that had real interest rates during the past two decades maintained the level of earlier years, the federal debt would have been well over $150 billion lower than it is today. Even today, only a 1-per-cent reduction in interest rates on the federal debt alone would save almost $6 billion a year!

Finally, a few words about poor Paul Desmarais. Here we have a man who became a multibillionaire in Canada and now whines about taxes in this country. Desmarais, who started out with a bankrupt bus company in Sudbury, now controls London Life, Investors Group, Great-West Life, and the Power Corporation, not to mention billions of dollars in overseas assets. Poor Paul now tells us that intelligent Canadians have no choice but to emigrate to the United States (Desmarais lives in

---

* April 1999.

a 12,000-square-foot house in a security controlled, drawbridge community in Palm Beach, Florida): "Anyone is better off in the U.S.," Diane Francis quotes him as saying.* According to Peter C. Newman, Demarais controls assets of some $100 billion and "he collects politicians like rare butterflies."†

Isn't it a terrible shame about what the awful taxes in Canada have done to Desmarais? Scott Feschuk summed it up nicely in the *National Post*:

> Very rich man gripes about high taxes in Canada but valiantly vows to persevere, much to the relief of ordinary Canadians who now will not have to pay overseas long-distance rates in order to pick up the phone and tell him personally just how little they care.**

And Charles Gordon of the *Ottawa Citizen* says that we really must study this remarkable paradox that "the more money you have, the more intolerable you find life in Canada."††

* *National Post*, March 12, 1999.
† *Titans*, Toronto, Viking, 1998.
** *National Post* March 13, 1999.
†† *Edmonton Journal*, March 28, 1999.

The Big Disconnect

Please go back for a moment and have a quick look at Figure 12 on page 87. Now, look at how Figure 61 heads downhill instead of up. Quite a difference between the two!

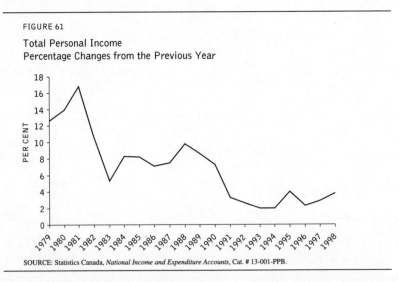

FIGURE 61

Total Personal Income
Percentage Changes from the Previous Year

SOURCE: Statistics Canada, *National Income and Expenditure Accounts*, Cat. # 13-001-PPB.

While GDP in Canada increased, average Canadians saw their incomes plunge from previous prosperous years.

Earlier I wrote about the severe deterioration in the rate of growth of personal income in Canada. Figure 61 even exaggerates that growth because it doesn't deduct inflation but simply measures *total* annual percentage changes for the entire population.

In the preceding chapter I mentioned that improving the overall economy was one of the most important ways to improve the situation of Canada's poor. At least, that's what we have always taken for granted. Why would we ever think otherwise?

Before we look at a key aspect of the Canadian economy, let's examine what has been happening in the United States. Economist Jared Bernstein of the Economic Policy Institute in Washington, D.C., writes:

> The theme of a growing, even booming economy leaving families behind is perhaps nowhere more relevant than in a discussion of American poverty. The fact that poverty did not fall . . . poses a stiff challenge to the highly touted recovery of the 1990s. . . . macroeconomic growth in and of itself is not likely to be enough to significantly reduce poverty. . . . A detailed exploration of the competing explanations strongly suggests that the growth of income and wage inequality and the decline in the real wages of low-income wage workers have been the key determinants of the growth of poverty in the 1980s and 1990s. . . . Wage and employment opportunities facing poor persons will have to expand considerably before we can reasonably expect the poor to work their way out of poverty. . . .
>
> Despite the long recovery . . . poverty was higher at the end of the 1980s than in the late 1970s. This pattern was repeated in the 1990s recovery. . . . Despite continued economic growth, average poverty rates were higher in the 1990s than in the 1980s.

Bernstein goes on to show that in virtually all categories, including persons, families, single heads of households, children, and so on, poverty in the U.S. increased as the American economy boomed, unemployment fell, and the stock market exploded.

Figure 62 is a look at an American calculation of child-poverty rates in seventeen countries. Bernstein points out that not only has poverty in the U.S. been increasing while the American economy booms, but the poverty gap has also been increasing: "In 1979, close to one-third (32.8%) of the poor were in 'deep poverty.' By 1983 . . . this proportion had approached two-fifths (38.5%), where it essentially held throughout the decade." By 1997, the percentage of poor people in the U.S. below 50 per cent of the poverty level had grown from under 30 per cent in 1975 to 41 per cent.

FIGURE 62

Relative Poverty Rates for Children, Mid-1980s to Mid-1990s

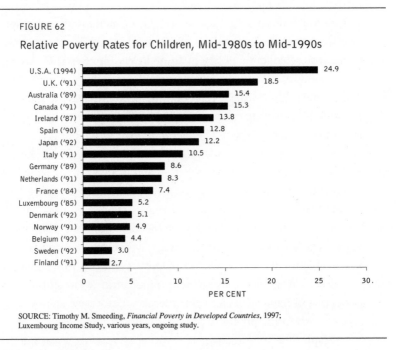

SOURCE: Timothy M. Smeeding, *Financial Poverty in Developed Countries*, 1997; Luxembourg Income Study, various years, ongoing study.

While the American economy boomed, child poverty rates in the U.S. were at disgraceful levels.

Several decades ago, economists thought that poverty would continually diminish (and virtually disappear) as the economy expanded. But, if economic growth is unequally distributed . . . the inverse relationship between growth and poverty is weakened. . . . [The result is a] disconnect between overall economic growth and poverty rates [while] American income inequality has been increasing real incomes at the top of the income scale and lowering them at the bottom.

In his conclusion, Bernstein writes:

> Despite long economic recoveries over the 1980s and 1990s, poverty rates remain significantly higher than would be expected given the overall economic growth. . . .
>
> This leads us to suspect that weak conditions in the low-wage labor market must be making it difficult for low-wage workers to generate family income levels that would lift them above the poverty line.*

I haven't read anything, anywhere, that so succinctly defines what has been happening in North America to produce such persistently high levels of growing and deepening poverty. Let me repeat two key points. First, there is now a "disconnect" between growth in the economy and poverty rates. Second, "income inequality has been increasing real incomes at the top of the income scale and lowering them at the bottom."

Both of these things are exactly what we've seen happening in Canada in this book.

Previously, we all took for granted that with an improving economy, more GDP, and lower unemployment, there would be more and better jobs for the poor and the standard of living for most of the population would rise. But, it hasn't worked that way. I have said for years that our basic economic policy should be as close as possible to a full-employment strategy. But, as Bernstein points out, if there is a basic disconnect and if income inequality inhibits poverty reduction, don't we then end up with the terribly unjust and frustrating situation of an improving economy failing to benefit those who most require an improvement in their standard of living? Look at the very low unemployment rates in the U.S. and look at their very high poverty rates. Look at the growth of GDP in Canada and our own continuing high poverty rates.

I can think of a dozen different ways in which the Canadian economy has been badly mismanaged during the past quarter-century, and a dozen ways in which we could improve our overall economic performance,

---

* *The State of Working America*, Cornell University Press, 1999.

including a low real interest-rate monetary policy, investing much more in research-and-development and high-tech industries, curtailing rapidly growing foreign ownership and corporate concentration in Canada, more and better education and job training funding, encouraging more value-added instead of exporting unfinished resources as quickly as possible, using our energy resources to create jobs in Canada instead of pipelining them in ever-increasing volumes out of the country so that our chief trade competitor can better afford to sell more labour-intensive finished products to Canadians, and other policies already mentioned in this book.

But given what has happened in our country since the mid-1980s, why would any improved economic strategy do very much to help the poor? As long as the country is led by the likes of Brian Mulroney, Michael Wilson, Jean Chrétien, and Paul Martin, the poor will not only always be with us, but they will likely suffer even more. Just wait until the next recession. This is a harsh analysis, but I see nothing in the record of our recent political leaders that leads me to conclude otherwise.

There are two major reasons for this forecast of continuing indifference. First, our political system has become more and more Americanized, more and more dependent on the big bucks from the corporations (a growing number of which are American-controlled) that finance our politicians and our political process. The second is the growing impact of globalization. A joke that's been around for about three years is "The good news is that the economy is creating hundreds of thousands of new jobs. The bad news is that to support your family, you need three of them." Globalization has hurt employment in Canada and suppressed wage increases. It has increased the need for money for social spending, while at the same time hampering government's ability to raise the money.

The *Toronto Star* in a December 1998 editorial asked whether globalization has gone too far.

In a recent book . . . Dani Rodrik, a Harvard University professor of international political economy, blames globalization for increasing the income disparity in the U.S. by keeping wages low.

He claims that there are various channels through which the international economy impinges on domestic labour markets:

- By giving corporations a great deal more bargaining power over their workers.
- By changing norms and institutions.
- By undermining social support systems.

But as Rodrik asks, how can labour expect to win when employers can credibly say: "Don't ask for wage increases, don't ask for improvements in labour standards or in work conditions, because if you do, we can go elsewhere."

Recognizing that some Canadians would lose because of its free trade deal, the Mulroney government promised in 1988 to bring in the best adjustment package "in the world."

But there never was an adjustment package.

And our governments subsequently have forgotten about the impacts of free trade – and globalization generally – when they cut welfare, unemployment insurance and money for training.

Critics of the Canada–U.S. free trade deal no doubt would find many parallels between Rodrik's analysis and the concerns they raised a decade ago.

As Rodrik's book reminds us, those concerns, unfortunately, have not gone away.[*]

In my previous book, *At Twilight in the Country,* I wrote about what I perceive to be a growing backlash against neo-conservatism and globalization: "The backlash can and must turn into a political revolt. The public is now beginning to understand that the elite's neoconservative globalization . . . represents a massive transfer of power and wealth from citizens and employees to corporations and the already wealthy." But the top political and economic leaders in both the United States and Canada like what has been happening. Why wouldn't they? Many of

---

[*] December 28, 1998. Rodrik's book is *Has Globalization Gone Too Far?* Institute for International Economics, 1997.

them have already received or will receive a huge direct personal benefit.

In the United States a new Yale University study shows that since 1979 a remarkable 97 per cent of all income increases has gone to the top 20 per cent of families, while the millions of poor have become even poorer.* In Canada, the ten wealthiest families have assets greater than the combined annual employment earnings of all the men and women in the labour force in Newfoundland, Prince Edward Island, Nova Scotia, New Brunswick, Manitoba, and Saskatchewan put together.

In Canada, just as in the U.S., the big disconnect is clearly both economic and political. The economic disconnect results in hunger, homelessness, despair, suffering, and abundant human tragedy. The political disconnect that causes this misery is the gigantic disconnect between our political leaders and most of the rest of the population.

---

* The *Economist*, May 15, 1999. Study by Bruce Ackerman and Ann Alstott, Yale University.

Conclusion

There is no excuse for the high levels of poverty in Canada. None. None whatsoever.

Through inept, uncaring, hypocritical government we have badly failed our own people.

Through selfishness, greed, indifference, and cruelty we have forced millions of men, women, and children to struggle through lives of misery, despair, and suffering.

Instead of comprehensive political, social, and economic solutions to the decades of excessive poverty in our country, we have offered pious, self-righteous rhetoric and Band-aid, patchwork, inconsequential and totally inadequate cosmetic improvisations.

In the past, over and over and over again, year after year, decade after decade, we've been told that the poor will have to wait until the government's financial situation has improved. Now the federal government is expecting large surpluses. How much longer will the poor have to wait?

Let us consider one last table. Here is a look at our national per capita net worth.

1979	$39,246	1989	75,959
1980	44,450	1990	77,599
1981	49,001	1991	77,907
1982	51,802	1992	77,937
1983	53,523	1993	79,182
1984	55,901	1994	81,969
1985	57,900	1995	84,078
1986	61,460	1996	85,681
1987	65,688	1997	88,565
1988	71,001	1998	90,934

In 1979, there were 3.9 million Canadians living in poverty. By 1997 the number had grown to over 5.2 million.* So, while our per capita net worth increased by more than 125 per cent, the number of poor people in Canada, instead of falling, increased by a third.

Given the above, and given what we've already seen in this book, is there really any reason to believe that there will be much change for the better in the future?

Now, yet again, we're hearing how well Canada is doing. Today, as I'm writing these words, the *Globe and Mail* tells us, "The Canadian economy is on a roll these days, giving economists and business owners reason to hope the country could be settling in for some long term growth."† A *Toronto Star* business reporter is equally enthusiastic: "Our economy is just too good to be true. It's an economic portrait that appears almost utopian; strong job creation, surging consumer confidence, booming markets, low inflation, falling interest rates and predictions of a glistening road ahead."** But given its performance since the election in 1993, is there any reason to believe that the Chrétien government will introduce policies that will allow Canada's poor to walk down that glistening road?

In their concluding remarks at Geneva, NAPO pulled no punches: "The Canadian federal government . . . bears much of the responsibility for the injustices and persecution that exists today. . . . We have poverty

* Statistics Canada, *The Daily*, April 1, 1999, and Cat. #13-214 PPB. Net worth table is in current dollars.
† May 5, 1999.
** May 5, 1999.

because of the failure of government. . . . There is every indication that the failure of governments to act is grounded in a class bias."

Where, then, are the compassion, humanity, and leadership that we need to come from? We already know that charity can offer only a small part of the help that must be provided every day. Thank God for all the caring and kind people who do donate to charities or directly to the poor. I know one man who quietly, privately, gives tens of thousands of dollars every year, year in and year out, to school lunch programs, to poor schools, to shelters, to poor families, and to others. He is a marvellous, compassionate, self-effacing, humble human being whose heart is full of love.

All across Canada there are countless acts of benevolent charity every single day. But, charity can hardly be a substitute for the national public programs that are needed to help the poor. In recent years, new corporate charity amounted to only about 2 per cent of the federal government's spending cutbacks to our already inadequate social programs.

Remarkably, the richest 20 per cent of Canadian households, with average incomes of $110,000, contribute a smaller portion of their income to "gifts and contributions" than the poorest fifth. Meanwhile, economist Jim Stanford points out: "Before-tax corporate profits grew by $47 billion between 1992 and 1997. But during the same period, the rate of corporate giving declined by about one-quarter to just over one per cent of before-tax profits."* Yet, incredibly, according to the far right in Canada, charity can be relied on to look after the needy, with little government intervention.

In January 1999, the Canadian Press reported a new study under the title "POOR DONATE MORE THAN BETTER-OFF CANADIANS":

> Canadian charities would bring in $8 billion more each year if well-off families donated as generously as do low-income families, says the president of the Canadian Centre for Philanthropy.
> Canadians who make less than $20,000 a year donate more than three times more of their income to charities than those families taking in $80,000 a year.

---

* "The Spirit of Giving" from Jim Stanford's newsletter *Facts from the Fringe*, December 1998.

I'll leave you to contemplate for yourself the meaning of the above. Let's leave our economic elite now and return to our political leaders.

What do you call a politician who, in opposition, passionately pleads for increased spending to help the poor, but then, when elected to power, drastically cuts funds for the poor? A hypocrite? Worse? Here is the same man, Paul Martin, in a 1997 interview: "The level of child poverty in this country is a disgrace and there has got to be a great national effort to directly deal with that."* Then, a few months later, in his February 1998 budget address:

> Our goals today remain what they were when Canadians placed their trust in us in 1993: first, to build a country of opportunity – of jobs and growth – one where every Canadian has equal access to the avenues of success that will ensure a better standard of living; and second, to safeguard and strengthen a caring, compassionate society.

Equal access to the avenues of success? A caring, compassionate society?

Let us now consider our prime minister. In 1996, the U.N. secretary-general, Boutros Boutros-Ghali, wrote to Jean Chrétien, expressing concern about Canada's high poverty rates and requesting information about Canada's intention to live up to its pledge to reduce poverty under our commitments to the World Summit for Social Development. The prime minister replied:

> Dear Mr. Secretary-General:
>
> Allow me first to reaffirm the importance we attach to the goals of the Social Summit.
>
> In Canada, government initiatives are being taken at both federal and provincial levels, and in collaboration with business and local communities, to create and strengthen policies and programmes aimed at reducing the number of people living in poverty, while at the same time providing effective social safety nets.

---

* *World Economic Affairs*, Autumn 1997.

Important measures include: new Employment Insurance legislation to help unemployed Canadians return to the labour force; measures to assist low-income families with children; programmes for youth geared to enhancing work opportunities; and more flexible transfer payments to provinces to support the development of innovative social programmes.

Yours sincerely,
Jean Chrétien.

Surely, one must view with contempt such disinformation. The Chrétien government's "new Employment Insurance legislation" has brought misery to large numbers of Canadians across the country, forcing many, who should qualify, to rely on terribly inadequate welfare. The "measures to assist low-income families with children" have ignored the needs of a large percentage of the most needy families. "Programmes aimed at reducing the number of people living in poverty" have been either non-existent or largely inadequate and ineffective. "More flexible transfer payments to provinces to support the development of innovative social programs" have meant the loss of billions of dollars in badly needed provincial social funding.

Judge for yourself if the prime minister is a hypocrite or worse.

In the 1998 Throne Speech the Chrétien government indicated that

a country that has decided to invest in its children is a country that is confident of its future. A country that invests in its children successfully will have a better future. One of our objectives as a country should be to ensure that all Canadian children have the best possible opportunity to develop their full potential.

The experiences of Canada's children, especially in the early years, influence their health, their well-being, and their ability to learn and adapt throughout their entire lives. By investing now in the well-being of today's children, we improve the long-term health of our society.

Similar sanctimonious, empty rhetoric has been uttered in Throne Speeches for decades while child poverty in Canada has grown to disgraceful levels.

Two other Chrétien ministers have offered their views on this topic. In an astonishing response to the U.N.'s criticism of the high poverty levels in Canada, Justice Minister Anne McLellan told Canadians, "The pressures of the global economy make it harder for Canada and other governments to close the gap between rich and poor. . . ."* And, with almost 1.5 million Canadian children living in poverty, Industry Minister John Manley told us it would be "a tragedy" if any Canadian NHL teams moved to the United States, so we had better lower Canadian taxes to U.S. rates. "As much as possible we need to be trying to bench-mark ourselves to the United States."† The real tragedy would be if the likes of Anne McLellan and John Manley were allowed to influence future government poverty policy.

Do we or do we not care about Canadian children? So far the answer seems to be that we care very little.

What kind of country lets so many children live lives in such deprived circumstances? Surely if we indeed really do care, we must do much, much more in the future to help poor families with better job training, better education opportunities, adequate affordable housing, quality child care, and, urgently, adequate income support until they can become self-sufficient.

As David Ross and the CCSD have asked, "What if producing healthy children was the main objective of anti-poverty efforts in Canada? It would mean that far more would have to be taken into con-sideration beyond simply providing the 'basic necessities' of life – typ-ically identified as minimum levels of food and shelter."**

For many years now we Canadians haven't been bothered to provide even the minimum levels of assistance to our poor. Somehow in Canada we have either forgotten or intentionally ignored the abundant international evidence that well-planned social assistance allows people to lead much better, healthier, more productive lives. Proper social assistance provides a chance for the poor, a life-saver during critical periods, an opportunity to become contributing, respected full members

---

* *Edmonton Journal*, November 27, 1998.

† *National Post*, May 1, 1999.

** *Income and Child Well-being: A new perspective on the poverty debate* by David P. Ross and Paul Roberts, CCSD, May 1999.

of the community. Good social programs will lead to more productivity, more tax revenues from workers, reduced welfare payments, and less crime and violence. And a happier, healthier population.

On May 10, 1999, I spoke to the students at three inner-city schools. There were kids of every size, colour, and religion. In a grade-one class I met two dozen beautiful poor children, most from single-parent families, some from group or foster homes. I met a wonderful seven-year-old immigrant boy who was in an hour-long one-on-one remedial session with a teacher. The boy beamed as he showed me how he was learning to read. Later, the principal told me the funds for this program expire this year and will not be renewed. I met a pretty, sad-faced fourteen-year-old girl with dark circles under her eyes. She was being abused at home, the principal told me. The intervention-program funds had been cut back. She wasn't getting the help she needed. A bright-eyed aboriginal girl came up to me after my talk and asked me how she could go to university when it looked like there wouldn't be enough money in the family to allow her to continue on to high school. Everywhere I turned I saw kids you wanted to hug, to sit down and talk with. And I saw overloaded, heroic teachers just barely able to cope with the problems they faced every day: poor kids in trouble, poor junior-high kids who were already giving up, poor kids who desperately needed help. All the teachers stressed the same thing: the government cutbacks were hurting poor children badly. "It's a tragedy," they said.

One of the schools is even selling its computers in the face of inadequate funding and soaring deficits.

Don't for a moment believe the nonsense that a globalized economy makes it impossible for us to reduce the levels of poverty in Canada. If any government apologist offers you that limp excuse, show them the charts of international poverty comparisons in this book. It *is* true that globalization has been increasing the gap between rich and poor. And it is true that globalization makes it more difficult for countries to manage their own affairs. But it is also true that *many other countries* have limited the impact of globalization and have radically reduced poverty to levels far below our own.

And don't accept the relentless right-wing selling job that so often appears in our daily press. There *are* much better, much fairer, much more egalitarian, practical, realistic ways of running a country. And there are benevolent and beneficial ways of reducing poverty to produce a more civil, more just society.

However, as we have seen, the Americanization of Canada, a political system that is more and more dependent on big money, terrible levels of corporate concentration and foreign ownership, all combine to make real change more difficult. Ultimately, there can be only one real solution to our problems of poverty and social injustice. To expect our political and economic elite to make the necessary changes without very strong political pressure is naïve in the extreme.

Our goal should be clear. Let's ensure that we deal with the prevention of poverty in Canada, not simply engage in attempts to alleviate poverty after it is solidly entrenched in concrete in our society. To achieve this goal many more men and women must become directly involved in politics. If even one-fifth of the poor in Canada became directly involved in the political life of our country, they could change the future. If even 5 per cent of adult Canadians were to become active in federal politics, they could completely dominate the political power structure of our country. If even 5 per cent of adult Canadians were to contribute $100 to the political party of their choice, they could overwhelm the dominance of corporate political contributions.

As much as anything, this book is about the kind of country we want to have. Let's reread Article XXV of the U.N.'s Universal Declaration of Human Rights:

> Everyone has the right to a standard of living adequate for health and well-being of himself and of his family, including food, clothing, housing and medical care and necessary social services, and the right to security in the event of unemployment, sickness, disability, widowhood, old age and other loss of livelihood. . . . Motherhood and childhood are entitled to special care and assistance.

How far we Canadians have strayed from these goals. How hypocritical we've become in our lip service to human rights. How disgraceful and tragic that we have, in Gro Bruntland's words, allowed "a policy failure that degrades people – those who suffer it, and those who tolerate it."

In the 1998 U.N. *Human Development Report* there are two special sentences: "But trend is not destiny. None of these outcomes is inevitable."

We *can* change things in Canada. We *can* have a much better, fairer country. We *can* stop cheating our children of their lives. There *are* viable solutions to the injustices we have been tolerating.

My own decades of travel all across our country tell me that the vast majority of Canadians are compassionate, caring people, concerned with social justice. The polls show that most Canadians consider themselves to be religious and conscientious. Let's then see what the religions say.

Compassion is one of the central messages of Christianity:

> For Jesus, compassion was the central quality of God. . . .
> Compassion is associated with feeling the suffering of some-
> body else and being moved by that suffering to do something.*

And in Judaism, Proverbs 29:7 in the Holy Scriptures:

> The righteous taketh knowledge of the cause of the poor; the
> wicked understandeth not knowledge.

In Deuteronomy 15:7-11:

> Thou shall not harden thy heart, nor shut thy hand from thy
> needy brother; but thou shalt surely open thy hand unto him,
> and shalt surely lend him sufficient for his need in that which he
> wanteth.

In the Quran 51:19:

> True charity in the highest sense includes all the help that can
> be provided to the needy. . . . In the wealth of the rich, the poor
> and the outcast has a due share.

---

* Marcus J. Borg, *Meeting Jesus Again for the First Time*, Harper, 1994.

In the Hadith:

> The humanity of the Prophet Muhammad is central to Islam. He said, "No man is a true believer unless he desires for his fellowman that which he desires for himself."

From the Dalai Lama of Tibet:

> My message is the practice of compassion, love and kindness. Compassion can be put into practice if one recognizes the fact that every human being is a member of humanity and the human family regardless of differences in religion, culture, color and creed. Deep down there is no difference.

Buddha taught that

> compassion is the mind of benevolence, rescuing and liberating ... without discrimination.

We Canadians *can* alleviate the suffering. We can open our hearts and our hands and take up the cause of the poor and provide them with their due share. We can and we must.

Our first goal should be to see that every poor child in Canada is treated as we would treat our very own children.

Nothing less will do.

Appendix One
Measuring Poverty

One of the best of the many articles and papers on the measurement of poverty in Canada comes from the excellent organization, the National Council of Welfare. *A New Poverty Line: Yes, No or Maybe?* is a discussion paper published by the council in March 1999. The National Council of Welfare was established by the Government Organization Act, 1969, as a citizens' advisory body to the federal government. It advises the Minister of Human Resources Development on matters of concern to low-income Canadians.

The council consists of members drawn from across Canada and appointed by the governor-in-council. All are private citizens and serve in their personal capacities rather than as representatives of organizations or agencies. The membership of the council has included past and present welfare recipients, public-housing tenants, and other low-income people, as well as educators, social workers, and people involved in voluntary or charitable organizations.

I am grateful to the council for allowing me to publish the following extracts from *A New Poverty Line*.

The debate in Canada on poverty lines goes back at least a decade and has produced much more heat than light. Most of the attacks on Statistics Canada's "low income cut-offs" or LICOs are ideologically motivated and ignore the four most basic facts about poverty and poverty lines:

- All poverty lines are relative.
- All poverty lines are arbitrary.
- Poverty lines are a research tool for measuring the incomes of *groups* of people, not a measure of *individual* need.
- Some poverty lines are better than others, but none of them is perfect.

All poverty lines are relative. Our view of poverty in Canada is profoundly different than it was a century ago, and it is profoundly different from current views of poverty in Greece, Peru, Nepal, Somalia and most other countries of the world.

A century ago, people in Canada would have considered someone poor if they did not have a horse or some other beast of burden for their work and basic transportation. Today, poverty is more likely to be measured in terms of reasonable access to buses or subways in cities or access to an automobile or truck in rural areas.

Poverty is also relative in the sense that every culture has its own ideas about what is needed to be part of the mainstream of society. Being able to afford meat products is considered necessary in many western cultures, but it would not be considered very important in a country where most people are vegetarians because of their religious beliefs. Warm winter clothing and central heating are vital in a country like Canada, and anything but a necessity in Honduras or Tahiti.

All poverty lines are arbitrary. Some poverty lines are drawn statistically and some are drawn by measuring the cost of a "market basket" of essential goods and services. Both types of lines are equally arbitrary.

In lines which are drawn statistically, someone has to decide what raw data to use and what methodology to use to get from the data to the poverty lines. One measure that is used in some international studies of poverty is one-half of median income or the half-way point for family income in each country. The decisions to use one-half rather than one-third of median income and to use median income rather than average income are both arbitrary.

In lines which are drawn from market baskets of goods and services, someone has to decide what goes in the basket and what does not. That is not nearly as easy as it sounds. How many rolls of toilet paper would a family of four reasonably use every week? How much clothing, new or used, would that same family need to buy in a typical month? What is a reasonable budget for school supplies over the course of a year? The answers to these and a host of other questions determine the overall cost of the market basket.

Poverty lines are a research tool for measuring the incomes of groups of people, not a measure of individual need. The primary limitation of both statistical poverty lines and market baskets of goods and services is that they cannot cover all the exceptions to the rule. Poverty lines work best when they are used to measure the incomes of large groups of people. They work worst when people try to apply them to individuals.

Take the cost of housing, for example. Some people have mortgages and others do not. Some people live in government-subsidized housing. Some people live in well-insulated apartments where the rent includes heating, while others rent houses which are poorly insulated and have to pay sizable heating bills on their own. A couple with two young children might be able to manage with two bedrooms, but a couple with a teenage boy and a teenage girl would need three bedrooms.

The people who draw poverty lines have to make compromises to keep the number of lines down to a reasonable total. The idea is to have poverty lines that cover the most common type of families in different parts of the country. All poverty lines are based on the number of people in the family, and some of them also take account of the size of the community where they live. Most poverty lines do not vary with the type of housing or the age of the people in the household.

There will always be individual cases where family needs are not well covered by any given poverty line. This is the reason welfare programs use a "needs test" for each individual case. With a needs test, all the family's needs and all its source of incomes are considered. Welfare entitlements can be increased to cover the added cost of prescription drugs for a child with asthma or additional transportation costs in a very remote area or the cost of child care to allow parents to work full-time in the paid labour force.

Some poverty lines are better than others, but none of them is perfect. No matter how hard the experts try, they cannot escape the first three facts about poverty lines. Poverty lines will always be relative, poverty lines will always be arbitrary, and they will always be suitable for research and unsuitable as a measure of individual well-being. The most we can hope for is a useful research tool that is easily understood and widely accepted.

Some poverty lines are better than others at measuring changes in poverty over time. That is a very desirable feature, because it allows researchers to see the impact of changes in economic conditions or changes in government policy. Statistics Canada's low income cut-offs are very good in reflecting the ups and downs of the economic cycle. However, poverty lines based on average or median income tend to change very little from year to year and are much less useful in measuring poverty over time.

Some poverty lines are better than others because they focus on disposable income or cash on hand. The low income cut-offs are based on income *after* government transfer payments such as welfare, unemployment insurance or the Canada Child Tax Benefit but *before* income taxes. Most market basket poverty lines are after-tax measures that reflect the cost of sales taxes as well as income taxes. That is because people actually purchase the items in the market basket, and they have to pay any federal, provincial or territorial sales taxes on taxable items when they make their purchases.

Some poverty lines are better than others because they are easily understood and therefore easily accepted. One of the problems that has dogged the low income cut-offs is the fact that the methodology used to derive the lines is not easily explained. Lines based on a market basket of goods and services are much more straight-forward and much more likely to be accepted as reasonable by the general public.

Why Have Poverty Lines At All?

Given all the limitations and shortcomings, why should Statistics Canada or anyone else go to all the trouble of developing poverty lines? The answer to that question goes to the heart of our existence as a political and economic democracy.

Canadians have a well-honed sense of fair play that dates from our beginnings as a nation. In politics, we accept the principle of one person, one vote and the principle that governments derive their mandate to govern from the collective will of voters. In economics, we pride ourselves on the ideal of equal opportunity for all and in making it possible for everyone to share in the vast bounty that is Canada.

Simply put, poverty lines are one measure of how well our democracy is working. They delineate that minority within the population that stands apart from the mainstream of Canadian life because of meagre income.

The statistics that come from poverty lines are every bit as valuable as widely accepted statistics such as the unemployment rate and Consumer Price Index, yet they always seem to instill fear in the hearts of governments. Governments are loath to admit that poverty exists in a country like Canada, but everyone knows that poverty exists – with or without official government sanction.

Poverty lines also give us the ability to take concrete steps to reduce the risk of poverty and to measure how good a job we are doing. The watershed in social policy is between the people who are content simply to count the number of poor people and those who use poverty statistics to champion better programs and policies for disadvantaged Canadians.

The National Council of Welfare's biggest complaint with the very low poverty lines supported by the Fraser Institute of British Columbia, for example, has been that the institute's apparent interest in poverty lines is to show that poverty is not a problem in Canada and does not warrant action by government.

Our Council has maintained from the beginning that poverty statistics are only a first step. Having identified groups of people who are poor or most likely to be poor, we follow through by putting forward policy options to ease the burden of poverty and by promoting our proposals through our reports and our representations to government.

Our annual *Poverty Profile* report tracks how well or how poorly Canada is doing in the fight against poverty and identifies the groups of people who face the highest risks of poverty. Our other reports build on this data with detailed policy recommendations to government.

The Search for Alternatives

Statistics Canada published a discussion paper in 1989 on alternatives to the LICOs that included a technical review of many of the shortcomings of LICOs. The paper led to interest in a poverty line known as a "low income measure" or LIM. LIMs were equal to one-half of median income adjusted for family size, but there was only one set of LIMs for all parts of Canada.

Many social policy groups were enthusiastic about LIMs at first. The methodology was simple and in line with some of the international research on poverty. Unfortunately, the big disadvantage with LIMs turned out to be that poverty statistics based on LIMs were relatively flat over time – that is, poverty rates during the worst part of the economic cycle were not very different from poverty rates during the best part of the cycle. Statistics Canada has published several years' worth of poverty data based on LIMs, but there has been little sustained interest in LIMs from social policy groups.

A number of social planning and research agencies have done market baskets for their own areas over the years. Some of the baskets could probably double as poverty lines, but others are more like guides to reasonable living standards. The lines developed by the Montreal Diet Dispensary reflect a bare-bones approach to daily needs, for example, while the basket of the Community Social Planning Council of Toronto includes items that go beyond what most people would consider necessities.

Each of the planning and research groups has chosen particular family types as the focus of its work. That often makes it difficult to compare the totals from one city to another. It also leaves a number of large cities and smaller population centres without any guidelines at all.

One researcher who has done extensive work on market basket measures of poverty is Christopher A. Sarlo of Nipissing University in North Bay, Ontario. Professor Sarlo has developed poverty lines for all provinces and all major cities with the support of the Fraser Institute, a right-wing think tank based in Vancouver.

Professor Sarlo's work has attracted the interest of other right-wing groups, some government officials and some media editorialists. The salient feature of his poverty lines is that they are far lower than the LICOs and almost all of the other lines used from time to time by social policy researchers and therefore produce poverty rates that are very low.

For example, the Sarlo food basket contains no coffee or tea. There are no health care items in the basket on the grounds that poor people should be able to get charity dental services from dentists in the community and they should be able to pick up free eyeglasses from the local Lions Club.

Finally, researchers at Human Resources Development Canada are taking the lead in efforts to develop "market basket measures" of poverty as a special project for the federal, provincial and territorial governments. The project is an attempt to develop a "consensus definition" of poverty as an alternative to existing measures, and it arose in part from the collective efforts of governments that went into the new Canada Child Tax Benefit.

A paper on the market basket measure or MBMs was published in March 1998 and distributed to a very limited number of people inside and outside government. A more public release in December 1998 prompted charges that governments were trying to get rid of poverty by lowering the lines rather than doing anything of substance. British Columbia's Minister of Human Resources bluntly told the federal government that the market basket approach to measuring poverty was not acceptable. "The Government of British Columbia's commitment is to reducing, resolving, and eliminating child poverty, not redefining it," the Minister said in a letter to the federal Minister of Human Resources Development.

The March 1998 paper said the MBMs are not a final product, but many social policy groups believe that the eventual and inevitable result of the exercise will be some kind of market basket poverty line to replace the LICOs.

Some anti-poverty groups consider the push for market basket poverty lines a form of poor-bashing. They say that many of the statistical measures used by governments – including the unemployment rate and the Consumer Price Index – are difficult to understand and are fraught with methodological shortcomings. Yet the only statistical measures that governments really do not accept and really want to change are the low income cut-offs.

Other excellent papers on defining poverty are Maryanne Webber, *Measuring Low Income and Poverty in Canada: An Update*, Statistics Canada, Income Statistics Division, May 1998; Richard Shillington, *What Do We Mean by Poverty?* http://home.istar.ca/~ers2/poverty/ MBM.htm January 15, 1999; *The Market Basket Measure*, Applied Research Bulletin, vol. 4, no. 2, 1998. Human Resources Development Canada. See also the Winter 1997 issue of the Statistics Canada, *Perspectives*. On the question of the validity of the LICOs measurement, here are Statistics Canada's own words:

Low-income cutoffs (LICOs) are established using data from Statistics Canada's Family Expenditure Survey. They are intended to convey the income level at which a family may be in straitened circumstance because it has to spend a greater portion of its income on the basics (food, shelter and clothing) than the average family of similar size. The LICO varies by family size and by size of community.*

Note again the words "straitened circumstance."

---

* *The Daily*, July 7, 1997.

Appendix Two

Canada's Trade Balance and the Free Trade Agreement

The FTA has been only one of several factors in the poor performance of the Canadian economy described in this book. But the picture we get from our business press is so blinkered that it's difficult for most Canadians who read the papers to believe that the FTA has been anything but a smashing success. According to the *Financial Post*, "The Free Trade Agreement with the U.S. has led to nearly a decade of prosperity and a much more competitive economy."[*] Some prosperity! Diane Francis calls free trade "demonstrably the best public policy ever adopted by Canada."[†] Francis goes on to suggest, if you can believe it, that "voters who don't know the facts should be weeded out until they grasp them." A third world dictator would be proud. According to Brian Mulroney, "free trade has been the best thing ever for Canada."

Almost every time the proponents of the FTA or NAFTA brag about how enormously successful the agreements have been for Canada, they focus exclusively on the huge increase in exports. As we've already seen in this book, exports are only one part of the economic landscape that needs to be examined in evaluating the impact of the agreement.

---

[*] October 24, 1998.

[†] *National Post*, November 19, 1998.

It is true that exports have almost doubled during the first FTA decade. But most economists will tell you that a Canadian dollar that plummeted from 84 cents (U.S.) in 1988 to as low as 63 cents in 1999, was probably the most important factor in increased exports. According to the Conference Board of Canada, "Were it not for the low C$, our trading industries would be in deep trouble."*

I asked Statistics Canada to run some numbers for me from their Canadian Socio-economic Information Management System (CAN SIM) database. Here are exports of goods and services in constant 1992 dollars, and imports as well.

Exports and Imports of Goods and Services
At 1992 Prices (millions of dollars)

	Exports	Imports
1979	98,092	88,772
1980	99,897	93,296
1981	103,568	103,147
1982	102,305	86,865
1983	108,822	96,247
1984	129,078	113,709
1985	136,229	123,759
1986	143,359	134,335
1987	148,093	141,920
1988	162,162	161,382
	$1,231,605	$1,143,432
1989	164,203	171,580
1990	171,977	175,482
1991	175,926	181,120
1992	189,784	192,393
1993	210,537	206,575
1994	238,141	223,710
1995	259,188	238,101
1996	274,504	250,956
1997	296,364	284,434
1998	320,301	302,576
	$2,300,825	$2,226,927

* *Financial Post*, October 16, 1998.

In the ten years before the FTA, 1979 to 1988, Canada's surplus of exports over imports came to $88.173 billion. During the first decade of the FTA, our surplus dropped by $14.275 billion, down to $73.898 billion.

Let me repeat: our trade balance *dropped* by over $14 billion.

If anyone has read these trade-balance results in any Canadian newspaper or magazine before this book was sent to the publisher, mail me the clipping and I'll send you a nice present.

Sergio Marchi, when he was minister for International Trade, and Industry Minister John Manley and their staffs are very fond of telling Canadians that every billion dollars of exports creates or sustains 11,000 jobs. On that basis, the drop of over $14 billion in our trade balance means a loss of over 157,000 Canadian jobs.

In May 1999, without mentioning the information above or the disastrous employment figures detailed earlier in this book, I asked Sergio Marchi what importance he attached to Canada's trade balance. He replied that it was an "important barometer of how well our country is doing" and "a sign of a competitive economy that provides the opportunity for jobs and prosperity for an ever-greater number of Canadians."*

---

* Letter to the author, June 1, 1999.

Appendix Three

Measuring Poverty in the United States

Jared Bernstein of the Economic Policy Institute in Washington, D.C., writes,

> A common criticism of the official poverty lines (in the U.S.) is that they no longer reflect even minimal levels of consumption and thus underestimate the extent of poverty. The original consumption data was collected in 1955. . . . If the poverty lines were recalculated today, they would be higher (as would poverty rates) since the food budget would be multiplied by a number larger than three.

For example, whereas the official poverty rate in the U.S. in 1992 was only 14.5 per cent, a U.S. National Research Council alternative updated measurement showed the rate to be 18.1 per cent. For children under eighteen, the rate went from 21.9 per cent to 26.4 per cent. Overall, the number of people living in poverty in the U.S. would have increased by about nine million. In 1997, the official U.S. poverty rate was 13.3 per cent. Using less than half of the median income as a measurement, the rate would have jumped to 22.3 per cent. Meanwhile, Bernstein calculated that family income "of prime-age families in the bottom 20%" in 1996 dollars fell from an average of $15,465 in 1979 to $12,628 in 1996, while the percentage of the working poor with full-time, year-round jobs *grew* from 13.6 per cent in 1974 to 16.9 per cent in 1997.

Appendix Four
Avoiding Paying Taxes in Canada

Roger Gordon is a noted tax expert from the University of Michigan. Here are his words from the *Canadian Tax Journal*:

There are many mechanisms that firms have available to shift taxable income across countries. One is use of debt. Firms can do all their borrowing in Canada and then use equity finance to help finance operations elsewhere. By concentrating their interest deductions in their Canadian subsidiary, they would reduce their Canadian taxable income while raising taxable income abroad. Another means of income shifting is manipulation of transfer pricing. In intrafirm transactions, the Canadian subsidiary could be paid a low price for the goods it sells and charged a high price for the goods it buys, thereby reducing taxable income in Canada and raising taxable income elsewhere. These are only a few examples of the mechanisms that firms can use to reduce their Canadian tax base.

In addition the report* proposes restricting the deductibility of interest when the borrowing is done for the purpose of

---

* "The Mintz Report," *Report of the Technical Committee on Business Taxation* chaired by Jack M. Mintz, December 1997.

financing capital abroad. The intent is to prevent firms from doing all their worldwide borrowing here and to allow the deduction of interest only on funds borrowed to finance Canadian investment.*

Bill Tieleman, president of West Star Communications in Vancouver, commented on auditor-general and Public Accounts Committee reports:

The 1993 report states that the auditor-general, who operates independently from government, found that "Canadian corporations have received nearly $600 million in the form of tax-exempt dividends from Barbados, Cyprus, Ireland, Liberia, the Netherlands and Switzerland that represents a loss of about $240 million in tax revenues for Canada, since the other countries have not collected any tax on those amounts.

The May 1996 auditor-general's report states that

large corporations, particularly those with extensive domestic and foreign operations, have significant opportunities and resources to enter into tax avoidance schemes.

However,

the Department of Revenue's large business tax auditors referred only 27 cases to the tax avoidance unit in 1994-95. Only one referral was made by its large business tax auditors in Toronto where many large businesses are located.

In the two years ended March, 1995, the Department's records indicated that it audited about 325 tax shelters and found most of them abusive. In 1995-96 the Department increased its audit coverage. The complete audits resulted in assessment of $161 million in additional taxes.

Tieleman continues,

* Vol. 46, No. 6, 1998.

Not bad, until you note that between just 1992 and 1994, taxpayers invested close to $5 billion in shelters. How many more millions should have gone to fund public services?

The May 1996 auditor-general's report notes that the mere 150 auditors allocated to combatting tax avoidance produced about $365 million in reassessments . . . or about $2.6 million per tax avoidance auditor.

So, with results like that, one might presume government would be hiring more auditors to increase corporate tax investigations. But last December, Denis Desautels, the Auditor-General, expressed concern that tax revenue was being lost due to staff shortages.

"Revenue Canada's staffing problems in the International Tax Directorate are troublesome because they may be limiting the government's ability to collect revenues that are due to Canadians from international transactions."*

---

* *National Post*, April 26, 1999.

Appendix Five
Organizations and Abbreviations

Applied Research Branch, Human Resources Development Canada
The Applied Research Branch is a division of the Strategic Policy and Planning Group within Human Resources Canada in Ottawa. The division focuses on research related to short- and medium-term federal-government policy development.

British Columbia Social Planning and Research Council (SPARC)
The British Columbia Social Planning and Research Council is a non-profit organization formed in 1966 and based in Vancouver. SPARC has nine thousand members from all parts of B.C. The organization advocates principles of social justice, equality, and dignity for all people, including social, economic, and environmental well-being for citizens and communities.

Business Council on National Issues (BCNI)
The Business Council on National Issues, founded in 1977 to coordinate corporate participation in government policy formulation, is the voice of big business in Canada and is unquestionably the most successful lobby group in the country. The BCNI is made up of 150 large Canadian and foreign corporations administering total

assets in excess of $1.9 trillion. Since the election of Brian Mulroney's government in 1984, the BCNI has been very successful in influencing federal-government policies in a more conservative and continentalist direction.

Caledon Institute of Social Policy

Founded in 1992, the Caledon Institute of Social Policy is an independent social-policy think tank that produces quality research and analysis and proposals for reform in all areas of social policy, including poverty, child benefits, pensions, employee and employer payroll taxes, the role of government and the voluntary sector. The institute is based in Ottawa.

Campaign 2000

Campaign 2000 is an umbrella organization founded in 1991 and headquartered in Toronto. The organization is made up of some thirty national and forty community, religious, medical, educational, social, child care, trade union, anti-poverty and other Canadian groups concerned about poverty in Canada. The organization was formed due to concern about the lack of government progress in addressing child poverty.

Canadian Association of Food Banks (CAFB)

The Canadian Association of Food Banks was incorporated in 1989 as a national umbrella group for food banks in Canada. Headquartered in Toronto, its main activities include distribution of large-scale industrial food donations to its members across the country, the co-ordination of national transportation of food, providing information to members, public-education activities and advocacy on behalf of food-bank clients. The organization has members in every province and operates its food-distribution system from warehouses in Toronto and Montreal.

Canadian Association of Independent Living Centres

The Canadian Association of Independent Living Centres is a national umbrella organization for independent-living resource centres across Canada. These organizations are run by and for people with disabilities. The centres work to enable persons with disabilities to integrate into and contribute to society. The association, founded in 1985, has a national office in Ottawa and twenty-three centres across Canada, located in all provinces except P.E.I.

Canadian Council on Social Development (CCSD)
The Canadian Council on Social Development, founded in 1920 by Charlotte Whitton, is based in Ottawa and is one of the of the most authoritative voices promoting better social and economic security for Canadians. The national, self-supporting organization's main product is new information and research focusing on concerns such as child well-being, economic security, employment, poverty, pensions, and federal and provincial social policies.

Canadian Tax Foundation
The Canadian Tax Foundation, headquartered in Toronto, established in 1945, provides the public and government with a steady stream of valuable comparative information and new research into current problems of taxation and public finance. The centre has a highly qualified permanent staff and commissions outside experts for special studies. The aim of the foundation is the establishment of an equitable tax system that fosters growth and productivity in Canada.

Centre for Social Justice
The Centre for Social Justice, founded in 1997 and headquartered in Toronto, conducts research and educational activities designed to strengthen the movement for social justice. The organization focuses on issues such as economic inequality, corporate power and democratic alternatives, and carries on the work of the former Jesuit Centre for Social Faith and Justice.

Centre for the Study of Living Standards
The Ottawa-based Centre for the Study of Living Standards was established in 1995 to undertake standard-of-living research. The centre's main objectives are to contribute to a better understanding

of trends and conditions through research papers and conferences, advocating policies and seeking expert consensus.

Childcare Resource and Research Unit at the Centre for Urban and Community Studies, University of Toronto

The Childcare Resource and Research Unit at the Centre for Urban and Community Studies at the University of Toronto began operations in the early 1980s and focuses on early childhood care and education research and policy. Its mandate is to advance the idea of publicly funded, universally accessible, comprehensive, high-quality, non-profit child care and education in Canada.

Economic Policy Institute, Washington, D.C.

The Washington, D.C.–based Economic Policy Institute, founded in 1986, is a non-profit, non-partisan think tank that seeks to broaden the public debate about strategies to achieve a prosperous and fair economy in the U.S. The institute produces research and educational material, much of which relates to the living standards of working families.

European Union (E.U.)

The European Union comprises fifteen member states whose goal is "an ever closer union among the peoples of Europe" and the promotion of economic and social progress through balanced and sustainable policies, as well as asserting the European identity on the international scene. Member countries are Austria, Belgium, Denmark, Finland, France, Germany, Greece, Ireland, Italy, Luxembourg, the Netherlands, Portugal, Spain, Sweden, and the United Kingdom.

Fraser Institute

The Fraser Institute, established in 1974 and headquartered in Vancouver, is a well-organized, well (but secretly) funded right-wing lobby organization. In recent years it has been increasingly successful in promoting its policies of less government, lower social spending, privatization, deregulation, and other pubic policies that more closely resemble those in the United States.

G-7

Beginning in 1975, the leaders of six major industrial democracies began annual meetings to review political and economic issues. The six – the United States, Britain, France, Germany, Japan and Italy – were joined by Canada in 1976. The G-7 continues to function today; full Russian participation in 1998 produced the G-8. The summit meetings now cover a broad range of international issues.

C.D. Howe Institute

The C.D. Howe Institute is an influential conservative and continentalist lobbying and research organization established in 1973 and headquartered in Toronto. The institute produces a steady stream of publications which are widely reported in the media. Among other topics, the institute commissions studies on fiscal and monetary policy, trade, social policy, federal-provincial relations, and constitutional reform. Like the Fraser Institute, the C.D. Howe's funding is substantial, but secret.

National Anti-Poverty Organization (NAPO)

NAPO is a national membership-based organization whose goal is the elimination of poverty in Canada. Since its founding in 1971 it has been directed by local activists who have personal experience with poverty. NAPO conducts research and engages in advocacy on national issues of concern to low-income Canadians and it works with local activists and organizations to strengthen efforts to reduce and eliminate poverty.

National Council of Welfare

The National Council of Welfare, headquartered in Ottawa, was created in 1969 as a citizens' advisory group to the federal government. Its mandate is to advise the Minister of Human Resources and Development on matters of concern to low-income people. For the past thirty years the council has provided Canadians with a steady output of valuable information relating to poverty in Canada.

Organization for Economic Co-operation and Development (OECD)
The Organization for Economic Co-operation and Development was established in 1961 and is headquartered in Paris, France. The OECD aims to promote policies designed to achieve the highest sustainable economic growth and employment and a rising standard of living in member countries. The OECD publishes an abundance of important economic and social information on a regular basis. There are now twenty-nine developed member countries.

Vanier Institute of the Family
The Vanier Institute of the Family, headquartered in Ottawa, was established in 1965 under the patronage of their Excellencies Governor General Georges Vanier and Madame Pauline Vanier. It is a national voluntary organization dedicated to promoting the well-being of Canadian families through research, publications, public education, and advocacy.